编委会

高等学校"十四五"规划酒店管理
与数字化运营专业新形态系列教材

总主编
周春林　全国旅游职业教育教学指导委员会副主任委员，教授

编　委（排名不分先后）

臧其林　苏州旅游与财经高等职业技术学校党委书记、校长，教授
叶凌波　南京旅游职业学院校长
姜玉鹏　青岛酒店管理职业技术学院校长
李　丽　广东工程职业技术学院党委副书记、校长，教授
陈增红　山东旅游职业学院副校长，教授
符继红　云南旅游职业学院副校长，教授
屠瑞旭　南宁职业技术学院健康与旅游学院党委书记、院长，副教授
马　磊　河北旅游职业学院酒店管理学院院长，副教授
王培来　上海旅游高等专科学校酒店与烹饪学院院长，教授
王姣蓉　武汉商贸职业学院现代管理技术学院院长，教授
卢静怡　浙江旅游职业学院酒店管理学院院长，教授
刘翠萍　黑龙江旅游职业技术学院酒店管理学院院长，副教授
苏　炜　南京旅游职业学院酒店管理学院院长，副教授
唐凡茗　桂林旅游学院酒店管理学院院长，教授
石　强　深圳职业技术学院管理学院副院长，教授
李　智　四川旅游学院希尔顿酒店管理学院副院长，教授
匡家庆　南京旅游职业学院酒店管理学院教授
伍剑琴　广东轻工职业技术学院酒店管理学院教授
刘晓杰　广州番禺职业技术学院旅游商务学院教授
张建庆　宁波城市职业技术学院旅游学院教授
黄　昕　广东海洋大学数字旅游研究中心副主任/问途信息技术有限公司创始人
汪京强　华侨大学旅游学院国家级旅游实验教学示范中心
　　　　国家级旅游虚拟仿真实验示范中心主任，教授级高级实验师
王光健　青岛酒店管理职业技术学院酒店管理学院酒店管理与数字化运营专业负责人，副教授
方　堃　南宁职业技术学院健康与旅游学院酒店管理与数字化运营专业带头人，副教授
邢宁宁　漳州职业技术学院酒店管理与数字化运营专业主任，专业带头人
曹小芹　南京旅游职业学院旅游外语学院旅游英语教研室主任，副教授
钟毓华　武汉职业技术学院旅游与航空服务学院副教授
郭红芳　湖南外贸职业学院旅游学院副教授
彭维捷　长沙商贸旅游职业技术学院湘旅学院副教授
邓逸伦　湖南师范大学旅游学院教师
沈蓓芬　宁波城市职业技术学院旅游学院教师
支海成　南京御冠酒店总经理，副教授
杨艳勇　北京贵都大酒店总经理
赵莉敏　北京和泰智研管理咨询有限公司总经理
刘懿纬　长沙菲尔德信息科技有限公司总经理

高等学校"十四五"规划酒店管理
与数字化运营专业新形态系列教材

总主编 ◎ 周春林

酒店英语

主　编　屠瑞旭　曹小芹
副主编　袁　榕　张　媛　宋锦波
参　编　熊馨玉　卢奕彤　刘馨柳
　　　　刘寒雨　肖顺菊　谷芸子

HOTEL
ENGLISH

华中科技大学出版社
http://press.hust.edu.cn
中国·武汉

内 容 提 要

本教材是基于项目化、任务化设计理念编写的新形态教材,主要内容包括酒店服务概论、前厅服务、客房服务、餐饮服务、其他常见酒店服务及投诉和突发事件处理等方面的内容,共 16 个学习单元。每单元围绕一个典型职业相关主题展开,单元主题分别为:酒店服务概论、预订服务、入住登记服务、礼宾服务、结账办理服务、客房清扫及洗衣服务、客房其他服务、中餐服务、西餐服务、客房服务、宴会及酒水服务、总机服务、商务中心、销售服务及购物中心、会展及康乐服务、投诉和突发事件处理。

通过以上的体例安排,达到相应主题的岗位任务目标和语言学习任务目标,切实提升学生的高端酒店涉外工作能力。

图书在版编目(CIP)数据

酒店英语/屠瑞旭,曹小芹主编. —武汉:华中科技大学出版社,2022.5(2024.8 重印)
ISBN 978-7-5680-8163-4

Ⅰ.①酒… Ⅱ.①屠… ②曹… Ⅲ.①饭店-英语 Ⅳ.①F719.3

中国版本图书馆 CIP 数据核字(2022)第 068370 号

酒店英语　　　　　　　　　　　　　　　　　　　　　　　　屠瑞旭　曹小芹　主编
Jiudian Yingyu

策划编辑:李家乐　王　乾
责任编辑:陈　然
封面设计:原色设计
责任校对:谢　源
责任监印:周治超

出版发行:华中科技大学出版社(中国·武汉)　　电话:(027)81321913
　　　　　武汉市东湖新技术开发区华工科技园　　邮编:430223
录　　排:华中科技大学惠友文印中心
印　　刷:武汉市籍缘印刷厂
开　　本:787mm×1092mm　1/16
印　　张:13.75
字　　数:410 千字
版　　次:2024 年 8 月第 1 版第 3 次印刷
定　　价:49.80 元

本书若有印装质量问题,请向出版社营销中心调换
全国免费服务热线:400-6679-118　竭诚为您服务
版权所有　侵权必究

总序

2021年,习近平总书记对全国职业教育工作作出重要指示,强调要加快构建现代职业教育体系,培养更多高素质技术技能人才、能工巧匠、大国工匠。同年,教育部对职业教育专业目录进行全面修订,并启动《职业教育专业目录(2021年)》专业简介和专业教学标准的研制工作。

新版专业目录中,高职"酒店管理"专业更名为"酒店管理与数字化运营"专业,更名意味着重大转型。我们必须围绕"数字化运营"的新要求,贯彻党中央、国务院关于加强和改进新形势下大中小学教材建设的意见,落实教育部《职业院校教材管理办法》,联合校社、校企、校校多方力量,依据行业需求和科技发展趋势,根据专业简介和教学标准,梳理酒店管理与数字化运营专业课程,更新课程内容和学习任务,加快立体化、新形态教材开发,服务于数字化、技能型社会建设。

教材体现国家意志和核心价值观,是解决"为谁培养人、培养什么样的人、如何培养人"这一根本问题的重要载体,是教学的基本依据,是培养高质量优秀人才的基本保证。伴随我国高等旅游职业教育的蓬勃发展,教材建设取得了明显成果,教材种类大幅增加,教材质量不断提高,对促进高等旅游职业教育发展起到了积极作用。在2021年首届全国教材建设奖评审中,有400种职业教育与继续教育类教材获奖。其中,旅游大类获一等奖优秀教材3种、二等奖优秀教材11种,但高职酒店类获奖教材只有3种。当前,酒店职业教育教材同质化、散沙化和内容老化、低水平重复建设现象依然存在,难以适应现代技术、行业发展和教学改革的要求。

在信息化、数字化、智能化迭加的新时代,新形态高职酒店类教材的编写既是一项研究课题,也是一项迫切的现实任务。应根据酒店管理与数字化运营专业人才培养目标准确进行教材定位,按照应用导向、能力导向要求,优化设计教材内容结构,将工学结合、产教融合、科教融合和课程思政等理念融入教材,带入课堂。应面向多元化生源,研究酒店数字化运营的职业特点及人才培养的业务规格,突破传统教材框架,探索高职学生易于接受的学习模式和内容体系,编写体现新时代高职特色的专业教材。

我们清楚,行业中多数酒店数字化运营的应用范围仅限于前台和营销渠道,部分酒店应用了订单管理系统,但大量散落在各个部门的有关顾客和内部营运的信息数据没有得到有效分析,数字化应用呈现碎片化。高校中懂专业的数字化教师队伍和酒店里懂营运的高级技术人才是行业在数字化管理进程中的最大缺位,是推动酒店职业教育数字化转型面临的最大困难，这方面人才的培养是我们努力的方向。

高职酒店管理与数字化运营专业教材的编写是一项系统工程，涉及"三教"改革的多个层面，需要多领域高水平协同研发。华中科技大学出版社与南京旅游职业学院、广州问途科技公司合作，在全国范围内精心组织编审、编写团队，线下召开酒店管理与数字化运营专业新形态系列教材编写研讨会，线上反复商讨每部教材的框架体例和项目内容，充分听取主编、参编老师和业界专家的意见，在此特向这些参与研讨、提供资料、推荐主编和承担编写任务的各位同仁表示衷心的感谢。

该系列教材力求体现现代酒店职业教育特点和"三教"改革的成果，突出酒店职业特色与数字化运营特点，遵循技术技能人才成长规律，坚持知识传授与技术技能培养并重，强化学生职业素养养成和专业技术积累，将专业精神、职业精神和工匠精神融入教材内容。

期待这套凝聚全国高职旅游院校多位优秀教师和行业精英智慧的教材，能够在培养我国酒店高素质、复合型技术技能人才方面发挥应有的作用，能够为高职酒店管理与数字化运营专业新形态系列教材协同建设和推广应用探出新路子。

全国旅游职业教育教学指导委员会副主任委员
南京旅游职业学院党委书记、教授　周春林
2022 年 3 月 28 日

　　国家"十四五"规划明确提出:加快发展现代服务业,推动生活性服务业向高品质和多样化升级。随着2020年新冠肺炎疫情的暴发,酒店业受到相当大的冲击,将促进酒店加快产品服务转型,而同时在消费端,安全健康或者数字消费需求将有更大增长。研究发现,近两年来,随着人们对美好生活需求的提升,高端酒店出现回归,预计发展会进入一个黄金期。因此,高端酒店的发展对于员工的跨文化交际与服务能力、数字化技术应用能力提出更高要求。

　　为顺应新时代酒店业发展趋势,以及教育立德树人的宗旨,本团队编写了新形态教材《酒店英语》。本教材打破以知识传授为主要特征的传统模式,编写了基于工作流程的项目化、任务化教学内容,并且遵循任务型和项目化外语教学规律,工作岗位任务与语言任务并列设置。首先,教材注重酒店服务数字化的发展趋势,将相关知识融入每一项学习任务。并积极结合信息化教学技术,每单元均可扫码学习相应单元内容的音频。其次,教材在学习任务中融入课程思政,培养学生职业责任感及文化自信。最后,教材秉承赛教融合,以赛促学的原则,将全国职业院校技能大赛对酒店英语技能的要求融入相关教学环节。通过以上内容设置,教材旨在培养和训练学生的酒店英语会话技能和服务技能,使学生具备从事高端酒店服务工作的基本英语交际能力、跨文化沟通服务能力,具备数字化素养、酒店职业精神及家国情怀。

　　本教材包括六个学习模块:酒店服务概论(第1单元)、前厅服务(2—5单元)、客房服务(6—7单元)、餐饮服务(8—11单元)、其他常见酒店服务(12—15单元)及投诉和突发事件处理(第16单元)。每个学习模块又细分为一至多个任务,形成16个学习单元。每个单元均严格按照任务场景导入、词汇学习、任务情景对话、服务流程、功能表达及文化要素分析、听力能力提升练习、口译能力提升练习、情景模拟、专业知识拓展阅读的体例安排,达到相应主题的岗位任务目标和语言学习任务目标,切实提升学生的高端酒店涉外工作能力。其中,每单元情景对话(Task Three)的Note是对前面情景对话的注释和拓展。

　　本教材的编写得到了多家院校和合作企业的支持,形成了强有力的编写团队。团队具有较丰富的教材编写经验,团队中既有海外留学及访学经历的专业英语教师,又有担任全国职业院校技能大赛指导老师的酒店管理专业教师,还有来自行业企业的一线专家。本教材不仅可作为本科及高职院校的英语学习教材,还可以作为酒店一线员工的培训教材及自学教材。全书编写分工如下。第1、3单元:曹小芹;第2单元:屠瑞旭;第4单元:卢奕彤;第5单元:袁榕;第6、7单元:肖顺菊;第8、9单元:张媛;第10、11单元:刘馨柳;第12、13单元:谷芸子;第14单元:刘寒雨;第15单元:熊馨玉;第16单元:宋锦波。

  本教材的编写得到了南京旅游职业学院、郑州旅游职业学院、武汉民政职业学院、武汉外语外事职业学院、上海虹口三至喜来登酒店、上海漕河泾万丽酒店、深圳星河丽思卡尔顿酒店、深圳蛇口希尔顿酒店、杭州康莱德酒店、南宁鑫伟万豪酒店的大力支持,在此我们表示衷心的感谢。本教材在编写过程中还参考了许多同行、前辈的经验和成果,在此一并致谢。

  由于编者水平有限,疏漏在所难免。希望使用者不吝赐教,以便我们后续的改进和提升。

编 者
2022 年 2 月

Unit 1	General Knowledge of Hospitality	/ 001
Unit 2	Reservation Service	/ 014
Unit 3	Check in Service	/ 027
Unit 4	Concierge Service	/ 040
Unit 5	Check out Service	/ 054
Unit 6	Room Cleaning and Laundry Service	/ 067
Unit 7	Other Services in Housekeeping Department	/ 081
Unit 8	Chinese Restaurant Service	/ 094
Unit 9	Western Restaurant Service	/ 109
Unit 10	Room Service	/ 123
Unit 11	Banquet and Beverage Service	/ 135
Unit 12	Telephone Service	/ 144
Unit 13	Business Center	/ 156

Unit 14   Sales and Shopping Center service   / 168

Unit 15   Events and Recreational Services   / 180

Unit 16   Handling Complaints and Unexpected Affairs   / 193

Unit 1
General Knowledge of Hospitality

Unit Objectives

After studying this unit, you should be able to do the following:

Knowledge & Ability Objectives

1. grasp the general knowledge of the famous hotels;
2. be familiar with the terms and sentence patterns to describe hotels;
3. know certain international rules in receiving guests;
4. receive guests based on international rules;
5. know the hotel digitization development.

Quality Objectives

1. identify the significance of receiving guests based on international rules;
2. have the awareness of forming global horizon.

Task One Lead-in

1. Brainstorming

Look at the following pictures, they are all world-famous hotels, do you know their names?

2. Discussion

Nowadays, there are increasing number of hotels with high-tech, please discuss with your classmates to find out the features of hotels with high-tech, and write them down.

Features: _____

(1)

(2)
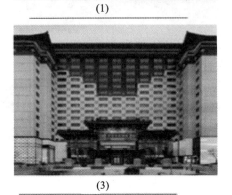
(3)

(4)

(Note: the above pictures are quoted from the following websites
https://www.smartmeetings.com/tips-tools/technology/96753/top-10-high-tech-hotels-world;
https://magazine.tablethotels.com/en/2017/05/the-next-dynasty/;
https://www.planetware.com/china/best-hotels-in-shanghai-chn-1-14.htm.)

Task Two Words and Expressions

historic	[hɪˈstɒrɪk] adj. 有历史意义的；历史上著名（或重要）的	adaptability	[əˌdæptəˈbɪləti] n. 适应性；适应
politician	[ˌpɒləˈtɪʃn] n. 从政者；政治家；政客，善于玩弄权术者	characteristic	[ˌkærəktəˈrɪstɪks] n. 特征；特点；品质
European	[ˌjʊərəˈpiːən] adj. 欧洲的 n. 欧洲人	empathy	[ˈempəθi] n. 同感；共鸣；同情
apartment	[əˈpɑːtmənt] n. 公寓；公寓套房	tolerance	[ˈtɒlərəns] n. 容忍；公差

Unit 1　General Knowledge of Hospitality

Continued

concession	[kən'seʃn]n. 让步；妥协	respect	[rɪ'spekt]n. 尊敬；敬意
luxurious	[lʌɡ'ʒʊərɪəs]adj. 奢侈的	flexible	['fleksəb(ə)l]adj.（人）适应力强的；柔韧的；有弹性的；灵活的
gallery	['ɡæləri]n. 陈列室；展览馆；画廊	interact	[ˌɪntər'ækt]v. 互动；相互作用
style	[staɪl]n. 风格；方式	greet	[ɡriːt]v. 问候；迎接；打招呼
restaurant	['restrɒnt]n. 餐馆；餐厅	attitude	['ætɪtjuːd]n. 态度；看法
fitness	['fɪtnəs]n. 健身；健康	business	['bɪznəs]n. 商业；买卖
establishment	[ɪ'stæblɪʃmənt]n. 建立；设立	acknowledge	[ək'nɒlɪdʒ]v. 接受；承认……的存在（或真实性）
dignitary	['dɪɡnɪtəri]n. 显贵；要人	digitalize	['dɪdʒɪtəlaɪz]v. 数字化；数位化
royalty	['rɔɪəlti]n. 王室成员	headquarter	[ˌhed'kwɔːtə(r)]n. 总部
elegance	['elɪɡəns]n. 优美；高雅	automated	['ɔːtəmeɪtɪd]adj. 自动化的
sensibility	[ˌsensə'bɪləti]n. 敏锐；敏感性	access	['ækses]v. 访问
savor	['seɪvə(r)]v. 品味	artificial	[ˌɑːtɪ'fɪʃl]adj. 人造的，人工的
setting	['setɪŋ]n. 环境；背景	intelligence	[ɪn'telɪdʒəns]n. 智力；才智
awareness	[ə'weənəs]n. 知道；认识	robot	['rəʊbɒt]n. 机器人
QR code	n. 二维码；二维条码		

Task Three　Sample Dialogues

1. Dialogue 1　Talking about Famous Hotels in China

Student: Professor Smith, can you share with me the famous hotels in China?

Professor: Sure. Today, we'll know something about expeditionary hotels in China. Firstly, let's get familiar with Jinjiang Hotel① of Shanghai.

Student: Why is Jinjiang Hotel so famous?

Professor: This historic hotel, popular with politicians and world leaders, is made up of three early 20th-century, European style apartment buildings, surrounded by green lawns.

Student: Where is Jinjiang Hotel?

Professor: As one of Shanghai's central hotels, it's located within the French

扫码
听听力

Concession area on Maoming Road near the great shopping area of Huaihai Road.

Student: What are the rooms and suites like in Jinjiang Hotel?

Professor: Rooms and suites are large and luxurious. The accommodations and the public areas ooze old Shanghai, and you really should check out the historical photo gallery in the lobby. However, the rooms are modern with nice luxury features like marble bathrooms, big flat-screen TVs, and big bathtubs. Room size, style, and features differ depending on which of the three buildings that the guests are in.

Student: What are the restaurants like in the hotel?

Professor: When you get hungry, there are more than 10 different restaurants and dining options at the hotel, including Indian, Western, Chinese, Japanese food and more.

Student: So cool. What about other facilities in the hotel?

Professor: The hotel has a large fitness center and spa, with a sauna, whirlpool baths, and a big indoor pool.

Student: Wow! I'm going to have a trip to Shanghai recently, and I will definitely go to visit Jinjiang Hotel.

> **Useful Expressions for Better Understanding of Dialogue 1**

(1) This historic hotel, popular with politicians and world leaders, is made up of three early 20th-century, Europeanstyle apartment buildings, surrounded by green lawns.

这家历史悠久的酒店深受政治家和世界领导人的欢迎,由三座20世纪早期的欧式公寓楼组成,四周环绕着绿色草坪。

(2) The accommodations and the public areas ooze old Shanghai.

住宿和公共区域散发着老上海的气息。

(3) The rooms are modern with nice luxury features like marble bathrooms.

这些房间都很现代,有大理石浴室等豪华设施。

(4) When you get hungry, there are more than 10 different restaurants and dining options at the hotel, including Indian, Western, Chinese, Japanese food and more.

当你饿了的时候,酒店里有10多家不同的餐厅和用餐选择,包括印度菜、西餐、中国菜、日本菜等。

2. Dialogue 2　Talking about Famous Hotels in the World

Student: Professor Smith, I really hope I can visit those famous hotels in the world.

Professor: I know. Today, let's get familiar with some famous hotels.

Student: Professor Smith, what do you know about The Plaza, New York②?

Professor: Since its establishment on October 1, 1907, The Plaza Hotel has remained a New York icon. It has hosted world leaders, dignitaries, legends, and

扫码
听听力

Hollywood celebrities. As an established staple for lavish society affairs and blockbuster films, The Plaza has welcomed guests from around the world to enjoy its magic for more than 100 years.

Student: Where is the hotel exactly?

Professor: Situated on Fifth Avenue③, The Plaza's prestigious address continues to define elegance with unmatched service and a modern sensibility.

Student: What are the particularities of The Plaza, New York?

Professor: The Plaza can offer you refined experiences. You can enjoy the magic of the afternoon tea in The Palm Court, savor the drinks in the elegant Champagne Bar, transport in time through the magic of The Rose Club, and embark on a culinary journey throughout The Plaza Food Hall. The Plaza offers 282 distinctive guestrooms including 102 luxurious suites. The hotel served as a setting for Kay Thompson's first book *Eloise*, Alfred Hitchcock's movie *North by Northwest*, and his second movie *Home Alone*.

Student: Wonderful! I really can't wait to have an experience in this hotel.

Professor: Be patient. One day, you can have the opportunity. Maybe in the future, you will work there.

> Useful Expressions for Better Understanding of Dialogue 2

(1) It has hosted world leaders, dignitaries, legends, and Hollywood celebrities.
它接待了世界领导人、政要、传奇人物和好莱坞名人。

(2) Situated on Fifth Avenue, The Plaza's prestigious address continues to define elegance with unmatched service and a modern sensibility.

纽约广场酒店坐落于第五大道,其享有盛誉的地点继续以无与伦比的服务和现代感来定义优雅。

(3) You can enjoy the magic of the afternoon tea in The Palm Court, savor the drinks in the elegant Champagne Bar, transport in time through the magic of The Rose Club, and embark on a culinary journey throughout The Plaza Food Hall.

您可以在棕榈园感受下午茶的魔力,在优雅的香槟酒吧品酒,在神奇的玫瑰俱乐部穿越时光,并在美食厅开启美食之旅。

3. Dialogue 3　International Service Expectations

Staff: Excuse me, Linda. You mentioned the Triple-A global services, could you please tell me their specific connotations?

Chief: They are "Awareness" "Attitude" and "Adaptability".

Staff: What does "Awareness" mean?

Chief: It means being aware of differences in culture, and gaining knowledge of other cultures and their characteristics.

Staff: Then what does "Attitude" imply?

Chief: It implies that the staff should be aware of his own attitude, embracing

扫码
听听力

empathy, tolerance and respect for others.

Staff: Thank you. But how should we do for "Adaptability"?

Chief: We should be flexible in how to react to different situations, and modify the way that we interact across cultures without hesitation.

Staff: I heard that welcoming guest is an important part in receiving guests. Could you share with me the important rules in welcoming guests?

Chief: Firstly, we should greet our guest warmly, sincerely and with a smile. This is very important because people can tell if you are faking it. We need to check our attitude, and express gratitude that our guest is at our business. They are the reason why we have a job in the hotel.

Staff: What is the second rule?

Chief: The second rule is that we should have eye contact. Greeting customers while doing something else is very disrespectful behaviour. Unless you are assisting another customer, drop what you are doing, look at the customer in the eye, and greet them.

Staff: That is a very helpful suggestion. What is the third rule?

Chief: The third rule is that we should acknowledge the guest immediately. We shouldn't wait. Even 15 seconds can be too long to acknowledge recognition or a guest who is nearby. A simple nod of the head or a brief comment will let the person know that you have seen them and will be with them soon.

Staff: These are really important rules to meet our guests'expectations. I'll try to put them into my work practice.

> **Useful Expressions for Better Understanding of Dialogue 3**

(1) They are"Awareness""Attitude" and "Adaptability".
它们是"意识""态度"和"适应性"。

(2) It means being aware of differences in culture, and gaining knowledge of other cultures and their characteristics.
它意味着了解文化差异，了解其他文化及其特征。

(3) It implies that the staff should be aware of his own attitude, embracing empathy, tolerance and respect for others.
这意味着员工应该了解自己的态度，拥有同理心，宽容和尊重他人。

(4) We should be flexible in how to react to different situations, and modifying the way that we interact across cultures without hesitation.
我们应该灵活应对不同的情况，毫不犹豫地改变我们跨文化交流的方式。

(5) Firstly, we should greet our guest warmly, sincerely and with a smile.
第一，我们应该热情、真诚、微笑地迎接客人。

(6) The second rule is that we should have eye contact.
第二条规则是我们应该有眼神交流。

(7) The third rule is that we should acknowledge the guest immediately.
第三条规则是我们应该立即向客人致意。

4. Dialogue 4   Talking about Stay in a Digitalized Hotel

Staff 1: Have you heard of the digitalized hotel of Alibaba④?

Staff 2: I once stayed there and the experience is so different.

Staff 1: Is it the FlyZoo Hotel⑤ which is not far away from its headquarters in Hangzhou?

Staff 2: Yes. Almost everything there is automated.

Staff 1: What is the check in process there?

Staff 2: In the hotel lobby, they don't have traditional check in counter, and they don't have a concierge.

Staff 1: Then, how do the foreign guests check in?

Staff 2: Foreign guests will check in there as staff will come up and assist them. But for Chinese citizens, they'll check on the kiosks, or they can just check in on their phone if they have the App of the hotel.

Staff 1: Do you get the key card?

Staff 2: No, I didn't get the key card. The staff took a picture of me and I can open the door and get access to the hotel. To access to my floor, I have to scan my face in the elevator. I just use my face to open the door. To be honest, I feel a little bit lost without a key card or receipt or anything like that.

Staff 1: So, there are few staff there.

Staff 2: You won't see as many faces at reception as in a traditional hotel, but there is still some staff around. Like housekeeping, which Alibaba says still have to use a traditional key card to clean the room.

Staff 1: For the young generation, they absolutely love it.

Staff 2: The most amazing thing is the room. Each hotel room has a small artificial intelligence device. With the device, you can order what you can, like slippers, and you could even order room service. It can also open the curtains for you and turn on the TV, even dim the lights.

Staff 1: Are there robots in the hotel?

Staff 2: Yes. There are robots in the hotel. Many of the deliveries are made by robot butlers. One robot can even call an elevator itself. It doesn't need to actually press any buttons.

Staff 1: What about other facilities in the hotel?

Staff 2: For the vending machine, you just need to open the Alipay App, scan the QR code, and then it unlocks. You get a drink. Within seconds, the App recognizes the product that you picked up from this refrigerator and it has charged you.

Staff 1: It's so convenient! What about dining in the restaurant?

Staff 2: There are robots to deliver your dishes. However, for some special

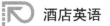

dishes, the staff member will serve the dish. When I go to the bar, I scan the QR code to order my drink. I see my drink is being made by a robot.

Staff 1: It's so cool and I'd like to go and experience it!

➢ Useful Expressions for Better Understanding of Dialogue 4

(1) In the hotel lobby, they don't have a traditional check in counter, and they don't have a concierge.

在酒店大厅,他们没有传统的登记柜台,也没有礼宾部。

(2) But for Chinese citizens, they'll check on the kiosks, or they can just check in on their phone if they have the App of the hotel.

但对于中国人来说,他们会在自助服务终端机上登记,如果他们有酒店的应用程序,他们也可以在手机上登记。

(3) Each hotel room has a small artificial intelligence device.

每个酒店房间都有一个小型人工智能设备。

(4) For the vending machine, you just need to open the Alipay App, scan the QR code, and then it unlocks.

对于自动售货机,您只需打开支付宝应用程序,扫描二维码,然后解锁。

(5) However, for some special dishes, the staff member will serve the dish.

但是,对于一些特殊的菜肴,工作人员会亲自上菜。

(6) When I go to the bar, I scan the QR code to order my drink. I see my drink is being made by a robot.

当我去酒吧时,我扫描二维码来点饮料。我看到机器人在制作我的饮料。

5. Notes Related to Check in Dialogues

①Jinjiang Hotel　锦江饭店,由中国女权运动先驱董竹君女士创办,坐落在上海市中心的茂名路上,是一家花园式饭店。开业至今已接待了一百多个国家的近三百位国家元首和政府首脑,以及众多商贾巨富。饭店北楼始建于1929年,建筑特色是将欧洲建筑风格和现代设施融为一体。1999年7月,修葺一新的北楼重新开业,设施按五星级标准配置,重新开业的还包括一个曾经见证《中美上海联合公报》签署的锦江小礼堂。装修后的锦江北楼,既保留了一些往日的风格,又增添了现代化的设施与装潢,成为上海的豪华级宾馆楼。

②The Plaza, New York　纽约广场饭店位于美国纽约第五十九街,它和中央公园隔街对望,东临大将军广场,广场饭店因此而得名。纽约广场饭店开业以来一直是名流要人下榻之地,被认为是名流的代名词。广场饭店作为纽约市的地标建筑之一,其实早已不是单纯的一个饭店,在许多纽约人心中,广场饭店见证了纽约的发展,承载了纽约市历史的变迁,已经成为纽约的一个标志。

③The Fifth Avenue　第五大道是美国纽约曼哈顿一条重要的南北向干道,南起华盛顿广场公园,北抵第138街。第五大道上景点众多,由南至北有帝国大厦、纽约公共图书馆、洛克菲勒中心、圣帕特里克教堂和中央公园等。此外,由于中央公园附近有大都会艺术博物馆、惠特尼美术馆、所罗门·古根海姆美术馆、库珀·休伊特设计博物

馆等著名的美术博物馆,因此第五大道又被称为"艺术馆道"。

④Alibaba 阿里巴巴集团控股有限公司经营多项业务,另外也从关联公司的业务和服务中取得经营商业生态系统上的支持。其主营业务和关联公司的业务包括淘宝网、天猫、聚划算、全球速卖通、阿里巴巴国际交易市场、1688、阿里妈妈、阿里云、菜鸟网络等。

⑤FlyZoo Hotel 菲住布渴酒店是阿里巴巴旗下的一家未来酒店,是全场景人脸识别酒店。隶属于浙江未来酒店网络技术有限公司,由阿里巴巴集团旗下飞猪、首旅酒店集团、石基信息三方共同出资成立。

Task Four Procedure, Functional Expressions and Service Culture Points of Check in

1. Triple-A Global Services

(1) They are "Awareness" "Attitude" and "Adaptability".

(2) "Awareness" means being aware of differences in culture, and gaining knowledge of other cultures and their characteristics.

(3) "Attitude" implies that the staff should be aware of his own attitude, embracing empathy, tolerance and respect for others.

(4) "Adaptability" means that we should be flexible in how to react to different situations, and modifying the way that we interact across cultures without hesitation.

2. Culture Points

Communication Culture in International Hotel Service

In international hotel service, there are a lot of cultural elements that we need to pay attention to. Firstly, we need to pay attention to cultural differences. Secondly, we need to break down stereotypes and know the rules of international service. Thirdly, we should make use of nonverbal communication and conscious communication. Fourthly, we should learn to use the proper language in a professional environment. In addition, we should know how to make requests and recommendations, how to deal with complaints with professional language. Lastly, we should try to exceed the expectations of the guests.

Task Five Listening Ability Enhancement

扫码
听听力

1. Listen to the dialogue of group check in and fill in the blanks

Student: Professor Smith, can you share with me the famous hotels in China?

Professor: Firstly, let's take a quick look at Aman at Summer Palace, Beijing. Just steps from the East Gate of the Summer Palace, ___(1)___ Aman at Summer

Palace, the ideal location from which to discover Beijing. Housed in a series of ___(2)___, some of which date back over a century. The ___(3)___ is only 15 km from Beijing's Forbidden City. A serene retreat, with peaceful internal ___(4)___ embracing traditional Chinese architecture, the property provides easy access to such cultural landmarks as the Great Wall, the Temple of Heaven and the Hutongs. Aman at Summer Palace is managed currently by ___(5)___, the world's most exclusive hotel brand.

Student: Professor Smith. Actually in Shanghai, there are also a lot of famous hotels.

Professor: ___(6)___ Pudong, Shanghai. Surrounded by the gleaming skyscrapers of Lujiazui, the hotel offers a unique blend of style and comfort with a stunning design, ___(7)___ restaurants and Mandarin Oriental's legendary service. More leisurely moments await at the historic ___(8)___—just ten minutes away—and other main attractions, all within easy reach by train. As sophisticated as they are spacious, the 318 rooms and 44 suites offer a sublime blend of ___(9)___ and contemporary design, all of them with sweeping views over the ___(10)___.

Student: The hotel is so amazing! Thank you for your information, Mr. Smith.

2. Listen to the passage and decide if the following statements are true (T) or false (F)

(　　)① The exterior of Eccleston Square looks divinely historic.

(　　)② Eccleston Square Pimlico holds 49 guest rooms and a Media Lounge which can sit up to 14 guests.

(　　)③ The interior of Eccleston Square Pimlico, pulses with technologies such as keypads that control the music and sound-controlled shower walls.

(　　)④ Aloft Cupertino is situated in Silicon Valley, the tech capital of the world.

(　　)⑤ A robotic butler distributes poolside towels and restaurant dishes.

(　　)⑥ Each room is decorated with trendy furniture, including an Apple TV.

扫码
听听力

Task Six　Interpretation

(1) This historic hotel, popular with politicians and world leaders, is made up of three early 20th-century, European style apartment buildings, surrounded by green lawns.

(2) The rooms are modern with nice luxury features like marble bathrooms, big flat-screen TVs, and big bathtubs.

(3) Room sizes, styles, and features differ depending on which of the three buildings that the guests are in.

(4) It has hosted world leaders, dignitaries, legends, and Hollywood celebrities.

(5) You can enjoy the magic of the afternoon tea in The Palm Court, savor the drinks in the elegant Champagne Bar.

(6) It means being aware of differences in culture, and gaining knowledge of other cultures and their characteristics.

(7) 第一，我们应该热情、真诚、微笑地迎接客人。

(8) 第二，我们应该有眼神交流。

(9) 对于中国人来说，他们会在自助服务终端机上登记。如果他们有酒店的应用程序，他们也可以在手机上登记。

(10) 每个酒店房间都有一个小型人工智能设备。

(11) 对于自动售货机，您只需打开支付宝应用程序，扫描二维码，然后解锁。

(12) 我看到机器人在制作我的饮料。

Task Seven Role Play

1. Make a situational conversation about a famous hotel

David Smith comes to the front desk of Jinling Hotel, Nanjing. You are the concierge, please make an introduction of your hotel to him.

2. Make a situational conversation about professional language used in greetings, goodbyes and determining guest needs

David Smith is the chief of the front desk of Jinling Hotel. Linda is a green hand in the hotel as a concierge. She is asking David Smith for suggestions about languages used in greetings, goodbyes and determining guest needs.

3. Make a situational conversation about a famous high-tech hotel

Anna Parker is going to visit Guangzhou. She would like to live in a high-tech hotel. You are her friend and you work in the hotel industry. Please give her suggestions.

Task Eight Extended Professional Knowledge Reading

Hi-tech Hotels

Generally, if you know the difference between a tablet and a desktop, a VCR and VR or how to program your watch to do everything other than make your breakfast, you're someone who finds life easier with more technology. Lucky for you, there are more and more high-tech hotels.

➢ The W Singapore at Sentosa Cove, Sentosa Island, Singapore

The W Singapore elevated the average dip in the pool with underwater speakers. Poolside music can also be enjoyed in a private cabana—loaner iPad included. The music technology extends to the hotel's WOW Suite, which comes with its own private DJ booth. LED lighting runs throughout the hotel, setting a stylish and futuristic tone. The hotel boasts 240 guest rooms and features special meeting amenities such as mood music and signature scents. The event space spans nearly 15600 sq. ft (about 1450.8 m^2).

➢ NH Collection Berlin Mitte Friedrichstrasse, Berlin, Germany

The NH Hotel is a business traveler's dream. Holographic technology is available to guests, making 3D image projections of meeting attendees or work presentations possible. The chain's other hotels, in Milan and Barcelona, also utilize this technology. If inspiration strikes, guitars and keyboards can be delivered to rooms upon request. The hotel has 268 guest rooms and planners can choose from 10 different meeting spaces with a maximum capacity of 350.

➢ The Hotel Silken Puerta América, Madrid, Spain

The Hotel Silken Puerta América surpasses all architecture standards. Each of the 12 floors in this rainbow-colored tower was carefully designed by nineteen top-notch architects. In an unprecedented endeavor, each floor exhibits an individual architect's vision. Concepts are materialized in designs such as white caves and red lacquered walls. Five flexible spaces on the ground floor offer 1000-person capacity for meetings and events. The hotel offers 315 guest rooms.

➢ The Peninsula Hotel, Tokyo, Japan

At The Peninsula Hotel of Tokyo, guests indulge in tech perks such as unlimited Internet radio with over 3000 stations, mood lighting pads, nail polish dryers and Skype-compatible wireless phones. The hotel's digitally-interactive Pokémon hunt serves as an amenity for the latest kid-friendly game. The hotel has 314 guest rooms and 10 meeting spaces that can host from 18 to 250 guests.

➢ Pengheng Space Capsules Hotel, Shenzhen, China

Pengheng Space Capsules Hotel has an entire staff of robots: doormen, waiters and front desk attendants. Glossy, neon surfaces, robo-waiters and banks of computers are just some features making this hotel a sci-fi reality. Beds are designed as innovative space station bunks. The minimalist design, lodging only 17 capsules, permits an affordable rate.

Unit 1 General Knowledge of Hospitality

> The Yotel, New York, United States

The Yotel provides a variety of advanced systems such as kiosk check ins and fold-up beds. Perhaps the most enthralling hotel feature is YOBOT, a robot that stores luggage in locked bins. Items can later be retrieved with a pin code and last name. Bedrooms come with techno walls and optimal Wi-Fi, audio streaming and motion-sensor air conditioning. There are 669 guest rooms and an event space for up to 400 attendees.

(1) Read the passage and write down the peculiarities of each hotel mentioned above.

_____
_____
_____
_____
_____

(2) Decide if the following statements are true(T) or false(F), according to the passage.

(　　)①LED lighting runs throughout the hotel, setting a stylish and classic tone for Sentosa Island, Singapore.

(　　)②Holographic technology in Hotel Silken Puerta América is available to guests, making 3D image projections of meeting attendees or work presentations possible.

(　　)③The Hotel Silken Puerta América surpasses all architecture standards. Each of the 12 floors in this yellow-colored tower was carefully designed by nineteen top-notch architects.

(　　)④Pengheng Space Capsules Hotel has an entire staff of robots: doormen, waiters and front desk attendants.

(　　)⑤Bedrooms come with techno walls and optimal Wi-Fi, audio streaming and light-sensor air conditioning in Yotel.

Unit 1
练习答案

Unit 2
Reservation Service

Unit Objectives

After studying this unit, you should be able to do the following:

Knowledge & Ability Objectives

1. grasp the steps in room reservations;
2. be familiar with the terms and sentence patterns of the reservation service;
3. develop communication skills in reservations;
4. communicate with guests and record their reservation information in English;
5. learn about online reservations.

Quality Objectives

1. be good at listening and grasping detailed information;
2. become an eligible and polite hotel employee.

Task One Lead-in

1. Brainstorming

Have you ever reserved a room at a hotel? How did you make your reservation? Please share your experience with your classmates.

2. Multiple Choice

What information is needed when making a reservation? Please tick and add other information below.

☐ guest name
☐ telephone number
☐ address
☐ room type
☐ length of stay

Unit 2   **Reservation Service**

Enter your details

Almost done! Just fill in the * required info

Are you travelling for work?
◯ Yes ⦿ No

First name *
Last name *

Email address *
Watch out for typos
Confirmation email goes to this address

Confirm email address *

Who are you booking for?
◯ I am the main guest
◯ Booking is for someone else

☐ date of arrival/departure
☐ payment
☐ _____
☐ _____

📖 Task Two   Words and Expressions

reservation	[ˌrezə'veɪʃn] n. 预订	reserve	[rɪ'zɜːv] v. 预订
extra	['ekstrə] adj. 额外的；外加的	charge	[tʃɑːdʒ] n. 费用
prefer	[prɪ'fɜː(r)] v. 更喜欢	suite	[swiːt] n. 套房
rate	[reɪt] n. 价格	confirm	[kən'fɜːm] v. 证实；确认
look forward to	期待	twin room	n. 双人间
record	['rekɔːd] n. 记录；记载 v. 记录	cancellation	[ˌkænsə'leɪʃ(ə)n] n. 取消；撤销
recommend	[ˌrekə'mend] v. 推荐	suburb	['sʌbɜːb] n. 郊区；城外
amusement park	n. 游乐场	appreciate	[ə'priːʃieɪt] v. 感谢
bath	[bɑːθ] n. 浴缸；洗浴	preferably	['prefrəbli] adv. 更好地
elevator	['elɪveɪtə(r)] n. 电梯	single room	n. 单人间
available	[ə'veɪləbl] adj. 可找到的；可获得的	adjustment	[ə'dʒʌstmənt] n. 调整

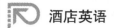

扫码听听力

Task Three　Sample Dialogues

1. Dialogue 1　Individual Guest Reservation

Staff: Good morning. International Hotel. What can I do for you?

Guest: I'd like to reserve a room.

Staff: Thank you, sir. For which date, please?

Guest: From Oct. 27th to Oct. 30th.

Staff: From Oct. 27th to Oct. 30th. That's three nights. How many guests will there be in your party?

Guest: Three. My wife, our daughter and myself.

Staff: Two adults and one child. Is your daughter over 16 years old? If she is over 16, we need to provide an extra bed and charge for it.

Guest: No. She's only 4.

Staff: What kind of room would you prefer?①

Guest: Well, we'd like a suite. How much is the rate?

Staff: A suite is 150 U.S. dollars per night, with 10% service charge.

Guest: OK. I'll take it.

Staff: Thank you, sir. May I have your name, please?

Guest: Yes, it's David White.

Staff: Mr. White, may I have your phone number, please?

Guest: Yes, my number is 15678902467.

Staff: Thank you, Mr. White. I'd like to confirm your reservation. A suite for your family at 150 U.S. dollars per night, from Oct. 27th to Oct. 30th, for three nights. Is that right?

Guest: Yes, that's right.

Staff: Thank you, Mr. White. We are looking forward to seeing you.

➤ **Useful Expressions for Better Understanding of Dialogue 1**

(1) I'd like to reserve a room.
我想要预订一间房。

(2) For which date, please?
请问您想订哪一天的房间呢？

(3) How many guests will there be in your party?
您一行几人？

(4) If she is over 16, we need to provide an extra bed and charge for it.
如果超过 16 岁，我们需要加床并且收费。

(5) What kind of room would you prefer?

您想要什么样的房间?

(6) How much is the rate?

房价是多少?

(7) A suite is 150 U.S. dollars per night, with 10% service charge.

套房每晚150美元,外加10%的服务费。

(8) May I have your name/phone number, please?

请问您的姓名/电话号码?

(9) I'd like to confirm your reservation.

我来确认一下您的预订信息。

(10) A suite for your family at 150 U.S. dollars per night, from Oct. 27th to Oct. 30th, for three nights.

一间每晚150美元的套房,10月27日至10月30日,预订3晚。

(11) We are looking forward to seeing you.

我们期待您的光临。

2. Dialogue 2　Group Reservation

Staff: Good afternoon, International Hotel. May I help you?

Guest: Yes, I'm David Smith calling from ABC Trading Company. I'd like to reserve rooms for my group.

Staff: What kind of rooms do you prefer?

Guest: We have 18 people. We'd like 9 twin rooms, please.

Staff: For which dates, Mr. Smith?

Guest: From May 23rd to 25th, for 2 nights.

Staff: Wait a moment, please. 9 twin rooms from May 23rd to 25th. Yes, the rooms are available.

Guest: What's the room rate?

Staff: It's 550 yuan per night.

Guest: OK. With breakfast?

Staff: Yes, that includes a Chinese breakfast.

Guest: Do you accept Visa?

Staff: Yes, we do. What time will you arrive?

Guest: We will be there around 4p.m..

Staff: OK. May I have your phone number, please?

Guest: Yes, it's 15567678989.

Staff: Thank you, Mr. Smith. Let me confirm your reservation. 9 twin rooms from May 23rd to 25th, for 2 nights, under the name of David Smith. Is that right?

Guest: Yes, that's right.

Staff: Thank you, Mr. Smith. We are looking forward to your coming.

➤ **Useful Expressions for Better Understanding of Dialogue 2**

(1) I'm David Smith calling from ABC Trading Company.

扫码
听听力

我是 ABC 贸易公司的 David Smith。

(2) We'd like 9 twin rooms, please.

我们想要 9 间双床房。

(3) The rooms are available.

有空房。

(4) Do you accept Visa?

可以用维萨卡支付吗?

(5) What time will you arrive?

你们什么时候到呢?

(6) We will be there around 4 p.m..

我们大概下午 4 点到。

(7) 9 twin rooms from May 23rd to 25th, for 2 nights, under the name of David Smith.

以 David Smith 的名义预订了 9 间双床房,5 月 23 日至 25 日,共 2 晚。

(8) We are looking forward to your coming.

期待您的到来。

3. Dialogue 3　Adjusting a Reservation

Staff: Good afternoon, International Hotel. How may I help you?

Guest: Good afternoon. This is Tom Smith from London. I have reserved a double room from Apr. 8th to Apr. 10th.

Staff: Wait a moment, Mr. Smith. I will check the reservation records. Yes, we do have a reservation for you on Apr. 8th. Are you calling to confirm it, Mr. Smith?

Guest: Not really. I'd like to make an adjustment to my reservation. I have another meeting in Beijing, so I have to stay for two more nights in your hotel.

Staff: Would you please hold the line for a second? I'll take a look at the hotel's reservation records.

Guest: Sure.

Staff: Yes, Mr. Smith. You can have the room for four nights, from Apr. 8th to Apr. 12th.

Guest: Wonderful. Thank you very much.

Staff: You're welcome. We are looking forward to seeing you soon.

> **Useful Expressions for Better Understanding of Dialogue 3**

(1) I have reserved a double room from Apr. 8th to Apr. 10th.

我预订了 4 月 8 日至 10 日的双人间。

(2) I will check/take a look at the reservation records.

我查看一下预订记录。

(3) Are you calling to confirm it, Mr. Smith?

史密斯先生,您打电话是确定预订信息吗?

扫码
听听力

(4) I'd like to make an adjustment to my reservation.

我想调整我的预订。

(5) I have another meeting in Beijing, so I have to stay for two more nights in your hotel.

我在北京有另一个会议，所以我要在酒店多住两晚。

(6) Would you please hold the line for a second?

请稍等，不要挂电话。

4. Dialogue 4　Fully Booked②

Staff: Good morning, International Hotel. How may I help you?

Guest: Yes, I'd like to book a room for Oct. 1st.

Staff: Wait a moment, please. I'm sorry, sir. We are fully booked on that day.

Guest: Really? That's awful.

Staff: Is it possible for you to change your booking date?

Guest: I'm afraid not.

Staff: I'm sorry. Would you like us to put you on our waiting list? We will call you in case we have a cancellation.③

Guest: Thank you very much. However, could you recommend another hotel that won't be fully booked?

Staff: Yes, of course. Where would you like to live, in the city center or in the suburb?

Guest: I prefer to live in the suburb near the amusement park.

Staff: Well, then I suggest trying Eden Hotel. It's not far from the park.

Guest: Thank you. Do you know the telephone number of Eden Hotel?

Staff: Yes. It's 4582904.

Guest: 4582904. Thank you. I really appreciate your help.

Staff: You're welcome. Thank you for calling us.

扫码
听听力

➢ **Useful Expressions for Better Understanding of Dialogue 4**

(1) We are fully booked on that day.

我们那天的房间已订满。

(2) Is it possible for you to change your booking date?

您可以更改预订日期吗？

(3) Would you like us to put you on our waiting list?

我们可以将您放进等待名单中吗？

(4) We will call you in case we have a cancellation.

如果有人取消预订，我们可以电话告知您。

(5) Could you recommend another hotel that won't be fully booked?

您可以推荐其他房间还没订满的酒店吗？

(6) Where would you like to live, in the city center or in the suburb?

您想住哪里呢？是市中心还是郊区？

(7) I prefer to live in the suburb near the amusement park.

我想住郊区，靠近游乐场的地方。

(8) I really appreciate your help.

很感激您的帮助。

(9) Thank you for calling us.

感谢致电。

5. Notes Related to Reservation Dialogues

①房间类型 Room types：

single room 单人间，配备一张单人床，适用于单身客人。

double room 大床房，配备一张双人床，适合夫妇居住。

twin room 双床房，配备两张单人床，又称标准间（standard room）。

triple room 三人间，配备三张单人床。

Suite 套房，分为 junior suite（普通套间）、business suite（商务套间）、deluxe suite（豪华套间）、presidential suite（总统套房）等。

②如果客人想要的房型已订满，不要只简单说"I'm sorry our ... rooms are all fully booked"，还要立即为客人推荐别的房型"What about ... ?"以抓住机会推销客房。如果所有的客房都满了，可以建议客人更改时间或查看附近酒店是否有房。同时，将客人的订房要求和预订人姓名、电话号码等记录在 waiting list（等候名单）上，一旦有客房，可以立即通知客人。

③酒店前台是酒店最早实现信息化的部分。Opera PMS 是目前国际上比较通用的酒店前台操作系统，它能满足不同规模酒店以及酒店集团的需求，为酒店管理层和员工提供全方位系统工具，以便其快捷高效地处理客户资料、客户预订、入住退房、客房分配、房内设施管理以及账户账单管理等日常工作。Opera PMS 系统的客房预订功能非常强大，可以进行建立、查询、更新客人预订和团队订房等操作，并提供了确认订房、等候名单、房间分配、押金收取、房间共享、团队客房控制及批房预留等功能，可用来帮助酒店简单快速地制订团队计划，实时监控可用房数并进行房价管理和自我控制预订以达到最佳出租率。

Task Four Procedure, Functional Expressions and Service Culture Points of Reservation

1. Greetings and Asking for Reservation Information

(1) Greet the guests.

Good morning/afternoon, ×× Hotel. What can I do for you? /May I help you?

(2) Ask for reservation information.

①Ask for room type.

What kind of room would you like?

②Ask for dates or length of stay.

For which date?

When will you arrive?

What's your departure date?

How long would you like to stay?

For how many nights, please?

③Ask for the number of guests/rooms in need.

How many people will be there in your party?

How many rooms would you like?

2. Search for Available Rooms

(1) Could you hold the line, please? Let me check if the rooms are available.

(2) Wait a moment, please. Yes, the rooms are available.

(3) I'm very sorry, sir/madam. We have no single room available as it's peak season.

3. Ask for Guest Information

(1) May I have your name, please?

(2) May I know the group name, please?

(3) May I have your phone number, please?

4. Accept and Confirm Reservation Information

(1) I'd like to confirm your reservation.

(2) Information about the reservation.

A double room for Mr. and Mrs. White at 200 yuan per night from Sept. 14th to Sept. 18th. Is that right?

5. Best Wishes and Record the Reservation Information

(1) Thank you for calling. We are looking forward to welcoming you.

(2) We are looking forward to seeing you soon.

6. Culture Points

Dealing with reservations through phone calls is not easy, because you and your guests cannot see each other. Therefore, when providing reservation service, try to be very careful, patient and polite. Do not ask several questions at a time. Ask your guests one question at a time, which is easier for them to remember and answer. Also, asking several questions at a time may lead to repetition of the questions, which is time-consuming and unpleasant. For important information, try to repeat again in order to avoid mistakes. What's more, do not assume your customer's answers. You can get answers by asking politely. For example, "Would you like a double room for you and your wife?" Answering phone calls is not easy at the beginning, but if you learn to be patient, careful and polite, your communication with guests will be smoother and more efficient.

Task Five Listening Ability Enhancement

1. Listen to the dialogue of individual reservation and fill in the blanks

Staff: Good morning, Edison Hotel. What can I do for you?

Guest: Good morning. This is Mary Morrison from the UK. I'm calling to __(1)__ a room from Jan. 6th to Jan. 10th.

Staff: OK. What kind of room would you like?

Guest: A __(2)__ with a bath, preferably facing the sea.

Staff: Wait a moment, please. A __(3)__ with a bath from Jan. 6th to Jan. 10th. Yes, the room is available.

Guest: Wonderful. What's the room __(4)__ ?

Staff: It's 800 yuan per night.

Guest: I'll take it. Please give me a room away from the __(5)__ . I hate the noise.

Staff: OK. May I have your __(6)__ , please?

Guest: Sure. 6554-7899.

Staff: Thank you, Ms. Morrison. I'd like to __(7)__ your __(8)__ . A __(9)__ room with a bath, away from the elevator and facing the sea, from Jan. 6th to Jan. 10th. Is that right?

Guest: That's right.

Staff: Thank you, Ms. Morrison. We are looking __(10)__ to seeing you soon.

2. Listen to the dialogue of canceling a reservation and fill in the missing information

Guest Name: _____

Room Type: _____

Date: _____

Reason of Cancellation: _____

Task Six Interpretation

(1) How many guests will there be in your party?

(2) I'd like to reserve a room.

(3) May I have your phone number, please?

(4) We are fully booked on that day.

(5) We are looking forward to seeing you soon.

(6) I'd like to confirm your reservation.

(7) 您想要什么样的房间呢？

(8) 您打算住几晚？
(9) 我查看一下预订记录。
(10) 双人间每晚500元，外加15%的服务费。
(11) 您什么时候到呢？
(12) 我们可以将您放入等待名单中吗？

Task Seven   Role Play

1. Make a situational conversation about an individual reservation

David Smith from Singapore is calling ABC Hotel to book a double room from March 16th to 18th. You are the receptionist. Please provide the reservation service.

2. Make a situational conversation about a group reservation

David Smith, the secretary of a business group from Singapore, is calling the hotel to book 10 twin rooms for the group. They will arrive in Shanghai on July 24th and leave on the 27th. You are the receptionist. Please provide the reservation service.

3. Make a situational conversation about adjusting a reservation

David Smith from New York is calling to adjust a reservation. He has booked a single room from Nov. 28th to 30th. However, his boss is coming with him, too. He wants to change the room type. You are the receptionist. Please deal with this adjustment.

Task Eight   Extended Professional Knowledge Reading

Hotel Reservation Service

Hotel Reservation Service is provided by the Front Office. The receptionists who work at the front desk in the lobby answer questions concerning reservations, booking and assigning rooms for guests. The receptionists also take reservations, cancellations and adjustments, and send out the hotel's letter of confirmation.

There are different ways of making reservations. You can go directly to the hotel and make reservations in person or call the hotel to make reservations. You can also sign up at the hotel website and book a room online. You can use a third-party App, such as Booking or Ctrip, to make a reservation. Nowadays, online reservations have become more and more popular because it is very convenient.

There are three forms of room reservations. The first one is "simple reservation", which refers to the reservation made by guests on the day of arrival or upon arrival. The hotel holds the right to cancel the reservation before 6 p.m.. The second one is "confirmed reservation". The hotel promises to reserve a room for guests up to a certain time. However, if the guests do not arrive at the cut-off time and they do not notify the hotel beforehand, the hotel may assign the room to other guests. The above two forms are non-guaranteed reservations. The third one is "guaranteed reservation". If guests want to ensure that the hotel will keep their rooms, they can use guaranteed reservations by credit card, advance deposit, or contracts. This method can ensure the hotel's due income while the hotel must guarantee to provide the guests with the rooms. Unless the hotel receives a notice from the guests to cancel the reservation, even if the guests do not arrive at the hotel, it should keep the room until the check out time limit the next day. Nowadays, many guests would choose to make a guaranteed reservation by credit card. They have to provide the card number and the card verification code, which is the three-digital number on the back of the credit card.

When a receptionist receives a reservation request, he/she first checks the hotel's booking situation to see if there are rooms available at the hotel. If there are rooms available, the receptionist would accept the reservation and record the information by the hotel management system, such as Opera PMS.

Please choose the best answer for each question

①Which department at the hotel provides reservation service?

A. Housekeeping Department

B. Food & Beverage Department

C. Recreational Department

D. Front Office

②Which is the way of making reservations?

A. Through phone calls

B. Going directly to the hotel and making reservations in person

C. Through the hotel website

D. All of the above

③Which one is not the form of hotel reservation?

A. Simple reservation

B. Difficult reservation

C. Confirmed reservation

D. Guaranteed reservation

④What does a receptionist do when providing reservation service at the front desk?

A. Answering questions concerning the reservation

B. Assigning rooms for guests

C. Taking cancellations and adjustments

D. All of the above

⑤When a receptionist receives a reservation request, what does he/she first do?

A. Check if the hotel has available rooms
B. Check the guests' information
C. Greet the guests
D. Record the information

Recent Development on China Hotel Booking Industry

Affected by the COVID-19 epidemic, China's tourism market and hotel booking industry have declined. However, after the lifting of the domestic tourism ban, domestic travel demand has increased, and the tourism market and hotel booking industry have clearly improved. The epidemic has promoted a further increase in the online rate of Chinese hotels. Although the shrinkage of the tourism and hotel market also has a negative impact on online hotel bookings, online bookings can reduce contact and are more convenient. In addition, the development trend before the epidemic is good. As the epidemic gradually eases, the online hotel market has recovered relatively quickly, compared to other channels. During the epidemic, the proportion of Internet users who chose OTA (Online Travel Agency) platforms to book hotels increased by 7.8%.

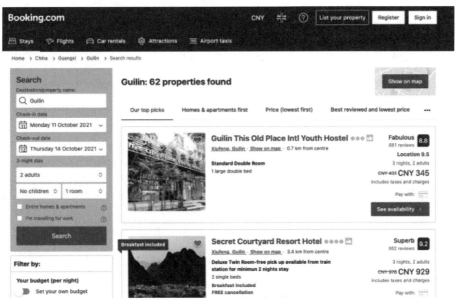

The OTA platform's help has become the most important support for hotels to fight the epidemic, and the preferential promotion and epidemic prevention publicity measures are the most recognized by hotels. In addition to self-rescue by adjusting the hotel's business, external assistance is also very important. Among them, the OTA platform is the most important source of orders during the epidemic. 65.5% of the surveyed hotels have received help from the OTA platform, and the effect is most recognized by them. Among the specific measures, the free discount promotion and epidemic prevention promotion launched by giant platforms such as Meituan and Ctrip are the measures that hotels believe are the best.

Decide if the following statements are true (T) or false (F), according to the passage

(   )①China's tourism market and hotel booking industry have declined before the COVID-19 epidemic.

(   )②Online bookings can reduce contact and are more convenient.

(   )③The development trend of hotel online booking before the epidemic is good.

(   )④The OTA platform is the most important source of hotel orders during the epidemic.

(   )⑤Compared to self-rescuing by adjusting the hotel's business, external assistance is not important.

Unit 3
Check in Service

Unit Objectives

After studying this unit, you should be able to do the following:
Knowledge & Ability Objectives
1. grasp the steps in checking in guests and online self check in;
2. be familiar with the terms and sentence patterns of check in;
3. know the qualifications for the receptionist;
4. check in guests in English in different situations;
5. deal with online self check in.

Quality Objectives
1. identify the significance of checking in guests professionally;
2. become an excellent receptionist with responsibility and the ability of active listening.

Task One Lead-in

1. Brainstorming
Look at the picture: the receptionist is receiving the guest at the front desk. What may be the situation? What are they saying? Please discuss with your group members and write down the sentences that they might say.

Receptionist: _____

Guest: _____

2. Sequencing
The following statements describe the job procedure of a receptionist. Discuss with your partner and put them in the correct order.

A. Greeting the guest;

B. Asking the guest to sign his name;

C. Confirming the guest's room type, rate and length of stay;

D. Asking the way of payment;

E. Asking if the guest has made a reservation;

F. Giving the key card to The guest;

Correct order：_____

Task Two　Words and Expressions

reservation	[ˌrezəˈveɪʃn] n. 预订	walk-in rate	n. 散客房价
reserve	[rɪˈzɜːv] v. 预订	arrival	[əˈraɪvl] n. 到达
arrange	[əˈreɪndʒ] v. 安排	departure	[dɪˈpɑːtʃə(r)] n. 离开
non-smoking	[ˌnɒnˈsməʊkɪŋ] adj. 禁烟的；不吸烟的	contact	[ˈkɒntækt] v. n. 联系；联络
passport	[ˈpɑːspɔːt] n. 护照	double room	n. 大床房
rate	[reɪt] n. 价格	registration	[ˌredʒɪˈstreɪʃn] n. 登记；注册
deposit	[dɪˈpɒzɪt] n. 押金；保证金	bar	[bɑː(r)] n. 栏
cash	[kæʃ] n. 现金	term	[tɜːm] n. 词语；术语
QR code	n. 二维码	scanner	[ˈskænə(r)] n. 扫描仪；扫描器
key card	n. 电子门卡	extension	[ɪkˈstenʃn] n. 延长的期限
luggage	[ˈlʌgɪdʒ] n. 行李	peak season	n. 旺季

Unit 3　Check in Service

Task Three　Sample Dialogues

1. Dialogue 1　Receiving Guests with a Reservation

Staff: Good afternoon, sir. Welcome to Jinling Hotel. How can I assist you?

Guest: I want to check in.

Staff: Have you made a reservation, sir?

Guest: Yes, I made a reservation 2 days ago under the name of John White.

Staff: Please wait a minute. Mr. White, you have reserved a double room for two nights, and the check out date is Oct. 7th. Am I correct?

Guest: Yes, you are right. Please try to arrange a non-smoking room with a higher floor.

Staff: No problem, sir. May I have a look at your passport?

Guest: Here you are.

Staff: Thank you, Mr. White. The room rate is 1000 yuan per night with breakfast for one. Please sign your name here.

Guest: OK.

Staff: Mr. White, how will you pay the deposit, in cash, by credit card, Wechat pay or Ali pay? The deposit is 3000 yuan for your entire stay.

Guest: I will use Alipay.

Staff: Let me scan the QR code for you. Mr White, this is your passport and key card. Please keep them well. Your room number is 2128. It is on the 21st floor.

Guest: Thank you. By the way, can you find someone to send my luggage to my room? It is so heavy.

Staff: No problem, Mr White. Our bellboy will help you with your luggage and show you to the room. If you have anything valuable, you could put them in the safe-box in your room or safe room on the first floor.

Guest: Nothing valuable, thanks.

Staff: Mr. White, this way, please. If you have any questions during your stay in our hotel, please call the hotline to contact us. We hope you will have a nice stay with us.

Guest: Thank you. Goodbye.

扫码
听听力

> **Useful Expressions for Better Understanding of Dialogue 1**

(1) Welcome to Jinling Hotel. How can I assist you?

欢迎光临金陵饭店，请问您需要什么服务？

(2) I want to check in.

我想办理登记入住。

(3) Have you made a reservation, sir?

先生，您有预订吗？

(4) Mr. White, you have reserved a double room for two nights, and the check out date is Oct. 7th.

怀特先生，您预订了一间大床房，住两晚，退房日期是10月7日。

(5) Please try to arrange a non-smoking room with a higher floor.

请尽量安排一间楼层较高的无烟房间。

(6) May I have a look at your passport?

请出示您的护照。

(7) The room rate is 1000 yuan per night with breakfast for one.

房价是每晚1000元，含单人早餐。

(8) Mr. White, how will you pay the deposit, in cash, by credit card, Wechat pay or Alipay?

怀特先生，您将如何支付押金，用现金、信用卡、微信还是支付宝？

(9) Our bellboy will help you with your luggage and show you to the room.

我们的行李员会帮您拿行李并带您去房间。

2. Dialogue 2   Receiving a Walk-in Guest

Staff: Good morning. Welcome to Hotel UNIC. How may I help you?

Guest: Good morning. I need a room in your hotel.

Staff: Do you have a reservation, sir?

Guest: No, I don't.

Staff: Then what kind of room would you like, sir?

Guest: A twin room, please.

Staff: All right. How long would you like to stay with us, sir?

Guest: Just one night. How much do you charge?

Staff: I can offer you a walk-in rate of 588 yuan, including breakfast.

Guest: It's somewhat expensive. Is that the cheapest rate you have?

Staff: I'm afraid so.

Guest: OK, I'll take it.

Staff: Sir, may I have your passport? I need to copy your passport. Just wait a moment and I will be right back.

Staff: Sir, how many guests will stay with you?

Guest: Just one.

Staff: Do you prefer a smoking or non-smoking room?

Guest: A non-smoking room.

Staff: Certainly. Sir, this is your registration form①. And this is your room rate. This is your room number, your arrival date and departure date. Our check out time is at 12 a.m.. If it is correct, please sign your name here and leave your contact number and email address.

扫码
听听力

Guest: Thank you.

Staff: We will charge you 1000 yuan for deposit. Would you prefer to pay in cash or by credit card?

Guest: By credit card.

Staff: This is your deposit amount. Please sign here.

Guest: Thank you.

Staff: Sir, your room is on the 10th floor and this is your key card. Your room rate includes one breakfast. It's buffet style. Our restaurant is on the 1st floor. It opens from 6 a. m. to 10 a. m.. Our hotel Wi-Fi is "Hotel UNIC" and no password is required. Our elevator is on your right side. Our bellman will carry your luggage to your room. If you have any needs, call our front desk, please.

Guest: OK.

Staff: Hope you will enjoy your stay with us.②

➤ Useful Expressions for Better Understanding of Dialogue 2

(1) What kind of room would you like, sir?
您想要什么种类的房间?

(2) How long would you like to stay with us, sir?
您打算在我们这里住多长时间?

(3) I can offer you a walk-in rate of 588 yuan, including breakfast.
我可以给您提供 588 元的散客价,包括早餐。

(4) I need to copy your passport.
我需要复印您的护照。

(5) This is your room number, your arrival date and departure date.
这是您的房间号、到达日期和离开日期。

(6) If it is correct, please sign your name here and leave your contact number and email address, please.
如果正确,请在此处签名,并留下您的联系电话和电子邮件地址。

(7) We will charge you 1000 yuan for deposit.
我们将向您收取 1000 元押金。

(8) Our hotel Wi-Fi is "Hotel UNIC" and no password is required.
我们的酒店 Wi-Fi 名称是"Hotel UNIC",不需要密码。

3. Dialogue 3   Receiving Guests with Online Check in③

Staff 1: Good afternoon, welcome to Jinling Hotel. How may I help you?

Guest 1: Good afternoon, I'd like to check in please.

Staff 1: Under which name is the booking?

Guest 1: Mike Taylor.

Staff 1: Welcome, Mr. Taylor. I see that you have done your E-check in. This is your key card, and your room number is 1106.

Guest 1: Thank you.

Guest 2: The E-check in is so convenient. I'd like to have a try.

Staff 1: That's great, our staff will show you how to do the E-check in with our Self Check In Kiosk.

Staff 2: Please come with me, sir. I'll help you do the self check in.

Guest 2: Thank you.

Staff 2: Sir, as you can see, this is the home page of our online system. Do you have a reservation?

Guest 2: No, I don't.

Staff 2: First, please click the "without reservation" bar. Then, you can see the terms and conditions. Please click to go on. Now, you can choose the days to stay. Then, please choose the room type.

Guest 2: OK, I'll click on the king size bedroom. Now, I should click on the number of rooms, right?

Staff 2: Yes. You are right. Now, the information of all your registration is here. You can read and then make a confirmation. Your room type is king size bedroom, two rooms for three nights, and the total amount is 4800 yuan.

Guest 2: Right.

Staff 2: Now, please click the "passport" bar. Please put the personal information page of your passport under the scanner. Now, you can confirm your name.

Guest 2: Thank you. Now, I should click to choose the method of payment, and I'll choose credit card.

Staff 2: Yes. You just need to click on the "credit card" bar. Please insert your credit card, or use the pay wave④. Now, the room card comes out automatically, please collect your room card.

Guest 2: OK.

Staff 2: Now, the receipt comes out. Please keep it well. All your self check in is done, sir. Your room numbers are 1106 and 1108. If you need anything, dial 0 from your room's phone and we'll be here to help you. In addition, you can download the Jinling Hotel App, and you can reserve our services online, such as restaurant reservation, fitness center reservation and so on.

Guest 2: Thank you!

Staff 2: My pleasure. Enjoy your stay!

➢ **Useful Expressions for Better Understanding of Dialogue 3**

(1) I see that you have done your E-check in.
我看到您已经完成了电子自助入住办理。

(2) First, please click the "without reservation" bar. Then, you can see the terms and conditions.

首先，请点击"无预订"栏。然后，您就可以看到相应的条款。

（3）I'll click on the king size bedroom.

我就点击大床房吧。

（4）The information of all your registration is here. You can read and then make a confirmation.

您所有的注册信息都在这里，您可以阅读并确认。

（5）Please put the personal information page of your passport under the scanner.

请把护照上的个人信息页放在扫描仪下面。

（6）You can download the Jinling Hotel App, and reserve our services online, such as restaurant reservation, fitness center reservation and so on.

您可以下载金陵饭店 App，在线预订多个服务项目，如餐厅预订、健身中心预订等。

4. Dialogue 4　The Guest Wants an Extension of the Stay

Staff: Good afternoon, madam. How may I help you?

Guest: I want an extension of my room.

Staff: How many nights do you wish to extend?

Guest: I'd like to extend my stay for 2 more nights.

Staff: Please wait for a moment. I will check if the room is available for the next 2 days.

Guest: OK, no problem.

Staff: Sorry, I'm afraid that there will be someone taking your room.

Guest: Are there any other rooms available?

Staff: Let me check. I'm afraid our hotel will be fully booked for next week. You see, it's the peak season now. We don't have any rooms available now.

Guest: Can you recommend some other hotels for me?

Staff: Maybe you can go to Sheraton, which is another famous five-star hotel with quality service. It's just ten minutes' walk from our hotel.

Guest: Thank you.

➢ **Useful Expressions for Better Understanding of Dialogue 4**

（1）I want an extension of my room.

我想办理房间延期。

（2）I will check if the room is available for the next 2 days.

我查一下接下来的两天这间房是否可用。

（3）I'm afraid that there will be someone taking your room.

恐怕您的房间会有新的客人入住了。

（4）It's the peak season now. We don't have any rooms available now.

现在是旺季，我们现在没有空房了。

（5）Can you recommend some other hotels for me?

你能给我推荐其他酒店吗?

5. Notes Related to Check in Dialogues

①对话中的 registration form 是纸质的登记表,上面标有入住、离店、退房时间和酒店的一些政策。根据酒店所使用系统的不同和客人所使用的证件,来区分是否需要手工填写。一部分酒店管理系统,如果客人使用的是身份证,所有的信息都能够扫描到系统里,不需要手工填写,客人只需签字确认即可。但如果是护照,相应的信息必须手工填写,然后客人签字确认。还有一类酒店管理系统,只能够扫出客人的姓名和出生日期,其他信息就需要客人手工填写,最后签字确认。

②客人登记(入住)时会被安排房间,这是与客人建立关系的重要时刻,可能是客人对酒店的第一印象。如果客人没有预订房间,前台接待人员就有机会为酒店出售房间。在确认付款方式和客人的离店日期后,登记流程即告完成。

③随着新冠肺炎疫情影响,以及客人对于高效和便利服务的要求,酒店开始提供电子自助入住登记服务,客人可以使用酒店的网站,或手机上的酒店应用程序及酒店前台处的智慧酒店自助机进行电子自助入住办理,从而接受酒店提供的无接触式服务。

④Visa pay wave 是用于 Visa 芯片卡的一项新增功能,使用通信技术中最新的近距离无线通信技术(NFC),支持在销售终端进行非接触式支付。该技术旨在使电子支付方式进入传统的以现金交易为主的零售行业,对这些行业的商户而言,如便利店、加油站、公交、快餐店和电影院等,支付的速度和便捷非常重要。

Task Four Procedure, Functional Expressions and Service Culture Points of Check in

1. Look for the Reservation Information

(1) Greet the guests, and check if they have a reservation.

Good afternoon sir/madam! Welcome to ABC Hotel! Do you have a reservation?

(2) Confirm the name of the reservation.

May I know the reservation name?

(3) Check the reservation, and request their passport/ID.

Mr.××/Ms.××, may I have your passport/ID card for registration?

(4) Scan or photocopy the passport/ID.

①Wait a moment Mr.××/Ms.××, I will scan your passport/ID card.

②Mr.××/Ms.××, could I have a copy of your passport/ID card for hotel retention?

2. Confirm the Reservation

(1) Confirm the general information.

Mr.××/Ms.××, you have booked a ×× room for ×× person, and you will be staying here for ×× days. The check out date will be on ××. Is that correct?

(2) Tell guests about their room rate, and confirm if they have made the payment.

①Payment has been made.

Mr. ××/Ms. ××, you've already paid the room rate on the website. If you want the invoice upon your check out, the booking website will send it to you.

②Rate has been negotiated.

Mr. ××/Ms. ××, you booked from our sales manager/×× company, and this is your rate after negotiation.

③Complimentary room.

Mr. ××/Ms. ××, your reservation is a complimentary room that our hotel offers to you. It is a ×× room valid from ×× to ×× (date) and can not be changed.

(3) Ask for the guest's signature.

Mr. ××/Ms. ××, could you double check your reservation? After that, could I have your signature and contact number on the registration form?

3. Collect the Deposit

(1) Mr. ××/Ms. ××, the reservation shows that you haven't paid the room rate yet, so I will charge your room rate plus ×× nights deposit. The total is ×× yuan. How would you like to pay?

(2) Mr. ××/Ms. ××, could you sign your name on the official receipt? And please bring back the white receipt when you check out. We will refund you.

(3) Mr. ××/Ms. ××, since you have paid the room rate, I will charge you ×× for deposit, total ×× yuan. In which payment would you prefer? Mr. ××/Ms. ××, may I have your name on the receipt for our retention?

4. Introduce Information about Hotel Facilities

(1) Information about breakfast.

Mr. ××/Ms. ××, your reservation includes ×× daily breakfast. The breakfast time is from 6 a.m. to 9:30 a.m.. On the weekend, it will be extended to 10:30 a.m.. The restaurant is in the lobby.

(2) Information about Wi-Fi.

Our hotel Wi-Fi is "Hotel UNIC", and no password is required.

(3) Related facilities.

①The pool, spa, and fitness center is on the first floor. They are open from 6 a.m. to 10 p.m..

② We have a shuttle service, and the information is available through the concierge.

The opposite red building is our club house. There is a gym.

③Swimming pool is free for our hotel guests.

(4) Way to contact the front desk.

If you have any questions, you can dial 1 to the front desk. We are at your service anytime.

5. Give Guest the Room Card

Mr. ××/Ms. ××, this is your room card. The elevator is over there. Our bellman will take your luggage to your room. Hope you will have a good stay with us.

6. Culture Points

In receiving guests, we also need to learn to be an active listener. Active listening is a skill. The Chinese symbol for the verb "listening" tells us we must focus, be attentive, and use all of our senses to truly listen. "耳", means ear, engages the ears and tunes out distraction. "王", means king, tells us to combine all the senses to actively listen. The right top part "十", means fully, and "目", means eye, tells us to watch the non-verbal gestures and maintain eye contact. The right middle part "一", means one, tells us to give undivided attention to guests. "心", means heart, tells us to be empathetic with our guests. Once we can do the above, we can be an active listener, and provide better communication and service, increasing our professionalism.

Task Five　　Listening Ability Enhancement

1. Listen to the group check in dialogue and fill in the registration form

Name ____	Surname ____	First/Middle name ____	Nationality ____	Certificate type ____
Mr. /Mrs. /Ms. ____			ID/Others No. ____	
Arrival date ____	Departure date ____		Expiry date ____	
No. of guest(s) ____	Member No. ____		Date of birth ____	
Room type ____	Advance deposit ____		Telephone No. ____	
My account will be settled by ____			Room No. ____	
Voucher　　Others ____			Room rate ____	

2. Listen to the passage of mobile check in and fill in the blanks

From Opera, the reservation can send the ___(1)___ of booking to guests by email. Upon receiving the confirmation ___(2)___ for online check in, the guests just need to ___(3)___ on the online check in link in the email. A guest can check in anytime, without having to ___(4)___ in line upon arrival at his or her hotel. Step one, enter the booking confirmation ___(5)___, and the guest's name. Step two, take a photo of ___(6)___, and provide a self-portrait as instructed by the system. Step three, the system will ___(7)___ the self-portrait and the photo on the ID. If the faces match, guest information will be picked up and automatically filled in the guest profile. Step four, display information for ___(8)___ and enter signature by the guest. Step five, the guest will immediately get a ___(9)___ email of successful check in with a QR code. Now, let's go to the hotel. At the check in counter, a guest will provide ___(10)___ sent to his or her email or stand face to face with the camera. The system will automatically ___(11)___ and display the guest details. The hotel staff will then provide the guest with their ___(12)___.

In case online check in is yet to be ___(13)___, the guest will have to check in at the front desk, where they will be ___(14)___, presenting their ID card and providing their e-signature on the iPad. More than that, using only the ___(15)___, the guest can use all hotel services, such as front desk check in, identity verification at the security gate, restaurants, spa entertainment and more.

扫码
听听力

 Task Six　　Interpretation

(1) Mr. White, you have reserved a double room for two nights, and the check out date is Oct. 7th.
(2) Please try to arrange a non-smoking room with a higher floor.
(3) What kind of room would you like, sir?
(4) How long would you like to stay with us, sir?
(5) I can offer you a walk-in rate of 588 yuan, including breakfast.
(6) I need to copy your passport.
(7) 我们的员工会向您展示如何使用智慧自助机进行电子自助入住办理。
(8) 首先，请点击"无预订"栏。然后，您就可以看到相应的条款。
(9) 您可以下载金陵饭店的 App，在线预订多个服务项目，如餐厅预订、健身中心预订等。
(10) 我想办理房间延期。
(11) 我查一下接下来的两天这间房是否可用/有人预订。
(12) 恐怕您的房间会有新的客人入住了。

Task Seven　　Role Play

1. Make a situational conversation about the check in with reservation
David Smith comes to the front desk of the Ritz-Carlton, Nanjing. He has

reserved a single room with a daily rate of 678 yuan per night. The dates for his stay are from May 2nd to May 6th, 5 days in all and the contact number of David Smith is 0028-3 3473 2768. You are the receptionist, please handle the check in.

2. Make a situational conversation about a group check in

David Smith, the tour leader of a business group from Italy, who will attend a business fair in Nanjing, came to the front desk of Jinling Hotel with his group members. They are going to check in. Gu Hua, a travel agent reserved 16 standard rooms for them for 6 nights. Gu Hua's telephone number is 5648 7790. You are the receptionist, please handle the check in.

3. Make a situational conversation about helping guests to deal with E-check in

Jason White is at the front desk of Jinling Hotel. He wants to try the E-check in with the hotel self check in kiosk. You are the receptionist, please help him handle the E-check in.

Task Eight   Extended Professional Knowledge Reading

Hotel Online Check in

The COVID-19 pandemic has forced hotels to dramatically evolve in a short space of time taking into account the latest health and safety guidelines as well as the changing needs of guests.

Putting guests first and creating an experience that makes them feel safe and secure while they still enjoy their stay is the key to the longevity of the hotel in these uncertain times. With everything up in the air, hotels have to adapt quickly to new solutions and new regulations that are required throughout the hospitality industry.

Technology is a huge help. Even before COVID-19 struck, hotels were tapping into ways they could communicate with their guests before, during, and after their stays, and they were turning to tech solutions to help them do this.

When it comes to the check in process, guests will jump on anything that makes it easier on them. Remote or online check in can save the guest a lot of time and appeals to those who are looking for a minimum of human contact before they settle into their room.

Here are the main reasons you should consider online check in at your hotel. It is convenient for the guest, reduces queues in the lobby, improves the customer relationship, showcases your website and other parts of your property, reduces staff workload, and enhances guest experience. Moreover, the twenty-four hour online check in could be used to increase marketing and direct bookings. Mobile check in is a great way to streamline property operations and the guest experience.

Online check in is not difficult. It's quick to set up and enables you to check

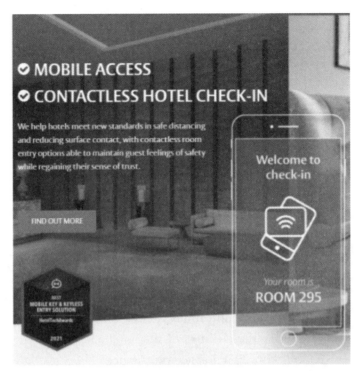

guests in safety right away. No training is needed! A range of integrations with property management systems, payment providers, and mobile key solutions ensures it ties in with your long-term holistic solutions.

(1) Read the passage and write down the benefits of online check in

_____

_____

(2) Decide if the following statements are true(T) or false(F), according to the passage

(   ) ① Many hotels start to launch the online check in only because of the COVID-19 pandemic.

(   ) ② Putting guests first and creating an experience that makes them feel safe and secure is the key to the longevity of the hotel in these uncertain times.

(   ) ③ Remote or online check in can save the guest a lot of time and appeals to those who are looking for a minimum of human contact.

(   ) ④ The twenty-four hour online check in could be used to increase marketing and reservations.

(   ) ⑤ Online check in can't improve the customer relationship, but can showcase your website and other parts of your property.

Unit 4
Concierge Service

Unit Objectives

After studying this unit, you should be able to do the following:
Knowledge & Ability Objectives
1. grasp the steps in offering bell service and information service;
2. be familiar with the terms and sentence patterns of concierge;
3. know the qualifications for the concierge;
4. describe the facilities of the hotel and places out of the hotel;
5. deal with digital concierge service.

Quality Objectives
1. identify the significance of helping guests with various needs professionally;
2. become an excellent concierge with responsibility and patience;
3. cultivate the ability to respect different cultures.

Task One Lead-in

1. Discussion

(1) What are the qualities to be a fine concierge?

(2) What duties does the concierge perform?

2. Brainstorming

Look at the picture, the concierge is helping the guest at the concierge desk. What may be the situation? What are they saying? Please discuss with your group members and write down the sentences that they might say.

Concierge: _____

Unit 4　Concierge Service

(Note: the above picture is quoted from the following website
http://europe.chinadaily.com.cn/world/2015-12/25/content_22808267_5.htm.)

Guest: _____

Task Two　Words and Expressions

concierge	[ˈkɒnsieəʒ] n. 礼宾部；礼宾员；礼宾服务	minibar	[ˈmɪnibɑː(r)] n. 客房小酒吧
luggage cart	行李车	A/C	空调
humid	[ˈhjuːmɪd] adj. 潮湿的	towel	[ˈtaʊəl] n. 毛巾
muggy	[ˈmʌgi] adj. 闷热的	remote control	遥控器
sticky	[ˈstɪki] adj. 黏性的；闷热的	directory	[dəˈrektəri] n. 指南；名录
elevator	[ˈelɪveɪtə(r)] n. 电梯	sightseeing	[ˈsaɪtsiːɪŋ] n. 观光
facilities	[fəˈsɪlətiz] n. 设施	mobile	[ˈməʊbaɪl] adj. 移动的
apparatus	[ˌæpəˈreɪtəs] n. 器械	convenient	[kənˈviːniənt] adj. 方便的
presume	[prɪˈzjuːm] v. 设想	transportation	[ˌtrænspɔːˈteɪʃn] n. 交通
city-view	城市景观	digital concierge	数字礼宾
deluxe	[dɪˈlʌks] adj. 豪华的	virtual	[ˈvɜːtʃuəl] adj. 虚拟的
insert	[ɪnˈsɜːt] v. 嵌入	status	[ˈsteɪtəs] n. 状态
slot	[slɒt] n. 狭槽	login	[ˈlɒgɪn] v. 登录
luggage rack	行李架	miscellaneous	[ˌmɪsəˈleɪniəs] adj. 混杂的；各种各样的

			Continued
safe	[seɪf] n. 保险箱	instant messenger	即时通信
the Confucius Temple		夫子庙	
Dr. Sun Yat-sen's Mausoleum		中山陵	

Task Three Sample Dialogues

1. Dialogue 1 Luggage Service

Staff: Good evening, sir. Welcome to Jinling Hotel. I am the bellman, let me help you with your luggage.

Guest: Thank you.

Staff: Are these all your luggage?

Guest: Yes, all together 4 pieces.

Staff: Please wait a minute, I will get a luggage cart. (After a while) Thank you for waiting, I will show you the way to the front desk.

Guest: Thanks.

(On the way to the front desk)

Staff: Do you like the weather here?

Guest: It's so hot and humid. I am hoping for a clear day.

Staff: What is the weather like in your country now?

Guest: Quite cool, and more importantly, it's dry.

Staff: It's probably pretty like the weather in the northern part of China. In Nanjing, it's quite hot, but it's very muggy because of the high humidity.

Guest: It's so sticky.

Staff: Here is the front desk. I will be here waiting for you.

(Mr. Allen finishes checking in)

Staff: Mr. Allen, your room is on the 18th floor. This way to the elevator please.

Guest: Yes, thank you. By the way, could you tell me something about the facilities in your hotel?

Staff: Certainly, sir. There is a full range of top-class restaurants and bars in our hotel.

Guest: But I want to know something about the fitness center. Is there a gym?

Staff: Oh, yes sir. We have a very well equipped body-building gym with all the latest apparatus. It is on the 10th floor.

Guest: Good, I presume you have a swimming pool?

Staff: Of course, we have a swimming pool, which is also on the 10th floor.

Guest: I see, thank you very much for the information.

Staff: Happy to help. Here we are and this is your room. You can open the door with your room card. Besides, you can open the door with our hotel's App. Have a nice day.

➢ **Useful Expressions for Better Understanding of Dialogue 1**

(1) Welcome to Jinling Hotel. I am the bellman, let me carry your luggage.
欢迎光临金陵饭店,我是行李员,我来帮您拿行李。

(2) It's so hot and humid. I am hoping for a clear day.
天气真是闷热,要是天气晴朗就好了。

(3) In Nanjing, it's quite hot, but it's very muggy because of the high humidity.
南京的天气很热,但是感觉闷主要是因为湿度太高。

(4) This way to the elevator please.
电梯在这边。

(5) By the way, could you tell me something about the facilities in your hotel?
顺便问下,你能给我介绍一下酒店的设施设备吗?

(6) I presume you have a swimming pool?
我估计你们酒店有游泳池吧?

(7) Besides, you can open the door with our hotel's App.
另外,您还可以通过我们酒店的 App 来开门。

2. Dialogue 2　Room Introduction

Staff: Here is your room, Mr. Allen. Let me help you open the door. May I have your room card, please?

Guest: Certainly, here you are.

Staff: (the bellman opens the door) After you, Mr. Allen.

Guest: Thank you.

Staff: Your room type is city-view deluxe double room. I hope you will like it.

Guest: The view of the room is perfect, and the room looks very nice too.

Staff: Your room key is inserted in the electricity slot to turn on the electricity. May I put your suitcase on the luggage rack?

Guest: Yes, thank you.

Staff: The room safe is in the closet. I recommend you put all your valuables in the safe.

Guest: Got it. Could you show me how to use it?

Staff: After you put your valuables in the safe and close the door, you need to enter a five number code to lock the safe. When you want to open the safe, just enter the same code.

Guest: OK, it's so easy.

Staff: The minibar is in the cabinet which is under the TV, and the price list is on the minibar. The complimentary tea and coffee are on the table. And the hotel room service is available 24 hours per day.

扫码
听听力

Guest: Very good.

Staff: Here is the master switch. And this is the A/C control, you can set the temperature as you want. If you need more pillows or towels, just call the front desk and they will help. The telephone number is on the phone.

Guest: Very convenient. Can you introduce the TV program?

Staff: No problem. Here is the remote control. And this is the program list, which includes 50 programs and 10 English programs. Besides, here is our hotel directory. You can find information about our facilities and service in it.

Guest: Thank you, you are so helpful.

Staff: I am always at your service. Is there anything I can do for you before I leave your room?

Guest: No more, you almost explained everything. You did a great job.

Staff: You are welcome. If you have any questions, you can call us and we are always at your service.

Guest: Got it, thank you so much.

Staff: It's my pleasure. Hope you will enjoy your stay with us.

➢ **Useful Expressions for Better Understanding of Dialogue 2**

(1) After you, Mr. Allen.

艾伦先生，您先请。

(2) Your room type is city-view deluxe double room.

您的房型是城市景观豪华大床房。

(3) Your room key is inserted in the electricity slot to turn on the electricity.

您的房卡插在卡槽以便通电。

(4) The complementary tea and coffee are on the table.

免费的茶叶和咖啡就在桌子上。

(5) Here is the master switch.

这是总控开关。

(6) If you need more pillows or towels, just call the front desk and they will help.

如果您需要更多的枕头或毛巾，您可以打电话给前台。前台的同事会帮助您。

3. Dialogue 3　Sightseeing Information

Staff: Good morning, sir. What can I do for you?

Guest: The front desk directed me here to ask you for sightseeing advice. I'd like to walk around the city tomorrow. Can you give me some suggestions?

Staff: No problem, sir. Would you like to see something natural or historical?

Guest: I heard that Nanjing is a city with a long history. So where do you think I should start my sightseeing?

Staff: The Confucius Temple is always a good place to begin.

扫码
听听力

Guest: But, I have already visited the Confucius Temple during my last visit here. So, do you have any other suggestions?

Staff: Have you been to Dr. Sun Yat-sen's Mausoleum? It is a world-famous scenic spot.

Guest: Can you tell me more about it?

Staff: Dr. Sun Yat-sen's Mausoleum is the tomb of Dr. Sun Yat-sen and is regarded as a masterpiece among all buildings of the former Republic of China. It is located in the Purple Mountain area, which is also a wonderful place for walking.

Guest: That's very interesting information. If I want to visit Dr. Sun Yat-sen's Mausoleum, can you help me arrange the transportation?

Staff: Sure, sir. Would you like me to arrange it now?

Guest: Not now and I will let you know if I want to go there. Thank you very much.

Staff: It's my pleasure. Enjoy your day.

> **Useful Expressions for Better Understanding of Dialogue 3**

(1) The front desk directed me here to ask you for sightseeing advice.
前台指引我到这边来问你关于旅游的建议。

(2) Would you like to see something natural or historical?
您是喜欢自然风光景点还是历史景点?

(3) So where do you think I should start my sightseeing?
那你认为我应该先去哪里游览呢?

(4) The Confucius Temple is always a good place to begin.
从夫子庙开始会是一个不错的选择。

(5) Have you been to Dr. Sun Yat-sen's Mausoleum?
您去过中山陵吗?

(6) It is a world-famous scenic spot.
这是一个举世闻名的旅游景点。

(7) Would you like me to arrange it now?
您需要我现在为您安排吗?

4. Dialogue 4　Digital Concierge[①]

Staff: Good evening, madam. What can I do for you?

Guest: I was told that there is a digital concierge. Can you tell me what a digital concierge is?

Staff: As your concierge, it is my pleasure to do this, madam. Digital concierge is a virtual concierge mobile platform.

Guest: What is the function of this platform?

Staff: By using our digital concierge, you can make requests on this platform. You can see the status of your requests on it. And you can also communicate directly with

扫码
听听力

the hotel concierge.

Guest: It sounds nice. Can you tell me more about it?

Staff: To use digital concierge on your phone, first download the App and then login with your username and password provided on your room card cover.

Guest: Great, then how to make a request?

Staff: Firstly, you need to enter the digital concierge, then select the MAKE A REQUEST button. Secondly, select a request category, such as sightseeing. Thirdly, select a specific request and enter your request details. Finally, select SUBMIT request. And that's all.

Guest: If the request I wanted is not listed on digital concierge, what should I do?

Staff: If you don't find the request you are looking for, you can make a miscellaneous request.

Guest: Got it.

Staff: You can view all your requests on the page. For details of your requests, you can enter that specific request.

Guest: Oh, I see. Can I reply to the digital concierge for further communication?

Staff: Of course. You can reply to the digital concierge through the instant messenger function.

Guest: That's convenient.

Staff: You will also receive an alert when your request has been completed.

Guest: That's so considerate.

Staff: Thank you. For more information, you can download our digital concierge App. Is there anything I can do for you?

Guest: No more, thank you.

Staff: It's my pleasure, goodbye.

➢ Useful Expressions for Better Understanding of Dialogue 4

(1) Digital concierge is a virtual concierge mobile platform.

电子礼宾是一个虚拟的移动端礼宾平台。

(2) Firstly, you need to enter the digital concierge, then select the MAKE A REQUEST button.

首先您需要进入电子礼宾,之后选择"提出请求"按键。

(3) If you don't find the request you are looking for, you can make a miscellaneous request.

如果您找不到您所需的请求,您可以选择其他请求。

(4) You can reply to the digital concierge through the instant messenger function.

您还可以使用即时通信的功能回复电子礼宾的信息。

(5) You will also receive an alert when your request has been completed.

当您的请求完成之后,您还会收到一条提示。

5. Notes Related to Concierge Dialogues

①concierge,酒店的礼宾员,负责行李搬运、解答客人在入住期间的咨询,在对客服务中起着相当重要的作用。他们会在客人到达酒店的时候迎接,为客人整理、搬运行李并引领客人到前台办理入住,同时解答客人提出的疑问。在客人离开的时候,他们会帮助客人把行李从房间运送到客人的车上。

此外,他们还负责传递相关物件给客人,为客人提供所需的信息,协助客人预订演唱会、剧院、餐厅或旅游行程。提供当地景点信息,包括购物、用餐等。同时为客人提供交通方面的帮助。他们的工作对于酒店的顺利运营非常重要,在打造酒店形象方面发挥着重要作用。

Task Four Procedure, Functional Expressions and Service Culture Points of Concierge

1. Procedure and Functional Expressions of Concierge

(1) Bellman service procedure.

Greet guest	Good morning/afternoon/evening, Sir/Madam. Welcome to ×× Hotel.
Offer luggage service	Sir/Madam, how many pieces of luggage do you have? Is there anything valuable or breakable in your luggage? Let me get a luggage cart for you, please wait for a moment.
Lead guest to the front desk	Sir/Madam, this way please. Our lobby is on the 20th floor. Please wait for the elevator. Sir/Madam, this way to the elevator, please.
Escort guest to check in	Sir/Madam, this is our front desk colleague ××. I will show you to your room when you finish check in.
Lead guest to the elevator	Sir/Madam, this way please. May I have your room card? To protect our guests' security, we need to swipe the room card to take the elevator.
Enter the room	Sir/Madam, after you. Sir/Madam, may I put your luggage on the luggage rack?

Continued

Introduce hotel services and facilities	Breakfast: our breakfast is served on 18th floor from 6:30 a.m. to 10:00 a.m.. And you need to tell your room number to the hostess. Restaurant: our Chinese restaurant is on the 19th floor, lunch time is from 11:00 a.m. to 1:00 p.m.. And dinner time is from 5:00 p.m. to 10:00 p.m.. Gym: our gym is on the 8th floor, it is equipped with a full range of the latest apparatus. It is open 24 hours. Spa: our spa is on the first floor, it is open from 6:00 p.m. to 10:00 p.m.. Recreation Center: the opposite white building is our recreation center. There is the swimming pool, which is free for our hotel guests. The rest of entertainment such as billiards and in-room golf needs to be reserved. For the other detailed information, you may dial 0 to the front desk in advance. They shall be happy to serve you.
Introduce room facilities	Sir/Madam, may I introduce our room facilities for you? This is the minibar/safe/remote control/switch. For Wi-Fi connection, the password is 88888888. This is the A/C control.
Say goodbye	Is there anything I can do for you? I am always at your service. Have a nice day. If you have any questions, you may dial 0 to the front desk, we are at your service anytime.

(2) Luggage storage and claim.

Upon guests' arrival	Good morning/afternoon/evening, Sir/Madam. How may I assist you?
Store luggage	Is there anything valuable or breakable in your luggage? Please write down your name/room number/phone number on the luggage tag.
Claim luggage	May I have your luggage tag? Sir/Madam, may I have your name/room number/phone number?
Confirm	Sir/Madam, you have stored 4 pieces of luggage, please confirm and sign your name here.

2. Service Culture Points of Concierge

Small talk is a good way to begin to communicate with our guests. In the customer service industry, this means we, as hotel concierge, should be comfortable when we talk with guests on a regular basis and let our guests feel welcome. It's easy to talk to someone you already know, but what about a stranger who speaks another language? In the hotel, you may often be in such a position where you'll need to talk to the guests and make conversation with them.

We should respect people with different cultures, especially when we, to some extent, are representing the image of China. Therefore, as the hotel concierge, we should, on the one hand, take advantage of having small talk with our guests while on the other hand, we should avoid inappropriate topics. The following table listed topics recommended as well as topics that should be avoided.

What is not suitable for small talk	What is okay for small talk
Are you single or married?	How long have you been in our hotel?
How old are you?	You come here for business or for pleasure?
How much money do you make?	What do you think so far?
What is your political views?	Are you enjoying the sights?
Do you believe in God?	Where are you from?
Do you have some health problems?	Do you get used to the weather here?

In general, we shouldn't talk about our guests' privacy, especially when some Chinese may regard this as acceptable talks. It seems that the topic of small talk is not a big deal, but it does represent the extent to which we are willing to take others into our considerations. If we can be aware of this, then we can improve not only our industry professionalism but also our inclusive culture.

Task Five Listening Ability Enhancement

1. Listen to the dialogue of luggage service and fill in the blanks

Staff: Good evening, sir. I'll show you to your room. Is this ___(1)___?
Guest: That's right.
Staff: Is there anything ___(2)___ or breakable in your bag?
Guest: Yes, there is a bottle of Brandy.
Staff: Would you mind taking the bottle? I'm afraid the contents might break.
Guest: Sure, no problem.
Staff: Thank you, sir. May I have your ___(3)___ please?
Guest: Yes, here you are.
Staff: Thank you sir. Your room is on the 15th floor. Please follow me.
(When they arrive at the guestroom, the concierge unlocks the door and switches on the light)
Staff: After you, sir. May I put your bags on the ___(4)___?
Guest: No, thanks. Just put them anywhere.
Staff: Here is your room key. Is this the ___(5)___ of your bags?

扫码
听听力

Guest: Let me see. Yes, that's correct.

Staff: May I hang your coat in the closet, sir?

Guest: Ah, yes. Please do.

Staff: Shall I ___(6)___ for you?

Guest: Yes, that's a good idea.

Staff: You can ___(7)___ the TV with this remote control. This is the ___(8)___, and the ___(9)___ is over there. This is the ___(10)___ and the ___(11)___ is here.

Guest: Thank you for your introduction.

Staff: Hope you will ___(12)___ here.

2. Listen to the dialogue of facilities and recreational items introduction, and tick off the facilities and recreational items mentioned in the dialogue

☐Health Center	☐Massage
☐Beauty Salon	☐Swimming Pool
☐Table Tennis	☐Yoga Class
☐Meditation Class	☐Chinese Restaurant

3. Listen to the passage of taking the elevator and fill in the blanks

Staff: The ___(1)___ is this way.

Guest: I see.

Staff: ___(2)___, sir.

Guest: Thank you.

Staff: ___(3)___?

Guest: Well, I don't like ___(4)___ and I felt tired when I arrived in Shanghai.

Staff: I hope you will have a ___(5)___ stay with us.

Guest: Thanks, I hope so too.

Task Six Interpretation

(1) By the way, could you tell me something about the facilities in your hotel?

(2) Your room type is city-view deluxe double room. I hope you will like it.

(3) The complementary tea and coffee are on the table.

(4) We advise you where to eat, visit, or shop during your stay here in Nanjing.

(5) Digital concierge is a virtual concierge mobile platform.

(6) 天气真是闷热，要是天气晴朗就好了。

(7) 您的房卡插在卡槽以便通电。

(8) 这是一个举世闻名的旅游景点。

(9) 您还可以使用即时通信的功能回复电子礼宾的信息。

(10) 当您的请求完成之后，您还会收到一条提示信息。

Task Seven Role Play

1. Make a situational conversation about the luggage service

Mindy Smith arrives at Marriott, Nanjing. The bellboy comes over to help her with her luggage. Mindy Smith gets several pieces of luggage. You are the bellboy, you are supposed to help Mindy Smith with her luggage. Besides, you need to show Mindy Smith the way to the front desk, as well as the way to her room after her checking in. Don't forget to have an appropriate small talk with Mindy Smith on the way to the front desk and to the guestroom.

2. Make a situational conversation about room introduction

You are the bellboy, you are going to escort Mr. Donald to his room. Please introduce the main room facilities to Mr. Donald.

3. Make a situational conversation about sightseeing

Cindy White wants to visit some scenic spots in her spare time. She goes to the concierge desk for some sightseeing advice. You are the concierge, please arrange a two-day tour plan for her.

4. Make a situational conversation about helping guests to deal with digital concierge

Mindy Smith is at the concierge desk of Marriott Hotel. She wants to try using digital concierge. You are the concierge, please help her handle the digital concierge.

Task Eight Extended Professional Knowledge Reading

What are the Benefits of Using a Digital Concierge in Hotels?

A digital concierge, also known as a virtual concierge, is a type of artificial intelligence that can be used to provide assistance to hotel guests. It is a customer-facing technology that is often used with mobile devices to provide information beyond what would traditionally be provided by a concierge, like flight status or weather forecast. In addition, it can also provide services a traditional concierge would, such as planning events, arranging to have flowers sent to the room, or booking a restaurant.

What are the benefits of using a digital concierge in hotels? There are a lot of benefits to using a digital concierge in hotels, such as saving on human resources, increasing customer satisfaction, promoting services, and the help guests more efficiently. So let's take a look one by one.

Save on human resources: one of the key benefits of a digital concierge is the fact

(Note: the above picture is quoted from the following website https://lp.ux-digital.co.uk/digital-concierge.)

that you can save on human resources. You essentially give guests the tools to educate themselves to help themselves rather than rely on staff to help them. In addition, guests can get instantaneous information such as directions and set their own wake-up calls.

Increase customer satisfaction: nothing is more disgruntling to a guest than having to wait in a long line to ask a simple question. This is where a digital concierge comes in. Simple questions can be answered in just a click, or via instant messages sent to their mobile application. Being able to resolve things quickly helps with guest satisfaction because they feel like they are being helped and having a personalized experience.

Help guests more efficiently: digital concierges also allow you to help guests more efficiently because the simple problems can be answered by their smart phones. They can request a wake-up call, make their own reservations for amenities such as spa services, or even request a table at the hotel restaurant. You no longer have to have dedicated staff to help with these simple requests.

Promotion of services: one of the most notable benefits of a digital concierge is the ability to promote services and cross-sell without being too obvious. The curious guest will browse through the digital concierge, and discover that they can easily book amenities and a table at the hotel's restaurant with the help of the assistant.

Question discussion based on the reading.
①How can digital concierge save on human resources?
②How can digital concierge increase customer satisfaction?
③How can digital concierge help guests more efficiently?
④How can digital concierge promote services?

Unit 4
练习答案

Unit 5
Check out Service

Unit Objectives

After studying this unit, you should be able to do the following:

Knowledge & Ability Objectives

1. know the different ways of making payment;

2. grasp the steps in checking out guests and online self-check out;

3. be familiar with the terms and sentence patterns of check out;

4. check out guests in English in different situations;

5. deal with online self-check out.

Quality Objectives

1. identify the significance of checking out guests professionally;

2. become an excellent cashier with responsibility and hospitality.

Task One Lead-in

1. Matching

(1)    A. Japanese Yen(JPY ¥)

(2)    B. Won(KRW ₩)

Unit 5　Check out Service

（3）　　　　　　C. United States dollar（USA＄）

（4）　　　　　　D. Russian Ruble（RUB ₽）

（5）　　　　　　E. Pound(GBP £)

（6）　　　　　　F. Euro(EUR €)

2. Sequencing

The following statements describe the procedures of check out. Discuss with your partner and put them in the correct order.

A. Asking for room card and confirming the guest's room type, rate and length of stay

B. Greeting the guest

C. Informing the room attendant to check the room

D. Preparing the bill

E. Asking the way of payment

F. Settling the bill

G. Giving the receipt and saying goodbye

Correct order：_____

Task Two　Words and Expressions

change	[tʃeɪndʒ]n. 零钱	receipt	[rɪˈsiːt]n. 收据；小票
ledger	[ˈledʒə(r)]n. 分类账簿	incidental	[ˌɪnsɪˈdentl]adj. 附带发生的；次要的
expense	[ɪkˈspens]n. 花费；费用	credit card	n. 信用卡
souvenir	[ˌsuːvəˈnɪə(r)]n. 纪念品	exchange rate	n. 兑换率

			Continued
exchange memo	n. 外汇兑换水单	denomination	[dɪˌnɒmɪˈneɪʃn] n. 面额
overcharge	[ˌəʊvəˈtʃɑːdʒ] v. 多收费	total	[ˈtəʊtl] n. 总数；总额；总计 v. 共计 adj. 全部的；总的
account	[əˈkaʊnt] n. 账号；账目	invoice	[ˈɪnvɔɪs] n. 发票
deduct	[dɪˈdʌkt] v. 扣去；减去	stand for	v. 代表
service charge	n. 服务费	luggage assistance	n. 行李协助
Pre-authorization	[ˌpriːˌθɔːraɪˈzeɪʃn] n. 预授权	be equivalent to	等于；相当于
look forward to	盼望	check out	结账；退宿

扫码
听听力

Task Three Sample Dialogues

1. Dialogue 1 Checking out Guest

Staff：Good morning. Can I help you?

Guest：Yes，I'd like to check out now.

Staff：Can I have your name and room number，please?

Guest：John Smith，room 1208.

Staff：May I have your room key，please?

Guest：Sure. Here you are.

Staff：Just a moment，please.

Mr. Smith. Here is your bill. Would you like to check it out?

Guest：I'm sorry. What does SC stand for?①

Staff：That's for service charge.

Guest：I see.

Staff：How would you like to make the payment②，Mr. Smith?

Guest：I'd like to pay in cash.

Staff：That'll be 2180 yuan.

Guest：Here you are.

Staff：Here's your change and receipt.

Guest：Thank you.

Staff：You are welcome. We are looking forward to serving you again.

➤ Useful Expressions for Better Understanding of Dialogue 1

(1) I'd like to check out now.
我想办理结账退宿。

(2) Can I have your name and room number, please?

请问您的姓名和房号。

(3) How would you like to make the payment, Mr. Smith?

史密斯先生,您打算如何付款呢?

(4) Here is your bill.

这是您的账单。

(5) What does SC stand for?

SC 是什么费用?

(6) That's for service charge.

这是服务费。

(7) I'd like to pay in cash.

我将使用现金结账。

(8) I'll send a bellboy up to help you with your luggage.

我让行李员帮助您拿行李。

(9) Here's your change and receipt.

这是您的找零和收据。

(10) I'm looking forward to serving you again.

期待能再次为您服务。

2. Dialogue 2 Checking out Group Guest

Staff: Good morning, Ms. Jane. How are you today?

Guest: Pretty good, thanks. I'm leaving today. Here is the room card.

Staff: Thank you. Have you enjoyed your stay?

Guest: Sure.

Staff: Thank you. As I know, your room charge is paid by the conference ledger?

Guest: That's right. I believe there are only a few incidental charges to settle.

Staff: Seems right. Do you have any last-minute expense such as a minibar?

Guest: I don't think so.

Staff: Great. Then here is your bill. If everything is correct, please sign here.

Guest: (Sign and give it back) Here you are.

Staff: Would you like me to put these charges on the credit card you gave us?

Guest: Actually, I shall pay them in cash.

Staff: No problem. (Take the money and give back changes) Here is your change and here is your copy of the bill. The shuttle bus your conference arranged to the airport is leaving from the right side of the main entrance. Do you need any luggage assistance?

Guest: Not really. But could you hold my luggage for two minutes? I want to grab a cup of coffee before I go.

Staff: Of course.

Guest: Thanks. (Leave, then come back with coffee) Now I'm ready for my

扫码
听听力

luggage.

Staff: Here you are, Ms. Jane. Have a safe trip and look forward to having you back.

> Useful Expressions for Better Understanding of Dialogue 2

(1) Have you enjoyed your stay?
您对这次的住宿满意吗？

(2) Your room charge is paid by the conference ledger?
您的房费由这次会议主办方支付吗？

(3) Do you have any last-minute expense, such as minibar?
您有即时消费吗，比如迷你吧？

(4) Would you like me to put these charges on the credit card you gave us?
您需要我把账记在您给我的信用卡上吗？

(5) The shuttle bus your conference arranged to the airport is leaving from the right side of the main entrance.
会议方安排的机场巴士从酒店大门的右边出发。

(6) Do you need any luggage assistance?
您需要行李服务吗？

(7) Could you hold my luggage for two minutes?
你可以帮我看管下行李吗？

(8) Have a safe trip.
祝您一路平安。

3. Dialogue 3　Changing Foreign Currency into RMB③

Staff: Good afternoon. What can I do for you, madam?

Guest: Good afternoon, I'd like to change some Euros into RMB for souvenirs.

Staff: My pleasure. According to today's exchange rate, 100 Euros are equivalent to 747 yuan. How much would you like to change, madam?

Guest: 500 Euros. Here you are.

Staff: Please fill in the exchange memo. Be careful to fill in your passport number, the total, your room number, and sign your name here as well.

Guest1: Here you are. Is that right?

Staff: That's right. What denominations would you like?

Guest: Any kind will be OK.

Staff: Here is 3735 yuan. Please count it. Here is your memo. Please keep it well. You are required to show it at the customs when you go back to your country.

Guest: No problem. By the way, how can I change my remaining RMB back into Euros when I go back to my country?

Staff: You can change it back here, or at the Bank of China and the Airport Exchange Counter. You'll be required to show the memo there, too.

扫码
听听力

Note

Guest: Thanks a lot.

Staff: You are welcome. Glad to have served you.

➢ **Useful Expressions for Better Understanding of Dialogue 3**

(1) I'd like to change some Euros into RMB for souvenirs.

我想把一些欧元兑换成人民币买纪念品。

(2) According to today's exchange rate, 100 Euros are equivalent to 747 yuan.

根据今天的外币兑换率，100 欧元可兑换 747 元人民币。

(3) How much would you like to change, sir?

您想兑换多少金额呢？

(4) Please fill in the exchange memo.

请填写外币兑换单。

(5) What denominations would you like?

您想要什么面额的呢？

(6) You are required to show it at the customs when you go back to your country.

当您回国的时候，海关需要您出示。

(7) How can I change my remaining RMB back into Euros when I go back to my country?

当我回国的时候，我怎么把剩余的人民币换成欧元呢？

(8) Of course, you can change it back here, or at the Bank of China and the Airport Exchange Counter.

当然您可以在这换回来，也可以在中国银行或者机场外币兑换处换回来。

4. Dialogue 4   the Guest Has Been Overcharged

Staff: Good morning, sir. How can I help you?

Guest: Good morning. I'd like to check out.

Staff: May I have your room card?

Guest: Sure.

Staff: Please wait for a moment. (After checking the information and the room)

Mr Johnson, here is your bill. It totals 2688 yuan. How would you like to make the payment?

Guest: Wait a minute. I think there is something wrong with my bill. I have been overcharged. What do they mean? (Pointing to the items on the bill)

Staff: L means laundry service, while RESTR stands for restaurant.

Guest: I didn't use any laundry service in my room. How did it happen?

Staff: I'm sorry, Mr Johnson. There must be some mistakes. Please wait a moment. I'll check it. (After a while …)

I'm terribly sorry, Mr. Johnson. We have charged another Mr. Johnson's bill into your account. I do apologize for the mistake.

扫码
听听力

Guest: It doesn't matter. Everyone makes mistake.

Staff: Thank you for your understanding. Your bill totals 2380 yuan, deducting 308 yuan for the laundry service. How would you like to pay?

Guest: By credit card.

➤ Useful Expressions for Better Understanding of Dialogue 4

(1) I have been overcharged.

我被多收了费用。

(2) There must be some mistakes.

肯定出错了。

(3) L means laundry service, while RESTR stands for restaurant.

L 指的是洗衣服务,RESTR 代表餐饮。

(4) We have charged another Mr Johnson's bill into your account.

我们把另一位 Johnson 先生的账单记到您的账户上了。

(5) Your bill totals 2380 yuan, deducting 308 yuan for the laundry service.

减去 308 元的洗衣服务费,您的账单一共是 2380 元。

5. Notes Related to Check out Dialogues

①SC 即 Service Charge,酒店根据星级不同在消费时将收取不同的服务费,比如五星级酒店一般收取 15%,四星级酒店一般收取 10% 左右的服务费。酒店收取服务费一般是用于抵充该笔收入对应的税款。

②Method of Payment,随着智慧酒店(Smart Hotel)的兴起,酒店触摸自助服务终端已经进入各大酒店大堂。通过自助服务终端,客人可以直接办理登记入住、结账退宿等业务。E-check out 主要分两个步骤:插入房卡和点击退房结算。常见的支付方式有 Alipay、WeChat Pay、Apple Pay、Union Pay、PayPal、VISA、Master 等。

③Changing Foreign currency into RMB 中国现行的外汇管理法规规定,在中华人民共和国境内,禁止外币流通并不得以外币计价结算。部分星级酒店、中国银行及机场外币兑换处可受理旅行支票、外币兑换业务。在外币兑换时需出示护照,填写兑换单。兑换单需妥善保管,一是在出海关回国时需要出示;二是将未使用完的人民币兑换回之前的外币也需要出示。

Task Four   Procedure, Functional Expressions and Service Culture Points of Check out

1. Look for the Staying Information

(1) Greet the guests, ask for the room card.

Good afternoon sir/madam! May I have your room card?

(2) Confirm the guest's name, room type, rate and length of stay.

Mr. ××/Ms. ××, you have been staying in deluxe single from May 10th to

May 15th for 5 days at a rate of 568 yuan per night.

(3) Check the last-minute consumption.

① Mr. ××/Ms. ××, do you have last-minute consumption?

② Mr. ××/Ms. ××, have you used a minibar this morning?

2. Preparing the bill

Mr. ××/Ms. ××, just wait a moment. I'll draw up your bill right now.

Mr. ××/Ms. ××, it's 800 yuan in total. Would you like to check it?

3. Make sure the way of payment

① Mr. ××/Ms. ××, how would you like to make the payment/settle your bill?

② Mr. ××/Ms. ××, may I know your way of payment?

③ Mr. ××/Ms. ××, how would you like to pay?

4. Settle the bill

The following are the procedures and functional expressions:

Procedure	Functional Expressions
Explain the bill	Mr. ××/Ms. ××, your bill totals 890 yuan, including 15% service charge. This 80 yuan is for laundry service. There might be some mistakes on the bill.
Foreign currency or cheque exchange service	① Foreign Currency. Mr. ××/Ms. ××, how much would you like to change? Today's exchange rate is 6.84 yuan for one U.S. dollar. ② Traveler's Check. Mr. ××/Ms. ××, according to the exchange rate, 100 U.S. dollars come to 684 yuan for traveler's check. Mr. ××/Ms. ××, please sign your name here again on the traveler's check and sign the memo. ③ Notes. Mr. ××/Ms. ××, please keep well of your exchange memo, you are required to show it at the customs when you go back to your country, or you want to change your money back. Mr. ××/Ms. ××, you can go to the Bank of China or Airport Exchange Counter to change your money back.
Provide additional service	① Luggage Assistance Mr. ××/Ms. ××, do you need luggage assistance? I'll send a bellman to help you with your luggage. ② Transportation Service Mr. ××/Ms. ××, shall I call a taxi for you to the airport? Or, you can take the hotel shuttle bus to the airport.

Continued

Procedure	Functional Expressions
Give receipt or invoice	Mr. ××/Ms. ××, here is your receipt. If you need an invoice, I'll change it to you right now.

5. Say Goodbye to the Guest

Mr. ××/Ms. ××, I hope you have enjoyed your stay with us. I wish you a good journey and look forward to serving you again.

6. Culture Points

Hospitality, as a fine tradition of the Chinese, has been changing in the forms in the long history, while the enthusiasm has not diminished. In history, China has had friendly co-communication with neighboring countries. When the foreign envoys came to China, the imperial court at that time showed great enthusiasm for them and gave thoughtful accommodation, without losing  the grace of a civilized country. Today, the hospitality tradition of the Chinese is still praised by all countries. The hotel front desk is an important place to show hospitality. From welcoming the guests to sending them away, we should make it all in a hospitable atmosphere.

How to be hospitable?

(1) Amiable.

(2) Helpful.

(3) Obliging.

(4) Informative.

Task Five   Listening Ability Enhancement

1. Listen to the dialogue of check out, and decide what each short dialogue is about and fill in the form with correct information

	Total Amount	Method of Payment	Deposit	Pre-authorization
Dialogue 1				
Dialogue 2				
Dialogue 3				
Dialogue 4				

Unit 5 Check out Service

2. Listen to the group check out dialogue and fill in the form

Name of the guest	
Requirement for the room	
Method of payment	
Parking place	
Time of coming back	
Last-minute consumption(Y/N)	
Where to go	
Luggage assistance(Y/N)	

3. Listen to the passage of check out and fill in the blanks

Staff: Good morning, sir. How may I help you?

Guest: Check out, please.

Staff: All right. ___(1)___ please?

Guest: Here you are.

Staff: (Check the computer and inform the floor to check the room) Mr. Porker?

Guest: That's right.

Staff: ___(2)___?

Guest: Quite nice.

Staff: Thank you very much. ___(3)___, Mr. Porker. And the total amount is ___(4)___. If it is correct, please sign here.

Guest: (Check the bill and sign) Here you are.

Staff: Thank you, sir. Would you like to ___(5)___ you provided at check in?

Guest: Yes, please. Here you are.

Staff: Thank you. (Swipe the card and provide the guest with the slip) ___(6)___.

Guest: OK.

Staff: (Print guest's copy of the bill) Here is your copy of the bill, Mr. Porker. Do you need any ___(7)___?

Guest: I'm fine. Just tell me ___(8)___.

Staff: ___(9)___ there is a stand. The doorman over there will take care of that for you, Mr. Porker. (Point the direction)

Guest: Great. Thank you very much.

Staff: You are welcome, Mr. Porker. Have a nice day and ___(10)___.

Task Six Interpretation

(1) How do you want to settle your bill, sir, in cash or by credit card?

(2) The total amount of pre-authorization is 400 pounds.

(3) According to today's exchange rate, 100 dollars is equivalent to 747 yuan.

(4) Please keep your exchange memo well, because you are required to show it when you want to change your money back.

(5) Your bill totals 2380 yuan, deducting 308 yuan for the laundry service.

(6) 您是我们酒店的 VIP 客户，可以给您打 8 折。

(7) 这 188 元是什么费用？

(8) 非常抱歉，账单出错了。

(9) 您可以自助办理结账退宿。

(10) 祝您旅途愉快，期待下次再为您服务。

Task Seven　Role Play

1. Make a situational conversation about checking out guests

Annie Clair comes to the front desk of the Hilton, Sanya to check out. Her bill totals 1800 yuan, including 15% service charge. She prefers to pay in cash and the invoice is needed. Besides, she needs a luggage assistant and transportation service to the airport. You are the cashier, please handle the check out.

2. Make a situational conversation about currency exchange service

Anna Jessie comes to the front desk of Marriott and asks for a currency exchange service. She wants to change 1000 dollars into RMB. You are the cashier. According to today's exchange rate, please help him change the money. Be sure to tell her the importance of the exchange memo.

3. Make a situational conversation about helping guests to deal with E-check out

Jason Smith is at the front desk of Ritz-Carlton Hotel. He wants to try the E-check out with the hotel self-check in kiosk. Please help him handle the E-check out.

Task Eight　Extended Professional Knowledge Reading

Check out Service

The duties of cashiers are a lot, such as settling guest's account, making changes, cashing traveler's checks, exchanging foreign currencies, balancing accounts at the close of each shift, and so on. Check out service means settling the account for the guest. Like the check in procedure, check out procedure takes only a few minutes when the system works efficiently.

Usually the hotel has an accounting system to maintain guest's consumption items within the hotel and keep them up-to-date. All charges must be entered or

Unit 5 Check out Service

posted on their accounts as soon as possible. In addition to the charges for the guests' rooms, there may also be charges resulting from the use of telephone, the laundry service, the restaurant, and room service. All the financial transactions not only must be posted, but also be checked for accuracy.

Many hotels have a check out time. The check out time is usually set at noon. Guests who check out after 12:00 a. m. normally will be charged half of the rate. Those who check out after 6:00 p. m. will be charged the full rate. Many commercial hotels receive a large number of guests in the late afternoon or early evening, between 4:00 p. m. and 8:00 p. m.. This is often a result of a heavy concentration of arriving airline flights during those hours.

With the development of the smart hotel, hotel self-service kiosk can allow customers to check in and check out by themselves in one minute. It can also greatly save labor costs. During the peak hour, one person at the hotel reception desk can easily handle the check in and check out, greatly improving work efficiency and saving labor costs.

Self-service check out process:

1. Insert room card
2. Click on the check out settlement
3. Print the receipt

The check out process is quite simple. In general, the whole operation is very convenient and fast. The hotel self-service kiosk not only improves the service quality of the hotel, but also gives consumers a good using experience. Based on it, the hotel's brand, reputation, and competitiveness has been improved.

(1) Answer and questions and write down your answer on the blanks

①What is check out service?

___

___

②What are the common regulations about check out time?

③What is the common procedure E-check out?

(2) Decide if the following statements are true(T) or false(F), according to the passage

(   )① Cashiers are only responsible for settling guest's account, making changes, cashing traveler's checks, exchanging foreign currencies and balancing accounts.

(   )② Usually the hotel has an accounting system to maintain guest's consumption items within the hotel and keep them up-to-date.

(   )③ All charges must be entered or posted on guests' accounts as soon as possible.

(   )④ The check out time is usually set in the afternoon.

(   )⑤ Hotel self-service kiosk can allow customers to check in and check out by themselves in one minute.

Unit 6
Room Cleaning and Laundry Service

Unit Objectives

After studying this unit, you should be able to do the following:

Knowledge & Ability Objectives

1. grasp the steps in basic housekeeping service;
2. be familiar with the terms and sentence patterns of room cleaning and laundry service;
3. know the qualifications for the room attendants;
4. know the hotel laundry service policy;
5. effectively offer basic housekeeping services in English.

Quality Objectives

1. identify the significance of the housekeeping department in a hotel;
2. become an excellent room attendant with responsibility, hardworking, being honest and keeping their words and taking good care of public property.

Task One Lead-in

1. Brainstorming

Look at the picture What room amenities and facilities do you know in it? Have a discussion with your partner.

Room amenities and facilities: _____

_____

2. Sequencing

The following statements describe the job procedure of cleaning a guest room. Discuss with your partner and put them in the correct order.

(图片来源:百度图片)

A. Cleaning the bathroom

B. Stripping the beds by stripping the sheets

C. Knocking the door twice and say "housekeeping"

D. Inspecting the bed for stains and making the bed

E. Dusting and sterilizing

F. Vacuuming the floor and removing any spots

G. Removing the dirty linen and rubbish from the room

H. Replace all other items provided by the hotel

I. Checking whether the pillows and curtains are in good shape and in the proper position

Correct order：_____

Task Two　Words and Expressions

housekeeping	[ˈhaʊskiːpɪŋ]n. 客房部	occupancy	[ˈɒkjəpənsi]n. 占有率；入住率
check out room	已结账房	doorknob	[ˈdɔːnɒb]n. 球形门把手
efficiency	[ɪˈfɪʃnsi]n. 效率	chambermaid	客房女服务员
room attendant	客房服务员	the turn-down service	夜床服务
convenient	[kənˈviːniənt]adj. 方便的	celebrate	[ˈselɪbreɪt]vt. 庆祝
boiled water	白开水	typical	[ˈtɪpɪkl]adj. 典型的
the drinking water	饮用水	draw the curtains	拉窗帘
cozy	[ˈkəʊzi]adj. 舒适的	drawer	[drɔː(r)]n. 抽屉
writing desk	写字台	laundry	[ˈlɔːndri]n. 要洗的衣服
laundry form	洗衣单	dye	[daɪ]v. 给……染色

Unit 6　Room Cleaning and Laundry Service

Continued

valet	['væleɪ]*n.* 服务员	charge	[tʃɑːdʒ]*n.* 费用
refund	['riːfʌnd]*v.* 退款	definitely	['defɪnətli]*adv.* 明确地
brand	[brænd]*n.* 品牌	receipt	[rɪ'siːt]*n.* 收据
replacement	[rɪ'pleɪsmənt]*n.* 代替者	inconvenience	[ˌɪnkən'viːniəns]*n.* 不便

Task Three　Sample Dialogues

1. Dialogue 1　Room Cleaning Service

Mr. White and his wife are going out for dinner and he encounters the room attendant in the corridor.

Staff: Good morning, Mr. and Mrs. White. You're looking great today!

Guest: Thank you! We are going out for dinner. Oh, it's nearly 11:30 a.m., and our room has not been made up yet.

Staff: I'm sorry, your room number is 1120, am I right, Mr. White? But when I got to your room this morning, the "Do Not Disturb" light was on.

Guest: Really? We forgot that.

Staff: It doesn't matter, Mr. White. I'll be there as soon as I finish this one. Every day I have a section of 14 rooms, and I usually do the check out rooms and the rooms with "Please Service the Room" sign hung on the doorknob first unless there is a request. As you may know, we have to get rooms ready for the new guests as soon as possible. And if you like, we can make up your room first next time.

Guest: Good, thanks a lot. I suppose there's a lot of work for you. Is the hotel full?

Staff: You are right, Mr. White. It is the peak season in Wuhan and the occupancy is very high.

Guest: I wonder how long it takes you to clean a room.

Staff: We usually finish cleaning one room in about thirty minutes.

Guest: What efficiency! Thank you, you've done a good job!

Staff: It's very kind of you to say so, Mr. White. Have a nice day, Mr. and Mrs. White.

> Useful Expressions for Better Understanding of Dialogue 1

(1) Oh, it's nearly 11:30 a.m., and our room has not been made up yet.
哦，快 11 点半了，我们的房间还没有打扫。

(2) It is the peak season in Wuhan and the occupancy is very high.
现在是武汉的旺季，入住率非常高。

(3) Every day I have a section of 14 rooms, and I usually do the check out rooms

and the rooms with "Please Service the Room" sign hung on the doorknob first unless there is a request.

我每天需要打扫14个房间，除非客人要求，我通常先打扫退房房间和门把手上挂有"请打扫房间"字样的房间。

(4) As you may know, we have to get rooms ready for the guests as soon as possible.

您可能知道，我们必须尽快把房间整理好以备新顾客使用。

(5) We usually finish cleaning one room in about thirty minutes.

我们打扫完一间客房大约需要30分钟。

(6) What efficiency! Thank you, you've done a good job!

效率真高！谢谢，你做得很好！

(7) It's very kind of you to say so, Mr. White.

您这么说真是太好了，怀特先生。

2. Dialogue 2　The Turn-down Service⑤

The Whites are having a rest in the room when a chambermaid knocks at the door.

Staff：Housekeeping. May I come in?

Guest：Yes, please.

Staff：Good evening, Mr. and Mrs. White, May I do the turn-down Service for you now?

Guest：Oh, thank you. But you see, we are having some friends to celebrate my birthday here. Could you come back later?

Staff：Happy birthday, Mr. White. What time would it be convenient for you?

Guest：Could you come again in 2 hours?

Staff：Of course, Mr. White. Is there anything else I can do for you?

Guest：Can you please bring us more bottles of pure water? We'd like to have typical Chinese tea in our room with friends later.

Staff：Mr. White, this is the electric kettle. Let me boil a pot of water for you.

(15 minutes later)

Staff：Housekeeping. May I come in?

Guest：Yes, please.

Staff：Mr. White, here is a cake specially designed by our chef. Happy birthday to you.

Guest：What a surprise! How sweet you are! Thank you so much.

Staff：My pleasure. It's growing dark. Would you like me to draw the curtains for you?

Guest：Why not? That would be so cozy.

Staff：May I turn on the lights for you?

Guest：No, thanks. I like this atmosphere.

扫码
听听力

Staff: Yes, sir. Anything else I can do for you?

Guest: No more. You're a smart girl indeed. Thank you very much.

Staff: I'm always at your service. Goodbye, Mr. and Mrs. White, and do have a very pleasant evening.

➤ **Useful Expressions for Better Understanding of Dialogue 2**

(1) Mr. and Mrs. White, May I do the turn-down service for you now?
怀特先生、怀特太太，我现在可以为你们开夜床服务吗？

(2) Certainly, Mr. White, What time would it be convenient for you?
当然可以，怀特先生，您什么时候方便？

(3) Could you come again in 2 hours?
你能在两个小时后再来吗？

(4) Can you please bring us more bottles of pure water?
能给我们拿几瓶纯净水吗？

(5) We'd like to have typical Chinese tea in our room with friends later.
待会我们会用地道的中国茶在房间招待朋友。

(6) Mr. White., this is the electric kettle. Let me boil a pot of water for you.
怀特先生，这是电热水壶，我来给您烧一壶水。

(7) It's growing dark. Would you like me to draw the curtains for you?
天色越来越暗了。需要我把窗帘拉上吗？

(8) May I turn on the lights for you?
我可以为您打开灯吗？

(9) Anything else I can do for you?
还有什么需要我做的吗？

(10) I'm always at your service.
随时为您服务。

(11) Goodbye, Mr. and Mrs. White, and do have a very pleasant evening.
再见，怀特先生、怀特太太，祝您们度过一个愉快的夜晚。

3．**Dialogue 3　Laundry Service**

A guest is calling for laundry service in the room.

Staff 1: Good morning, housekeeping. May I help you?

Guest: Yes. I have some laundry to do.

Staff 1: Well, would you fill in the laundry form, please? The laundry bag and laundry form are in the drawer of the writing desk.

Guest: Would you please send someone to pick up my laundry?

Staff 1: Your room number, please?

Guest: 1102.

Staff 1: OK, Mrs. White, a valet will be up in a few minutes.

(A few minutes later)

扫码
听听力

Staff 2: Housekeeping. May I come in?

Guest: Yes. Come in, please.

Staff 2: Good morning, Mrs. White. I came to collect your laundry.

Guest: Yes. Will you have the laundry done today?

Staff 2: Well, for regular service, laundry is collected before 11a. m. and returned at 6p. m. the same day. I'm afraid it's too late for today's laundry. We can deliver it tomorrow around 6p. m.

Guest: Oh, we're going to set off tomorrow morning.

Staff 2: Then if you have express service, we'll deliver it within four hours at a 50% extra charge.

Guest: That's all right. And there is a stain on this overcoat. I'd like it removed before it's dry-cleaned.

Staff 2: What kind of stain is it, Mrs. White?

Guest: I spilt some coffee on it.

Staff 2: We will do our best to remove the stain, but we cannot guarantee the result.

Guest: OK. And I'd also like to have this sweater washed by hand in cold water. It might shrink otherwise.

Staff 2: By hand in cold water. I understand. Please mark it on the laundry list. Is there anything else I can do for you, Mrs. White?

Guest: Nothing else at the moment. Thank you very much.

Staff 2: It's our pleasure to serve you.

➢ Useful Expressions for Better Understanding of Dialogue 3

(1) I have some laundry to do.

我有些衣服要洗。

(2) Well, would you fill in the laundry form, please?

好的,请您先填写洗衣单,好吗?

(3) The laundry bag and laundry form are in the drawer of the writing desk.

洗衣袋和洗衣单在写字台的抽屉里。

(4) Good morning, Mrs. White. I came to collect your laundry.

怀特太太,早上好。我来取您要洗的衣服。

(5) Will you have the laundry done today?

今天能把衣服洗好吗?

(6) Well, for regular service, laundry is collected before 11a. m. and returned at 6p. m. the same day.

一般是上午11点前取,当天下午6点送回。

(7) I'm afraid it's too late for today's laundry. We can deliver it tomorrow around 6p. m. .

Unit 6　Room Cleaning and Laundry Service

今天的洗衣时间恐怕太晚了。我们可以明天下午6点左右送到。

(8) Oh, we're going to set off tomorrow morning.

哦，我们明天早上就要结账离店了。

(9) Then if you have express service, we'll deliver it within four hours at a 50% extra charge.

如果您选择快洗服务，我们可以在4小时内送到，但要加收50%的费用。

(10) And there is a stain on this overcoat. I'd like it removed before it's dry-cleaned.

这件大衣上有个污渍。请先去除再干洗。

(11) What kind of stain is it, Mrs. White?

怀特太太，这是什么污渍？

(12) We will do our best to remove the stain, but we cannot guarantee the result.

我们会尽力去除污渍，但不能保证。

(13) And I'd also like to have this sweater washed by hand in cold water.

这件毛衣请用冷水手洗。

(14) It might shrink otherwise.

否则可能会缩水。

(15) Please mark it on the laundry list.

请在洗衣单上注明。

4．Dialogue 4　Laundry Damage

Staff: Good morning, Mr. Smith. I came here to deliver your laundry. Where would you like me to put it?

Guest: On the bed, please. Thank you.

Staff: My pleasure, Mr. Smith. You'd better have a check, please.

Guest: OK. Let me have a look. Oh, my goodness, my shirt is white, but now it's pink.

Staff: I'm awfully sorry your shirt has been dyed, Mr. Smith. We do apologize for that.⑥

Guest: And look at my sweater. It's shrunk after you cleaned it.

Staff: I'm terribly sorry, Mr. Smith. May I take the sweater back to the Laundry? They may be able to restore it.

Guest: OK, How long will it take?

Staff: About 2 hours for quick service.

Guest: How about my shirt?

Staff: According to our hotel policy, the hotel will be responsible for the damage only up to 10 times the amount of item charge. The laundry charge is 30 yuan, so you can get 300 yuan. Also, we will refund the laundry charge.

Guest: That's unfair. It was a birthday gift given by my wife. I'm not exactly sure

扫码
听听力

about the price, but it's definitely more than 300 yuan.

Staff: I'm terribly sorry, sir. Could you have a replacement here and give us the receipt? We will refund the cost of your new shirt.

Guest: I'm attending a meeting here and I have no time for shopping. I'm going back to the U. S. tomorrow.

Staff: In that case, could I get you a similar replacement here, the same brand if possible?

Guest: I have no choice.

Staff: We'll make it as soon as possible and try to meet your demand. And we'll send back your sweater as soon as possible. We apologize sincerely for the inconvenience again.

➢ **Useful Expressions for Better Understanding of Dialogue 4**

（1）I'm awfully sorry your shirt has been dyed, Mr. Smith.
非常抱歉，史密斯先生，您的衬衫被染色了。

（2）And look at my sweater. It's shrunk after you cleaned it.
看看我的毛衣。洗过之后缩水了。

（3）May I take the sweater back to the Laundry? They may be able to restore it.
我可以把这件毛衣送回洗衣房吗？他们也许能修复它。

（4）The hotel will be responsible for the damage only up to 10 times the amount of item charge.
酒店应负责赔偿最高 10 倍洗衣费的损坏费。

（5）The laundry charge is 30 yuan, so you can get 300 yuan. Also we will refund the laundry charge.
洗衣费是 30 元，所以您可以得到 300 元赔偿。我们也会退还洗衣费。

（6）I'm not exactly sure about the price, but it's definitely more than 300 yuan.
我不太确定这件衬衣的价格，但肯定超过 300 元。

（7）Could you have a replacement here and give us the receipt?
您能否去买一件新衬衣，然后给我们收据？

（8）We will refund the cost of your new shirt.
我们将返还您新衬衫的费用。

（9）In that case, could I get you a similar replacement here, the same brand if possible?
如果是这样的话，我可以帮您买一件衬衣，如果可以的话，同一个品牌的，可以吗？

（10）We'll make it as soon as possible and try to meet your demand.
我们将尽快去买，尽量满足您的要求。

5. Notes Related to Housekeeping Dialogues

①Room Cleaning Service 清理房间基本礼仪。
如门上有"请勿打扰（DND）"（Do Not Disturb）的字牌，则不应进房。进房前一定

要先按门铃，或轻敲房门，即使是空房也应如此，以防房内有客人（Housekeeping. May I come in?）。

如果客人在房间，则应礼貌地问好，询问客人是否可以清理房间（Housekeeping, May I clean your room now?）。

不要触摸客人的贵重物品，也不要随意移动客人的物品，必要时须先征得客人同意（May I move it?）。

②Good morning, Mr. and Mrs. White. You're looking great today!

"早上好，怀特先生、夫人。您们看上去气色不错。"在酒店服务规范中，要求员工为客人服务时要尽量使用客人的名字及适当地赞美客人。这样可以提高客人对酒店服务的满意度，从而对酒店留下难忘的印象。

③Every day I have a section of 14 rooms …

我每天要打扫 14 间客房。

一般来讲，客房部的员工每天的标准工作量是清理打扫 14 间客房。

④It is the peak season in Wuhan.

在武汉，现在是酒店的旺季。

一般来讲，旅游的旺季就是酒店的经营旺季。

peak season 旺季   high season 旺季
off season 淡季   low season 淡季

⑤The Turn-down Service

开夜床服务，它是和"ROOM SERVICE"同等重要的酒店服务，该项服务的内容包括：开地灯（switching on the floor lamp）、摆拖鞋（tidying the slippers）、检查小酒吧（checking the minibar）、清洁客房（cleaning up the room）、倒垃圾（emptying the waste bin）、铺床（making the bed）、清洁卫生间（cleaning the bathroom）、换布件（replacing the lines）、关闭窗帘（drawing the curtains）等。为 VIP 客人开夜床，还应包括加水果（replenishing fresh fruits）、小食品（refreshments）、浴袍（bathrobes）、报纸（newspapers）等服务。

夜床服务的时间，一般从下午 5:30 或 6 点开始或按客人要求做，一般夜床服务在晚 9 点之前做完，因为 9 点以后再去敲门为客人做夜床服务势必打扰客人休息。

⑥We do apologize for that.

道歉态度要诚恳，一般有以下句子表达：

… but I'm awfully sorry that …

I'm terribly sorry, sir.

We do apologize for that.

We apologize sincerely for the inconvenience.

Task Four Procedure, Functional Expressions and Service Culture Points of Room Cleaning and Laundry Service

1. Working Procedure of Room Cleaning Service

(1) Greet the guests.

Good morning. Housekeeping. May I help you?

Good afternoon, I am the room attendant. What can I do for you?

(2) Ask for information.

May I help you?

May I have your name, sir/madam?

May I have your room number?

When would you like me to clean your room, sir/madam?

Would you like me to clean up your room right now, sir/madam?. We will come and clean your room immediately.

(3) Express gratitude.

Thank you for your suggestion.

I am very/extremely grateful to you.

It's very kind of you to say so.

It's very thoughtful of you to remind me of that.

Thank you very much for everything. You have certainly made my stay a most pleasant one.

Thank you so much. You've been so helpful.

I appreciate your help very much.

I appreciate your consideration.

(4) Respond to gratitude.

You are welcome.

You are always welcome.

Not at all.

Don't mention it.

It was nothing ... That's all right ...

It's my pleasure.

I am always at your service.

Don't worry about it.

Forget it.

It's my pleasure. Just let me know if there's anything else I can do for you.

2. **Working Procedure of Laundry Service**

(1) Greet the guests.

Good morning. Housekeeping. May I help you?

Good afternoon. I am the valet. What can I do for you?

(2) Ask for information.

May I have your name, sir/madam?

Could you tell me your room number, please?

When would you like me to collect your laundry, sir/madam?

Please notify us on the laundry list whether you need your clothes ironed.

(3) Hotel laundry policy.

We charge 50% more for express service, but it only takes 4 hours.

If the clothes are damaged, the indemnity shall not exceed ten times the laundry charge.

Any complaints must be made within 24 hours of delivery.

Usually it takes two days to get the laundry done.

(4) Laundry English sentences.

Could you send someone up for my laundry, please?

A valet will be up in a few minutes.

I have a silk dress which I don't think is colorfast. Will the color run in the wash?

3. Culture Points

The upper left part of the Chinese character is the pronunciation of it; the upper right part is "力", the strength, meaning working hard and trying to do more; The bottom is "心", the heart, meaning that when working, you should think more and do your best to help others.

The service work of the housekeeping department is complicated, and the most basic requirement of the guest room is comfortable, tidy and safe. In order to meet the standard, staff need to make great efforts, bear hard work, observe and think carefully to improve skills and efficiency. With those, staff can provide guests with high-quality and personalized service.

Task Five Listening Ability Enhancement

1. Now listen to a passage and answer the following questions

(1) When the "Do Not Disturb" sign is on, what may the guests do according to the passage?

(2) What does the "Do Not Disturb" sign indicate?

(3) Does the "Do Not Disturb" sign mean the guest does not wish his room to be cleaned?

(4) What should the room attendant do when the "Do Not Disturb" sign is on?

(5) What should the room attendant do if the "Do Not Disturb" sign is off?

2. Listen to the dialogue and fill in the blanks

Room Cleaning

Staff: __(1)__ , may I come in?

Guest: Sure, come in.

Staff: Good morning, madam. My name is Susan, __(2)__ . May I clean up the room now?

Guest: Would you come back ___(3)___? I've not finished yet.

Staff: Certainly, madam.

(10 minutes later)

Staff: May I come in?

Guest: Yes, please. Excuse me, how long does it take to make up the room?

Staff: It takes ___(4)___ your room, madam. ___(5)___ will help to clean up everything in your room.

Guest: Can I stay in my room and ___(6)___ while you're working?

Staff: Certainly, Madam.

3. Listen to the dialogue and fill in the blanks

Laundry Service

Staff: Good morning, can I help you?

Guest: Would you please send someone up for my ___(1)___, please? Room ___(2)___, White.

Staff: Certainly, Mrs. White. A valet will be up in a few minutes.

Guest: I have ___(3)___, which I don't think is colorfast. Will the color run in the wash?

Staff: We'll ___(4)___ the skirt. Then the color won't run.

Guest: You're sure? Good! And the lining of my husband's jacket has come unstitched. It might tear over further while being washed.

Staff: Don't worry, madam. We'll stitch it before ___(5)___.

Guest: That's fine. Now, when can I have my laundry back?

Staff: Usually it takes ___(6)___ to have laundry done. All deliveries will be made before ___(7)___. And we also have express service.

Guest: I'd have the express because I'm going to a party this evening. How soon will they be done?

Staff: It only takes ___(8)___.

Guest: What is the difference in price?

Staff: We ___(9)___ for express, but it only takes 3 hours.

Guest: Well, thank you. Oh, I think your valet is at the door.

Staff: Please feel free to ask him anything. Also, please refer to your ___(10)___ for further information. Thank you for calling and have a nice day.

Task Six　Interpretation

(1) 您需要我什么时候打扫房间?

(2) 怀特先生、怀特太太,我现在可以为你们开夜床服务吗?

(3) 您能不能派人到2115房取我的送洗衣服呢?

Unit 6 Room Cleaning and Laundry Service

（4）现在恐怕已经过了今天的洗衣时间。

（5）洗衣单和洗衣袋在写字台右边第一个抽屉里。

（6）我们可以在4小时内送回，但需要多收50%的费用。

（7）I'd like this sweater dry-cleaned/washed by hand in cold water.

（8）The hotel should be responsible for the damage up to 10 times the laundry charge.

（9）Please call the housekeeping, when you want your room done.

（10）I usually do the check out rooms and the rooms with "Please Service the Room" sign hung on the doorknob first unless there is a request.

（11）Would you like me to draw the curtains for you?

（12）For clothes received before 11:00 a.m., we'll deliver them to your room by 9:00 p.m. the same day; and for those received before 3:00 p.m., you may get them back by noon the next day.

Task Seven   Role Play

1. Make a situational conversation according to the form

Mr. Smith	Valet
Wash s shirt	Name：_____
Do not starch	What：_____
Hand washing in cold water	How：_____
Tomorrow evening around 6 o'clock	When：_____

2. Make a situational conversation according to the information below

The room maid is offering a turn-down service. The guest asks what the turn-down service means.

Room maid：

（1）Knocks at the door.

（2）Offers to do a turn-down service.

（3）Explains what turn-down service is：switch on the floor lamp, tidy slippers, check the minibar, clean up the room, empty the waste bin, make the bed, clean the bathroom, replace the linens, draw the curtains, etc.

（4）Agrees to bring in a new bathrobe.

（5）Gives the paper to the guest.

（6）Agrees to refill the minibar.

（7）Agrees and asks for further help.

Guest：

（1）Responds with permission.

(2) Asks about the meaning of turn-down service.

(3) Says about the unavailability of a bathrobe in the bathroom.

(4) Asks if the maid has brought the evening newspaper.

(5) Says about the unavailability of refreshments in the minibar.

(6) Wonders about the possibility of having several extra chairs in the room, and gives the reason.

(7) Needs four cups of hot coffee.

Task Eight Extended Professional Knowledge Reading

Read the laundry list and fill in it according to the guest's request

Mr. Smith in Room 1218 wants to have his suit and sweater washed and pressed, suit light starched at 3:00 p.m. on October 14th. He will have a meeting at 8:00 p.m. that evening.

Regular service: Garments collected by 9:00 a.m. will be returned the same day after 6:00 p.m.;

Express service: Garments will be returned in 4 hours from the time of collection. A 50% express charge will be applied.

GUEST COUNT	OFFICE COUNT	ITEM (LAUNDRY - PRICES FOR INDIVIDUAL ITEMS ONLY)	LAUNDRY	COST	GUEST COUNT	OFFICE COUNT	ITEM (DRY CLEANING OR PRESS ONLY - PLEASE CIRCLE SERVICE REQUIRED)	DRY CLEAN	PRESS ONLY	COST
		SHIRT-Plain	4.65				SUITS	13.50	7.00	
		SHIRT-Sport or Dress	4.65				PANTS	8.00	4.00	
		PYJAMAS	7.00				JACKETS	9.00	4.50	
		UNDERSHORTS	2.60				SWEATERS	9.00	4.50	
		UNDERSHIRTS	2.60				COATS	17.25	8.00	
		NIGHT GOWNS	7.00				DRESSES	13.50	8.00	
		LADIES UNDERWEAR	2.60				BLOUSES	7.50	4.00	
		BLOUSES	8.00				TIES	4.50	2.25	
		SOCKS	2.60				SKIRTS	8.00	4.00	
		T-SHIRTS	4.00				SHIRTS	8.00		
		OTHER					SUB TOTAL			
		SPECIAL INSTRUCTIONS					GST			
							TOTAL			

SHIRTS: ☐HANGER ☐FOLDED
STARCH: ☐LIGHT ☐MEDIUM ☐HEAVY
NAME: _____
ROOM#: _____
DATE: _____

ALL CLAIMS MUST BE MADE WITHIN 24 HOURS. Articles requiring extra time & labour will be charged accordingly. We cannot be responsible for more than 10 times the cleaning price. Unless a list of articles accompanies the package, our list must be accepted as being the correct count. Claims for loss or damage must be made within 12 hours, limited to 10x the cleaning price. Please present this bill when making claims.

CALL FRONT DESK FOR INFORMATION
PICK UP BY 9:00 AM - RETURN BEFORE 6:00 PM

Unit 7 Other Services in Housekeeping Department

Unit Objectives

After studying this unit, you should be able to do the following:

Knowledge & Ability Objectives

1. Attend to guests' needs;
2. Fulfill babysitting service;
3. Fulfill adding a bed service;
4. Take care of sick guests;
5. Know what to do when a guest claims that someone has stolen his/her personal belongings/valuables;
6. Know hotel policy about offering special services, for example: borrowing items; changing a room; helping guests deal with the broken facilities in the rooms.

Quality Objectives

Become an excellent room attendant with integrity, and have the ability to offer specialized service.

Task One Lead-in

1. Brainstorming

A guest is calling the housekeeping department to ask for the babysitting service. What are they saying? Please discuss with your group members and write down the sentences that they might say.

Room attendant: _____

_____

Guest: _____

Babysitting Services

(图片来源:百度图片)

2. Discussion

If a registered guest is ill, what would you like to do? Can you bring medicine to him/her?

Task Two　Words and Expressions

wash basin	洗脸盆	stainless steel	不锈钢
leather	['leðə(r)]n. 皮；皮革	strap	[stræp]n. 带子
issue	['ɪʃuː]n. 问题	night stand	床头柜
babysitter	['beɪbɪsɪtə(r)]n. 临时照顾幼儿者	minimum	['mɪnɪməm] adj. 最小的；最低的
Pamper	['pæmpə(r)]n. 帮宝适（纸尿裤品牌）	extra	['ekstrə]adj. 额外的
blanket	['blæŋkɪt]n. 毯子	laptop	['læptɒp]n. 笔记本电脑
Engineering Department	工程部	access	['ækses]v. 使用；访问
install	[ɪn'stɔːl]v. 安装	anti-virus	['ænti'vaɪrəs]adj. 杀计算机病毒的

Task Three　Sample Dialogues

1. Dialogue 1　A Watch is Missing

(Mr. Bush couldn't find his watch, and the room attendant helped him search for it in the room.)

Staff: Housekeeping. May I come in?

Guest: Yes, come in.

Staff: Good morning. Mr. Bush. Could I clean the room for you now?

Guest: Oh, my god. I am going out for a meeting, but I couldn't find my watch. I'm sure I took it off and put it next to the wash basin last night.

Staff: Take it easy, Mr. Bush. I'm sorry about what happened to you. Did you lock your room last night?

Guest: Yes, of course.

Staff: Don't worry, Mr. Bush. The watch must be left in some corner. I will search for it in your room. What color is it?

Guest: Silver stainless steel case with black croco leather strap.

Unit 7　Other Services in Housekeeping Department

Staff: OK. I will look for it carefully in the bathroom.
...
Sorry, Mr. Bush. I didn't find it in the bathroom.
Guest: Then, who will be responsible for my loss?
Staff: Mr. Bush, wait a moment, I will go on searching for it in the bedroom. If your watch was stolen by someone, we'll report it to the police.
(10 minutes later)
Staff: Is this your watch, Mr. Bush?
Guest: Yes, great. Where did you find it?
Staff: It's under the night stand.
Guest: Oh, I made a mistake. Thank you so much.
Staff: I'm glad you have your watch back, Mr. Bush, hope you won't be late for the meeting.
Guest: Yes, I must go now, goodbye.
Staff: Have a nice day, Mr. Bush. If you have any other issues, please feel free to contact us.

➤ Useful Expressions for Better Understanding of Dialogue 1

(1) I'm sure I took it off and put it next to the wash basin last night.
我确定昨晚把它取下来放在洗脸盆旁边了。
(2) Silver stainless steel case with black croco leather strap.
银色不锈钢的表壳，黑色鳄鱼皮表带。
(3) If your watch was stolen by someone, we'll report it to the police.
如果您的手表被人偷了，我们会向警察报告的。
(4) Oh, I made a mistake.
我记错了。
(5) If you have any other issues, please feel free to contact us.
如果您有任何其他问题，请随时与我们联系。

2. Dialogue 2　Receiving a Babysitting Service

(A guest is not in the room this evening, so she needs a babysitter to take care of her children.)
Staff: Housekeeping. Good morning. May I help you?
Guest: I'm Kathy Jenkins at 212. I need a babysitter tonight.
Staff: (The housekeeper begins taking notes) At what time will you need a babysitter, Mrs. Jenkins? We charge 60 yuan for the service by the hour, for a minimum of one hour.
Guest: From eight until eleven.
Staff: OK, Mrs. Jenkins, but we don't take care of children under 18 months old. How old are the children?①

扫码
听听力

Guest: My little girl is two years old and the boy is three.

Staff: That's good. At what time would you like the babysitter to come to your room?

Guest: Just before eight.

Staff: Before eight, OK, Mrs. Jenkins, I will arrange everything for you.

Guest: Thank you very much.

Staff: Is there anything special that you would like the babysitter to do, Mrs. Jenkins?

Guest: The babysitter should just give them some milk and put them in bed.

Staff: Very well.

Guest: The little girl still wears Pampers. I'll leave some on the bed.

Staff: Is there anything else we should know, Mrs. Jenkins?

Guest: No, I think that's about everything.

Staff: I'll arrange for the babysitter right now.

Guest: Thank you very much.

➢ Useful Expressions for Better Understanding of Dialogue 2

(1) I need a babysitter for tonight.

我今晚需要看护婴儿服务。

(2) At what time will you need a babysitter, Mrs. Jenkins?

您什么时候需要看护婴儿服务，詹金斯太太？

(3) We charge 60 yuan for the service by the hour, for a minimum of one hour.

我们按小时收费60元，至少一个小时。

(4) OK, Mrs. Jenkins, but we don't take care of children under 18 months old.

好的，詹金斯太太，但是我们不照顾18个月以下的孩子。

(5) At what time would you like the babysitter to come to your room?

您希望保姆什么时候到您房间来？

(6) Is there anything special that you would like the babysitter to do, Mrs. Jenkins?

有什么特别的事情需要保姆去做吗，詹金斯太太？

(7) The babysitter should just give them some milk and put them in bed.

保姆需要给他们一些牛奶，然后让他们上床睡觉。

(8) The little girl still wears Pampers. I'll leave some on the bed.

小女孩仍然穿着帮宝适。我会留一些在床上。

(9) Is there anything else we should know, Mrs. Jenkins?

还有什么需要我们知道的吗，詹金斯夫人？

3. Dialogue 3　Arranging an Extra Bed

Mr. and Mrs. Smith have just checked in this morning. They are expecting their mother to come to the hotel to join them. Mr. Smith calls the housekeeper asking for

Unit 7 Other Services in Housekeeping Department

an extra bed.

Staff: Housekeeping. Li Feng speaking. How may I assist you?

Guest: Yes, I'd like to have an extra bed in our room. ②

Staff: May I have your name and room number, please?

Guest: I'm Tom Smith. Room 608.

Staff: And what kind of bed do you need? For child or adult?

Guest: What's the difference?

Staff: Mr. Smith, we could offer one baby-crib for child under 12 months free of charge. And one standard extra bed would charge 50% of your room rate. ③

Guest: OK, we will take one for adults.

Staff: When do you wish the bed to be placed in your room, Mr. Smith?

Guest: As soon as possible.

Staff: OK, Mr. Smith, we will have your request registered at the Reception Desk first, and half of one room night rate, that is 300 yuan per night, and will be billed to your room account.

Guest: No problem. Could you bring in one more blanket, please?

Staff: Certainly, Mr. Smith. We will also provide another set of guest supplies in the room.

➢ Useful Expressions for Better Understanding of Dialogue 3

(1) I'd like to have an extra bed in our room.

我想在房间里多加一张床。

(2) And what kind of bed do you need? For child or for adult?

您需要什么样的床？儿童的还是成人的？

(3) We could offer one baby-crib for child under 12 months free of charge. And one standard extra bed would charge 50% of your room rate.

我们可以免费为12个月以下的儿童提供一张婴儿床。加一张标准床的费用是房费的50%。

(4) When do you wish the bed to be placed in your room, Mr. Smith?

史密斯先生，您希望床什么时候放在您的房间里？

(5) OK, Mr. Smith, we will have your request registered at the Reception Desk first, and half of one room night rate, that is 300 yuan per night, and will be billed to your room account.

好的，史密斯先生，我们会先在前台登记，每晚一半的费用即300元将记入您的账户。

(6) Could you bring in one more blanket, please?

请再拿一条毯子进来好吗？

(7) We will also provide another set of guest supplies in the room.

我们还会在房间内再提供一套客人用品。

4. Dialogue 4　Handling Computer Problems

Mr. Taylor's laptop has stopped working in the guest room. He calls the Guest Service Center for help.

Staff 1：Good evening. Guest Service Center. This is Lily speaking. How may I help you?

Guest：Yes. I don't know why my computer, which I have just bought, stopped working. Would you please have someone come over to my room right now?

Staff 1：May I know your room number, please?

Guest：1106.

Staff 1：Yes, Mr. Taylor. You said you have a problem with your computer. I'll call the IT Department. The IT officer will come to your room very soon.

(Knocks on the door)

Staff 2：IT officer. May I come in?

Guest：Yes, please.

Staff 2：What is the matter with your computer, Mr. Taylor?

Guest：I was accessing on the web, but suddenly my computer became very slow, and it took a long time to open a web page or save a file.

Staff 2：Let me have a check. Have you checked the Internet?

Guest：Yes, the network works well and the signal is strong.

Staff 2：Oh, I remember! I heard a kind of computer virus attacked the networks last night. Have you installed anti-virus software on your computer?

Guest：Not yet.

Staff 2：Your computer might have been hit by a virus.

Guest：Can you help me solve the problem?

Staff 2：I'm afraid we couldn't. I suggest having it fixed in the local computer repair shop.

Guest：OK, thank you, can you recommend one?

Staff 2：I noticed your computer brand is Apple, Mr. Taylor. There's one Apple shop across the street downstairs. I can be your guide to the shop.

➢ Useful Expressions for Better Understanding of Dialogue 4

(1) Would you please have someone come over to my room right now?
你现在能派人到我房间来一下吗？

(2) I'll call the IT Department.
我给信息技术部打电话。

(3) The IT officer will come to your room very soon.
信息技术主管很快就到您房间来。

(4) It took a long time to open a web page or save a file.
打开一个网页或保存一个文件需要很长时间。

(5) Have you checked the Internet?

您检查网络了吗?

(6) Yes, the network works well and the signal is strong.

是的,网络运行良好,信号强。

(7) I heard a kind of computer virus attacked the networks last night.

我听说昨晚有一种电脑病毒攻击了网络。

(8) Have you installed anti-virus software on your computer?

您的电脑安装杀毒软件了吗?

(9) Your computer might have been hit by a virus.

您的电脑可能被病毒攻击了。

(10) I suggest having it fixed in the local computer repair shop.

我建议您去当地的电脑修理店修理一下。

5. Notes Related to Check in Dialogues

①But we don't take care of children under 18 months old.

但是我们不提供看护 18 个月以内婴儿的服务。

房务中心(Room Center)接到客人看护婴幼儿服务(child care/babysitting service)要求时,应热情介绍酒店该项服务内容、收费标准(charge)等。询问客人的看护要求,记下房号(room number)、姓名(name)、婴幼儿人数(number of children)、年龄(age)、看护时间(duration),然后向管理员(housekeeper)报告。

②I'd like to have an extra bed in our room.

我想在我们房间内加一张床。

客人在住店期间,无论是打电话到总台还是到房务中心要求加床,服务员都要热情提供服务,记录下房号、加床数量和时间。楼层服务员应在十分钟内铺好加床(make the beds),添加床上用品和房客用品。加床结束后,报告房务中心,并由房务中心反馈至总台,以便登记收费。

③We could offer one baby-crib for child under 12 months free of charge. And one standard extra bed would charge 50% of your room rate.

我们可以免费为 12 个月以下的儿童提供一张婴儿床。加一张标准床的费用是房费的 50%。

Task Four Procedure, Functional Expressions and Service Culture Points of Housekeeping Service

1. Greet the guests

Good morning. I'm the floor attendant. May I help you?

Good afternoon. I am the floor attendant, What can I do for you?

2. Ask for information

May I help you?

May I have your name, sir/madam?

May I have your room number?

3. Hear the guest's report of property loss or theft

I'm sorry to hear that. Would you mind coming with me to my office and telling me what exactly happened?

Could you describe what happened to your property, how it might have been stolen in detail? I'll keep a record.

Shall we check the room one more time again?

Don't worry, we'll try our best to find it in the shortest possible time.

Well, I understand how you feel and we'll try our best to help you. But …

I'm afraid I have to say that the hotel can't be held responsible for your loss.

Would you please calm down? We'll try our best to help you.

Would you please sign your name on the Lost and Found Form?

4. Deal with the situation when the facilities in the house are damaged

Don't worry, sir. I'll inform the Maintenance Department immediately.

But I'm afraid you'll have to pay for the damage.

We'll take care of that. I'll send someone from the Maintenance Department to your room. But I'm afraid you'll have to pay for the damage.

5. Deal with the situation when the guest complains about the malfunction of the facilities in the room

May I have a look at it?

I'll send an electrician from the Maintenance Department to your room.

Just a minute, please. I'll get a technician to come and fix it for you right now.

6. Deal with the situation when a guest is ill

I'm sorry to hear that you are not feeling well.

What's the matter, Mr. Scott?

I'm sorry to hear that. Should I send you to a doctor?

Is there anything I can do for you, Mr. White?

If you need help, just call me at any time.

Hope you'll recover soon.

7. Deal with the situation when items are lost or stolen

I'm sorry to hear that. Would you mind coming with me to my office and telling me what exactly happened, Mrs. Johnson?

Could you describe your bag in detail? I'll keep a record.

Shall we check the room once again?

Don't worry. We'll do our best to find it in the shortest possible time.

Well, I understand how you feel and we'll try our best to help you. But I'm afraid I must say that the hotel can't be held responsible for your loss.

Unit 7 Other Services in Housekeeping Department

8. Deal with the situation when the items are found

Will you please come to our office on the first floor?

You need to sign your name on the Lost and Found Form.

And remember to take your ID card.

9. Culture Points

The Chinese character "信" is a beautiful word that embodies the traditional virtues of our people. It can be seen early in the golden script, with "人" on the left and "言" on the right, "信" means to be honest, trustworthy, not hypocritical, and sincere. "信" is not only one of the important conditions for Confucians to realize the moral principle of "benevolence", but also one of the contents of Confucian moral cultivation. Confucianism regards "信" as the foundation of establishing and governing the country.

As a room service staff, he should be honest and trustworthy, and create greater value for the hotel.

Task Five   Listening Ability Enhancement

1. Listen to the following dialogues and fill in the special items in room form

Special Items in Room Form

Items	Room No.	Required No.	Items	Room No.	Required No.
extra blanket			bed sheet		
bath towel			pillow		
infant cot			ashtray		
heater			bathrobe		
ball pen			light bulb		
vase			toilet paper		
others			towel		
extra bed			remarks		

扫码
听听力

2. Listen to the passage of claim and damage and then fill in the blanks

Claim and Damage

(Mr. Lucas is calling the housekeeper about the broken reading lamp.)

Guest: Hello, operator? This is Lucas speaking.

Staff 1: Yes. What can I do for you?

Guest: I'd like to speak to ___(1)___. I'm in ___(2)___. I have some bad news to tell him.

(The operator puts the call through)

Staff 2: What's the bad news, sir?

Guest: This is Mr. Lucas. I went out this morning and the children were playing ___(3)___ in the room. They smashed ___(4)___ on the desk and ___(5)___. Could you send someone to fix the curtains and bring me another lamp?

Staff 2: Of course, Mr. Lucas. I'll send someone from ___(6)___ to your room. Thank you for calling.

Guest: I'm terribly sorry.

Staff 2: That's nothing. We'll take care of that, M. Lucas. But I'm afraid you'll have to ___(7)___

Guest: Oh, I will.

Staff 2: May I have your room number, sir?

Guest: Room 403.

Staff 2: Yes, Room 403, Mr. Lucas. Don't worry. I'll ___(8)___ it at once. Goodbye.

Guest: Goodbye.

3. Listen to the passage of changing the room and fill in the blanks

Changing the Room

(Mr White wants to change a room. He goes to the assistant manager.)

Staff: Good morning, sir. What can I do for you?

Guest: I'm White in Room 608. Can you ___(1)___ for me? It's too noisy. My wife was woken up several times by the noise ___(2)___ made. She said it was too much for her.

Staff: I'm awfully sorry, sir. ___(3)___. Room 608 is ___(4)___. It is possible that the noise can be heard early in the morning when all is quiet.

Guest: Anyway, I'd like to change our room.

Staff: No problem, sir. We manage it. How about ___(5)___? It's rather quiet. The room rate is ___(6)___ that of Room 608.

Guest: Very well.

Staff: Please fill in this ___(7)___.

(Mr. White goes through the formalities.)

Here's the key to ___(8)___. The bellman will help you ___(9)___. Please return the key to Room 608 to him.

Guest: What efficiency! I hope I'll ___(10)___ tonight.

Staff: Be sure, Mr. White. If there is anything more you need, please let us know.

Unit 7   Other Services in Housekeeping Department

Task Six   Interpretation

(1) We provide guests with laundry service, babysitting service, 24-hour room service and morning call service.

(2) We'll do our utmost to find the missing things.

(3) Our Housekeeping Department has a very good babysitting service.

(4) If your watch was stolen by someone, we'll report it to the police.

(5) The faucet in my room cannot be turned on.

(6) I'll ask the room attendant to put in a new bulb immediately and see if that solves the problem.

(7) We do apologize for the inconvenience.

(8) 我房间里的电视坏了，你什么时候派人来修理？

(9) 我会请电工过去修理空调。

(10) 一名客人把东西送到失物招领处了。

(11) 您希望保姆几点到您的房间？

(12) 您的电脑可能被病毒攻击了。

(13) 这是违反酒店规定的。我陪您去酒店医务室/诊所。

(14) 恐怕我们要收取房间一半的费用，也就是 300 元每晚。

Task Seven   Role Play

Make dialogues according to the situations

(1) There is something wrong with the TV in Mr. White's room. He asks a floor attendant for help.

(2) Mrs. Grace calls the housekeeping that her daughter's necklace is missing, which is a birthday gift. The room attendant tells her it's lucky because someone picked it up and sent it to the Lost and Found Office. In the locket, there is a photo of Mrs. Grace's daughter.

(3) In the evening, the room attendant comes to the guest room for turn-down service, and explains what it is to the guest. The guest requests to add snacks, bathrobes, newspapers and other services. He asked if he could have two more chairs because he will have some Chinese guests coming tonight. He also asks the room attendant to bring in four cups of coffee when the guests come.

(4) After knocking on the door, the room attendant comes in to find the guest in bed with a bad headache. The attendant sends for the doctor who asks him about his

illness. Then the doctor advises him to get plenty of rest and drink plenty of water and prescribes him some medicine.

Task Eight   Extended Professional Knowledge Reading

Modern Technology in Hotel Rooms

Hotel guests demand technology as well as the services offered. A decade ago, the latest technology in a hotel room was voicemail. Five or six years ago, it was luxurious to make reservation by means of the Internet. And today, it is not uncommon that high-tech amenities such as data-ports and Internet access, even food delivery robots and cleaning robots are available in a hotel room.

（图片来源：百度图片）

Almost all the hotels are now using wireless Internet connections into hotel rooms for the convenience of their guests.

Wireless communication system can meet the growing demand for Internet access. Therefore, this headache can be got rid of.

Business travelers are able to enjoy an interactive information and entertainment system in their guest rooms. A flat-panel, active-matrix screen is installed in the desk of the room. By simply touching on it, guests can find information about the hotel, business services available, and local dining, entertaining and recreation activities. The system includes commonly used business software and allows access to guests' e-mail. Guests don't have to take with them their laptops, which are sometimes a burden to them. Not only does the system service as a computer and info-desk, it also offers video games and allows a guest to interact with other players in other hotel rooms or even outside of the hotel. What is more, available in the guest room are reservation assistance, news, weather reports and a virtual jukebox of musical selections.

Unit 7 Other Services in Housekeeping Department

In-room modern amenities do not end there. Bedsides panels control the lighting, air conditioning, radio, television and curtains, there are also in-room signals that indicate incoming faxes. Guests may find it more convenient if all-in-one printer-copier-fax machines are placed in the rooms.

(selected from *21st Century Practical Situational Hotel English* by Wu Yun and Shao Hua)

Exercise 1: translate the following words into Chinese

interactive information _____ business service _____
virtual jukebox _____ video games _____
in-room signal _____ data-ports _____
flat-panel, active-matrix _____ reservation assistance _____
all-in-one printer-copier-fax machine _____ high-tech amenity _____

Exercise 2: answer the questions

(1) Can you list some of the high-tech amenities in a hotel room?
(2) How can a hotel solve guests' computer-related problems?

Unit 7
练习答案

Unit 8
Chinese Restaurant Service

Unit Objectives

After studying this unit, you should be able to do the following:

Knowledge & Ability Objectives

1. grasp the steps in Chinese restaurant service;
2. be familiar with the terms and sentence patterns of Chinese restaurant reservation, food ingredients, ways of cooking, communication, etc.;
3. know the qualifications for the waiters and waitresses;
4. deal with the daily service process of Chinese restaurant, such as reservation, seating the diners, taking orders, recommending dishes and checking the bill.

Quality Objectives

1. explain the basic responsibilities of food & beverage service;
2. implement diversified role plays for Chinese restaurant scenarios;
3. construct professionalism for Chinese cuisine and service culture.

 Task One   Lead-in

1. Brainstorming

Chinese food is very popular with foreign guests all over the world. Please think about what you should pay attention to when serving foreign guests. Try to consider the differences between Chinese and Western food, such as cooking techniques, taste preferences, eating habits, the use of tableware, the culture of paying bills, etc. Please write down your group opinion.

Notes on Chinese Restaurant Service

2. Sequencing

The following statements describe the job procedure of a waiter or waitress in a Chinese Restaurant. Discuss with your partner and put them in the correct order.

A. Greeting the guests;

B. Presenting menus to guests;

C. Serving the food and drinks;

D. Take orders from guests by writing food orders on slips or memorizing them;

E. Passing on the orders to the kitchen staff;

F. Preparing the checks;

G. Escorting guests to the door and performing cleaning duties;

Correct order: _____

Task Two Words and Expressions

vacancy	['veɪkənsi] n. 空房;空缺	celebrate	['selɪbreɪt] v. 庆祝
anniversary	[ˌænɪ'vɜːsəri] n. 周年纪念日	congratulation	[kənˌgrætʃu'leɪʃn] n. 祝贺
private	['praɪvət] adj. 私人的	absolutely	['æbsəluːtli] adv. 完全地
lobby	['lɒbi] n. 大堂	suitable	['suːtəbl] adj. 合适的

Continued

classic	['klæsɪk]adj. 典型的；经典的	Cantonese cuisine	[ˌkæntə'niːzkwɪ'ziːn]n. 广东菜，粤菜
quality	['kwɒləti]adj. 优质的	dim sum	[ˌdɪm 'sʌm]n. 点心
appetizer	['æpɪtaɪzə(r)]n. 开胃菜	ingredient	[ɪn'griːdiənt]n. 食材
sticky	['stɪki]adj. 黏性的	BBQ Pork	n. 叉烧
jellyfish	['dʒelifɪʃ]n. 海蜇	cucumber	['kjuːkʌmbə(r)]n. 黄瓜
nutrition	[nju'trɪʃn]n. 营养	brew	[bruː]v. 沏（茶），冲（咖啡）
flavor	['fleɪvə(r)]n. 风味	squab	[skwɒb]n. 乳鸽
quail	[kweɪl]n. 鹌鹑	oxtail	['ɒksteɪl]n. 牛尾
portion	['pɔːʃn]n. 一份（量）	poach	[pəʊtʃ]v. 水煮
lobster	['lɒbstə(r)]n. 龙虾	vegetarian	[ˌvedʒə'teəriən]adj. 素食的
loofah	['luːfə]n. 丝瓜	garlic	['ɡɑːlɪk]n. 大蒜
shrimp	[ʃrɪmp]n. 虾	considerate	[kən'sɪdərət]adj. 体贴的
steam	[stiːm]v. 蒸	turnip	['tɜːnɪp]n. 白萝卜
almond	['ɑːmənd]n. 杏仁	sago	['seɪɡəʊ]n. 西米
pomelo	['pɒmɪləʊ]n. 柚子	registered	['redʒɪstəd]adj. 已登记的
amount	[ə'maʊnt]v. 总计		

扫码
听听力

Task Three Sample Dialogues

1. Dialogue 1   Telephone Reservation①

Staff：Good morning，Panda Restaurant. How may I assist you?

Guest：Morning，I'd like to book a table for dinner tomorrow.

Staff：Great，please let me check our reservation record and may I have your name，sir?

Guest：James Brown.

Staff：Wonderful，Mr. Brown. We have some vacancies for tomorrow，Sep. 22. How many people are there in your party?

Guest：Two，my wife and I.

Staff：Mr. Brown，may I know if you have special reasons to celebrate?

Guest：Yes，it's our anniversary.

Staff：Congratulations. What time will you arrive?

Guest：Around 7:30 p. m..

Staff：Would you like a table in the hall or in a private room?

Guest：I prefer a private room.

Staff：Just a moment，please. We will have the Bamboo Hall reserved for you. Is that OK?

Guest: Perfect.

Staff: That's great! May I have your telephone number, please?

Guest: Sure. My number is 1593718××××.

Staff: Thank you very much, Mr. Brown. I'd like to confirm your reservation: Bamboo Hall for Mr. Brown's anniversary at 7:30 p.m., Sep. 22. The telephone number is 1593718××××. Am I right?

Guest: Absolutely correct. Thank you.

Staff: It's our pleasure, Mr. Brown. We are looking forward to serving you and your wife. See you tomorrow.

➤ Useful Expressions for Better Understanding of Dialogue 1

(1) Good morning, Panda Restaurant. How may I assist you?
早上好,熊猫餐厅,请问您需要什么服务?

(2) Please let me check our reservation record and may I have your name, sir?
请允许我来核对下我们的预约记录,请问您怎么称呼,先生?

(3) Mr. Brown, we have some vacancies for tomorrow, Sep. 22. How many people are there in your party?
布朗先生,明天9月22日,我们还有一些位子可以预订。请问您一共几位客人?

(4) Mr. Brown, may I know if you have special reasons to celebrate?
布朗先生,您订位子是有什么原因要庆祝吗?

(5) Congratulations. What time will you arrive?
祝贺你们,请问你们大概什么时候抵达餐厅?

(6) Would you like a table in the hall or in a private room?
请问您想坐大厅还是包间呢?

(7) Just a moment, please. We will have Bamboo Hall reserved for you. Is that OK?
请稍等,我们为您安排竹林厅可以吗?

(8) I'd like to confirm your reservation: Bamboo Hall for Mr. Brown for anniversary at 7:30 p.m., Sep. 22. The telephone number is 1593718××××. Am I right?
我来和您确认下预定信息:9月22日,晚上7:30,布朗先生为结婚纪念日预定的竹林厅,电话号码是1593718××××。请问信息是否正确?

2. Dialogue 2　Seating the Diners②

Staff: Good evening. Do you have a reservation?

Guest 1: No, we don't.

Staff: I'm afraid all our tables are taken, sir. Would you mind waiting for a while? If you are in a hurry, we also serve dinner at the coffee shop on the lobby floor.

Guest 1: Oh, no, we'll wait.

扫码
听听力

Staff: How many people, please?

Guest 1: A table for three, please. Well, by the window, if you have.

Staff: Here is your waiting card, a table for three. There are 3 parties in front of you. The expected waiting time will be about 20 minutes.

Guest 1: All right.

Staff: Thank you for your waiting, sir and madam. This way, please. Is this table satisfactory?

Guest 2: Yes. Thank you.

Staff: You are welcome. Please take your seats. Here is the menu. The waitress will come to take your order in a few minutes. Would you like a high chair for your baby?

Guest 2: Yes, please.

➢ **Useful Expressions for Better Understanding of Dialogue 2**

(1) Good evening. Do you have a reservation?

晚上好,先生,请问您有预约吗?

(2) I'm afraid all our tables are taken, sir. Would you mind waiting for a while? If you are in a hurry, we also serve dinner at the coffee shop on the lobby floor.

先生,对不起,现在正好没有位子,请您等一下可以吗?如果您赶时间的话,大堂的咖啡厅也供应晚餐。

(3) Here is your waiting card, a table for three. There are 3 parties in front of you. The expected waiting time will be about 20 minutes.

这是您的等待卡,三人桌,您前面还有三桌客人,你们预计等待20分钟。

(4) Thank you for your waiting, sir and madam. This way, please. Is this table satisfactory?

先生、女士,让你们久等了。请这边走,这个位子您满意吗?

(5) You are welcome. Please take your seats. Here is the menu. The waitress will come to take your order in a few minutes. Would you like a high chair for your baby?

请稍后片刻,服务人员会过来为您点餐。要为小朋友拿个高脚椅吗?

3. Dialogue 3 Taking Orders and Recommending Dishes[③]

Staff: Good evening, ladies and gentlemen. May I take your order now?

Guest 1: Er ... Can you give us some suggestions?

Staff: No problem, sir. Our restaurant offers classic Cantonese cuisine and quality dim sum. Which food ingredients would you like best?

Guest 2: I think I want vegetarian food, but my daughter and her friend would prefer some red meat. My husband likes seafood.

Staff: All right, madam. Let's start with cold dishes, just like appetizers. I would suggest Char Siu, Chinese BBQ Pork. It tastes a little sweet and sticky. And you can also try Cucumber and Jellyfish. It tastes fresh and natural.

扫码
听听力

Note

Unit 8　Chinese Restaurant Service

Guest 1: It's amazing! We will take that. Ah, we also want some soup. What soup do you have?

Staff: I will recommend Slow-cooked Soup, which is slowly brewed over a low fire for a long time. It has rich nutrition and a tasty flavor. Many kinds of ingredients can be used, like squab, quail and oxtail.

Guest 2: It sounds nice. We'll have 2 portions of Slow-cooked Soup with oxtail.

Staff: For hot dishes, I recommend Poached Lobster in Soup, with delicious taste and rich nutrition. Madam, if you like vegetarian food, you can also try Stir-fried Loofah with Garlic.

Guest 2: Wow, you are considerate. We love that.

Staff: Dim sum is a must for Cantonese food. We offer Shrimp Dumplings, Pan Fried Turnip Cake, Siu Mai-Steamed Pork Dumplings. It's not big, each portion only has 4 pieces. So it's suitable for you to share 2 or 3 kinds of dim sum.

Guest 2: We'd like Pan Fried Turnip Cake, Pork Dumplings.

Staff: Would you like some Canton desserts, Egg White Almond Tea, Chilled Mango Sago Cream with Pomelo?

Guest 2: 2 portions of each, please.

Staff: What would you like to drink?

Guest 1: We'd like two bottles of iced Tsingtao Beer.

Staff: OK, sir. Let me confirm what you will have.

➢ **Useful Expressions for Better Understanding of Dialogue 3**

(1) Good evening, ladies and gentlemen. May I take your order now?

晚上好，女士们、先生们，请问现在可以点单了吗？

(2) Which food ingredients would you like best?

您最喜欢哪种食材？

(3) I think I want vegetarian food, but my daughter and her friend would prefer some red meat. My husband likes seafood.

我想吃素，但我女儿和她的朋友更喜欢红肉。我丈夫喜欢海鲜。

(4) Let's start with cold dishes, just like appetizers. I would suggest Char Siu, Chinese BBQ Pork. It tastes a little sweet and sticky. And you can also try Cucumber and Jellyfish. It tastes fresh and natural.

让我们从凉菜开始，凉菜就像开胃菜一样。我建议点蜜汁叉烧（烤猪肉）。它吃起来有点甜和黏糯。您也可以试试黄瓜海蜇头，它尝起来很鲜美。

(5) I will recommend Slow-cooked Soup, which is slowly brewed over a low fire for a long time. It has rich nutrition and a tasty flavor. Many kinds of ingredients can be used, like squab, quail and oxtail.

我会推荐老火靓汤。这种广式汤是在小火上长时间慢慢熬制而成的，营养丰富，味道鲜美。食材也很多，像乳鸽、鹌鹑、牛尾。

(6) For hot dishes, I recommend Poached Lobster in Soup, with delicious taste and rich nutrition. Madam, if you like vegetarian food, you can also try Stir-fried Loofah with Garlic.

关于热菜，我推荐上汤焗龙虾，味道鲜美，营养丰富。女士，如果您喜欢素食，也可以尝试蒜蓉丝瓜。

(7) Dim sum is a must for Cantonese food. We offer Shrimp Dumplings, Pan Fried Turnip Cake, Siu Mai-Steamed Pork Dumplings. It's not big, each portion only has 4 pieces. So it's suitable for you to share 2 or 3 kinds of dim sum.

点心是广东菜必吃的。我们有虾饺、萝卜糕、烧麦。份量不大，每一笼只有四个。所以你们可以点两到三种尝试下。

(8) Would you like some Canton desserts, Egg White Almond Tea, Chilled Mango Sago Cream with Pomelo?

你们想品尝下广式甜品，蛋白杏仁茶和杨枝甘露吗？

(9) Let me confirm what you will have.

让我和您确认下您的点单。

4. Dialogue 4　Settling the Bill[④]

Guest: Bill, please.

Staff: One moment, sir. Sorry to have kept you waiting, sir. Your bill amounts to 1058 yuan, including the service charge.

Guest: How much is the service charge?

Staff: The service charge is 15% of the total, 920 yuan. That is 138 yuan.

Guest: I see. How should I pay for the bill?

Staff: You can pay in cash, by credit card, WeChat or Alipay. Or you may sign the bill if you are a registered guest.

Guest: No, I'm not registered. What card do you accept?

Staff: We honor UnionPay, American Express, Diners Club, JCB, MasterCard and Visa Card. Which card would you like to use?

Guest: MasterCard.

Staff: May I take a print of your card, sir?

Guest: Here you are.

Staff: Sir, here is your card and the receipt.

Guest: This is the tip for you.

Staff: Thank you, sir. I hope you've enjoyed your meal and hope to see you next time.

> **Useful Expressions for Better Understanding of Dialogue 4**

(1) Your bill amounts to 1058 yuan, including the service charge.

包括服务费，您的账单共计 1058 元。

(2) The service charge is 15% of the total, 920 yuan.

加收15%服务费，消费为920元。

(3) You can pay in cash, by credit card, WeChat or Alipay. Or you may sign the bill if you are a registered guest.

您可以用现金、信用卡、微信或支付宝支付。如果您是住店客人，也可以签单。

(4) We honor UnionPay, American Express, Diners Club, JCB, MasterCard and Visa Card.

我们接受银联、美国运通、大莱卡、JCB、万事达卡和维萨卡。

(5) May I take a print of your card, sir?

先生，我可以刷一下您的卡吗？

(6) Here is your card and the receipt.

这是您的卡和收据。

(7) This is the tip for you.

这是给你的小费。

5. Notes Related to Chinese Restaurant Service Dialogues

①餐厅提供订位服务对于餐厅和客户来说是一个双赢的策略。餐厅可以事先了解当天的来客情况，方便评估人力与食材；客户可避免长时间排队或可能扑空的风险。常见的订位方式包括：电话订位、现场订位、网络订位、（电子）信函订位。

②作为领位员一定要熟悉酒店的设施、规定、目前有什么促销活动、特色菜品等。需要清楚了解餐厅客人入座情况，不断与餐厅内联系，在生意繁忙时尽快为客人安排座位。一个出色的领位员要有很强的控场能力。

③在为外国客人提供中餐服务时，需要注意：a. 舒适性。外国客人的餐饮习惯和中国人有很多不一样的地方，如喜欢喝冰水，不喜欢吃全鱼，对于辣的食物的接受度也需要询问。b. 注意面部表情和目光交流。目光交流体现了一位服务员的专业度和服务意识，此外外国客人的面部表情比较丰富，喜欢用肢体语言。c. 要了解每个国家对于服务距离和礼貌的理解是不一样的。在餐饮服务过程中，要注意观察客人的满意程度，并利用服务间隙，进一步了解客人的需求。d. 注意中国文化的宣传和讲解。中国菜的特色、食材的选取、烹饪的方法与火候、调味的艺术都值得好好探究与传播。

④在为客人办理结账时，首先要问询客人对于饭菜和服务是否满意，并询问客人结账的方式，如移动支付、现金结账、银行卡结账、签单挂账、会员卡、优惠券等，要认真核对、高效服务、及时保存和更新相关的餐饮电子系统。

Task Four Procedure, Functional Expressions and Service Culture Points of Chinese Restaurant

1. Chinese Restaurant Service

The following are the procedures and functional expressions for restaurant service:

Procedure	Functional Expressions
Reserve a table	①Check the date and tables/private rooms. Wait a moment. Mr. ××/Ms. ××, let me check our reservation record. The private rooms are fully booked. Do you mind sitting in the hall? We still have some vacancies. ②Confirm numbers of guests. May I know how many people are there in your party? ③Inquire other information. Are you celebrating a special affair with us? Do you have a preferred server or table? Does anyone in your party have any special dietary needs or food allergies? ③Confirm the reservation details. I'd like to confirm your reservation: Bamboo Hall for Mr. Brown's anniversary at 7:30 p.m., Sep. 22; the telephone number is 1593718×××. Am I right?
Seating the diners	①Greet guests and ask if they have a reservation. Good evening, sir. Welcome to our restaurant. Do you have a reservation? ②Ask guests if they are willing to wait for a table. I'm afraid all our tables are taken, madam. Would you mind waiting until one is free? ③Ask if the guest is satisfied with the table. Is this table fine? /How about this table? ④Give the menu to guests and tell them a waiter will be right away. A waitress will come soon to take your order.
Taking orders	①Ask guests if they want to order. Mr. ××/Ms. ××/Sir/Madam, may I take your order, please? ②Suggestive selling. May I suggest…, which consists of …? Today's specialty is…, with a 20% discount. Excuse me, Mr. ××/Ms. ××/Sir/Madam, would you like to have a cold dish/appetizer to start with, may I suggest …? Which flavor would you prefer, sweet or salty? What would you like to drink with your meal?

Continued

Procedure	Functional Expressions
Serve dishes and refill glasses	Here is the Sweet and Sour Pork. It is hot, please be careful. Would you like me to refill your glass? This is the complete course, and a fruit plate to follow. It's complimentary.
Deal with the bill	Your bill amounts to 1058 yuan, including the service charge. You can pay in cash, by credit card, WeChat or Alipay. Or you may sign the bill if you are a registered guest. We honor UnionPay, American Express, Diners Club, JCB, MasterCard and Visa Card. Here is your card and the receipt. I hope you've enjoyed your meal and welcome you again.

2. Culture Points

The Value of Teamwork

Teamwork, simply stated, is less me and more we. Each member has a different role on the team. The strengths—and weaknesses—of each team member are unique, but they are all working towards the same goal. Individual efforts contribute to the team's success, but the team won't reach its goal unless everyone works together. The same is true of teamwork in a restaurant.

When teamwork is running effectively in your restaurant, the benefits are multi-faceted. First, each member of the team benefits. Working on a team helps employees learn important skills that not only make them better employees, but better people, too. Next up, managers benefit. Effective teamwork in a restaurant makes day-to-day operations run more smoothly. Finally, the business benefits from teamwork. When employees feel like they are part of a team, they're more supportive of each other and morale is higher. This, in turn, reduces turnover costs and improves the bottom line.

Task Five   Listening Ability Enhancement

1. Listen to the dialogue of apologizes for serving the wrong dish and fill in the blanks

Server: Good evening. May I serve your dinner now?
Guest: Yes, please.
Staff: This is the pork in brown __(1)__.
Guest: Pork? We didn't order pork. We ordered __(2)__ duck.

扫码
听听力

Staff: I am so sorry. Let me ___(3)___. Oh, you are right. Your order is crispy duck. I'm very sorry for the ___(4)___.

Guest: That's all right.

Staff: I'll change the dish for the duck and come back soon. Please wait a moment.

Guest: OK. Thank you.

Staff: Sorry to have kept you waiting. This is your crispy duck.

Guest: Thank you. The menu says we will have another two dishes.

Staff: For a Chinese ___(5)___, it will come to an end when ___(6)___ is served.

Guest: I am nearly full.

Staff: The following two dishes are the fried vegetable with ___(7)___ and ___(8)___ mandarin fish, and then the clear soup. Please take your time.

2. **Listen to the dialogue of seating guests and taking orders and fill in the restaurant order form**

Restaurant Order		
Table Number: ___(1)___		
Guests Number: ___(2)___		
	Type	Number
Cold Dishes	___(3)___ Cutlassfish	1
	Tossed Seasonal Vegetables with ___(4)___ Oil and ___(5)___	1
Hot Dishes	___(6)___ Pork Belly with Abalone in ___(7)___	1
	Shrimp with Pepper and ___(8)___	1
Pastry	Steam Bun with ___(9)___ Meat	1
Wines	Chinese Rice Wine	1 bottle
	Coke	1 ___(10)___

3. **Listen to the passage of restaurant POS systems and fill in the blanks**

When comparing restaurant POS systems, it's important to understand the functionality included in each. Here are the most common features of restaurant POS systems:

Order ___(1)___	Ensures that orders, including any special modifiers, are easily, quickly and correctly entered and received by the bar and/or kitchen, while enabling ___(2)___ checks
Inventory management	Helps monitor inventory use and costs while ___(3)___ portioned items to determine food costs. Produces management reports to help detect theft and over-portioning while setting thresholds for ___(4)___ product counts and assigning automatic reordering

	Continued
_(5)_ costing	Helps determine the monetary value of each batch and/or serving of a menu item to determine the actual costs and profitability for each _(6)_
Customer management	Track customer purchase histories and follow up with targeted offers to valuable customers through email and _(7)_ messages, while allowing for "opt outs" of future offers. Often supports a _(8)_ rewards program to build lucrative relationships with loyal customers
Tablet/iPad-based system	Provide an enhanced customer experience by reducing the amount of ordering and payment time. Staffs have the ability to send an order directly to the kitchen while customers can input tips on the iPad and _(9)_ their names on the spot

Task Six   Interpretation

(1) Just a moment, sir. I'll check our reservation list.

(2) I'm afraid all the private rooms are reserved. Would you mind a table in the main restaurant?

(3) Would you like your rice now or later?

(4) Do I pay here or at the register?

(5) I'd like some sort of beef or veal dish.

(6) I'd like to order something sweet. What do you have?

(7) 我们餐厅常常客满,所以我建议您事先预订比较好。

(8) 真对不起,大的桌子都没有了,不过如果您愿意的话,我可以将两张桌子并在一起。

(9) 先生,茉莉花茶是免费的。

(10) 您是要一张账单,还是分开结账?

(11) 我去厨房确认下您的点单。请耐心等候,我马上回来。

(12) 莲子是一种传统又健康的食材,也被当成中药使用。

Task Seven   Role Play

1. **Make a situational conversation about the telephone reservation with a Chinese restaurant**

Ryan Andrews would like to book a table for three people on Oct. 15th. His clients like Chinese food very much, especially spicy food. His party favors a private room and would like to arrive at the restaurant at 6:30 p.m..

2. Make a situational conversation about seating walk-in guests

You are the hostess of a Moose Restaurant. A young foreign couple ask you for a table without reservation. It's the peak time for your restaurant and there are no vacant tables. You would suggest that they could wait in line until a table is free, or you may introduce another restaurant nearby.

3. Make a situational conversation about taking an order in a Chinese restaurant

Vicky Gray and Kailey Lindberg walk into King' Joy Restaurant, which offers vegetarian cuisine using green and seasonal products that are sourced from local, organic farms. Vicky and Kailey are vegans. They don't know Chinese cuisine well. You may introduce your set menu for them.

4. Make a situational conversation about serving dishes and refilling the glasses

You are a waiter/waitress, who is in charge of Table 8. During your service, the bus boy delivers a wrong dish and you help guests change it and apologize for it. And you should also help guests refill drinks during their dining process.

Task Eight   Extended Professional Knowledge Reading

Food and Tea Pairing

Drinking tea is a lifestyle for us here in China, and we know that's the case with many of our international customers. Tea extends itself past the morning and afternoon cup into dinner, and of course, dessert. As with wine, pairing drinks with food is a fascinating, ever-evolving world, and tea is certainly part of it. The varieties of flavors and aromas tea offers make it a perfect candidate for culinary opportunity!

➢ White Tea

Because of the extremely subtle flavor of white teas, we recommend pairing them with only the mildest of flavors, so as to not miss the sweetness that is so loved in white tea.

Suggestions: Bai Mu Dan + rice, light fish and basic salads.

➢ Green Tea

In general, the subtle, vegetative flavor and aroma of most green tea is well suited to mild or subtly-flavored food, such as seafood, rice, salads, melon or chicken.

Suggestions: Dragon well + seafood or fish, salads, chicken; Gunpowder + Asian or Middle Eastern Food; Hojicha + turkey or potatoes; Sencha + arugula and lightly steamed vegetables.

➢ Oolong Tea

Many argue that the subtle complexity of flavor and aroma attributed to oolong tea demand drinking it on its own. However, because oolongs can range in character between green and black teas, many can be paired with food along the same lines as their green or black counterparts. For instance, greener oolongs tend to go well with scallops, lobster and other sweet rich food, while darker oolongs compliment somewhat stronger-flavored food such as duck and grilled meats.

Suggestions: High Mountain Oolong+fruits or lighter bread with butter; Ti Kuan Yin Oolong+desserts and fruits; Wu Yi Oolong+roasted vegetables and squash; Plum Oolong+wheat bread with jam.

➢ Black Tea

The more robust flavors and aromas of most black teas, as well as the most pronounced tannins, are well suited to pairing with full-flavored foods such as meat and spicy dishes.

Suggestions: Darjeeling + egg dishes, creamy dessert; Keemun + meat, fish, Chinese food, spicy Mexican, Italian, or Indian dishes; Yunnan + highly seasoned food; Lapsang Souchong+chicken, smoked salmon, lemony dessert; Assam+hearty food, breakfast food, chocolate, custard or lemon dessert.

➢ Pu-erh Tea

Worthy of special note, pu-erh teas are known for their digestive benefits. Not only do these teas pair well with meat and oily food, they can offer a welcome settling effect after large, multi-course meals!

Suggestions: Wild Tree Mini Tuo-Cha+after a large meal, red meat, stir-fries, oily food.

Experimentation is the best way to find out what works best for you. The suggestions above will act as a guide, but sometimes you will find an unexpected combination that works beautifully. For new tea drinkers, we suggest sampling at least one tea of each variety for comparison (i.e. white, green, oolong, black, and pu-erh)—you'll be amazed by the variety.

Decide if the following statements are true(T) or false(F), according to the passage.

(　　) ① Much like wine, tea and food pairings are now popular all over the world.

(　　) ② White tea is renowned for their digestive benefits.

(　　) ③ Every green tea is matched to subtly-flavored food, such as seafood, rice, or chicken.

(　　)④Oolongs are characterized by both green and black teas, which can be paired with food as their green or black counterparts.

(　　)⑤Black teas have strong flavors, aromas and tannins, which are suitable for spicy dishes and meat.

Unit 9
Western Restaurant Service

Unit Objectives

After studying this unit, you should be able to do the following:

Knowledge & Ability Objectives

1. grasp the steps in Western restaurant service;

2. be familiar with the terms and sentence patterns of Western restaurant reservations, food ingredients and sauces, a la carte, table d'hote, communication, etc.;

3. give examples of Italian food and Japanese food;

4. deal with the daily service process of Western restaurant, such as reservation, seating the diners, taking orders, recommending dishes, serving during the meal and checking the bill.

Quality Objectives

1. explain the basic responsibilities of food and beverage service;

2. implement diversified role plays for Western restaurant scenarios;

3. construct professionalism for Western cuisine, cooking and service culture.

Task One Lead-in

1. Brainstorming

The Western food service process describes the organization of dishes and beverages, customers, their chronological order and infrastructural planning. Food and drinks are the premise of the whole Western food service. Please classify the following words briefly and think about how these food and drinks are matched and served in a certain sequence.

Appetizer   Cocktail   Beer   Bread
Water   Liqueur   Tea   Entrée
Wine   Dessert   Coffee   Soup

2. Matching

The following pictures show different service types in Western restaurants. Discuss with your partner and match them.

（1）A la Carte Service　（2）Buffet Service　（3）Table d'hote Service
（4）Banquet Service　（5）Take-away Service　（6）Room Service

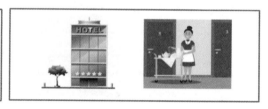

1 Menu
Fixed Time
1 Group

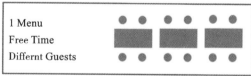

1 Menu
Free Time
Differnt Guests

Free Time
Free Time
Different Guets

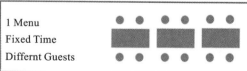

1 Menu
Fixed Time
Differnt Guests

Unit 9 Western Restaurant Service

Task Two Words and Expressions

separate	['seprət]adj. 单独的	calendar	['kælɪndə(r)]n. 日历
cocktail	['kɒkteɪl]n. 鸡尾酒	presentation	[ˌpreznˈteɪʃn]n. 演讲
package	['pækɪdʒ]n. 打包价	convenient	[kənˈviːniənt]adj. 方便的
appetizer	['æpɪtaɪzə(r)]n. 开胃菜	bacon	['beɪkən]n. 培根
grilled	[grɪld]adj. (铁扒)烤的	truffle	['trʌfl]n. 松露
tuna	['tjuːnə]n. 金枪鱼	prawn	[prɔːn]n. 对虾;明虾
scallop	['skɒləp]n. 扇贝	abalone	[ˌæbəˈləʊni]n. 鲍鱼
minestrone	[ˌmɪnəˈstrəʊni]n. 意大利蔬菜汤	pan-seared	['pæn-sɪəd]adj. 煎的
main course	主菜	wagyu	['wægjuː]n. 和牛
ribeye	['rɪbˌaɪ]n. 牛脊肉;肋眼	rare	[reə(r)]adj. 一成熟
medium	['miːdiəm]adj. 五成熟	champagne	[ʃæmˈpeɪn]n. 香槟
strawberry	['strɔːbəri]n. 草莓	Cabernet Sauvignon	['kæbəneɪ-ˌsɒˈvɪnjɒn]n. 赤霞珠
table d'hote	(法)套餐	a la carte	(法)按菜单点菜
tempura	['tempʊərə]n. 天妇罗	teppanyaki	[tepənjeɪˈkiː]n. 铁板烧
sashimi	[sæˈʃiːmi]n. 生鱼片;刺身	portion	['pɔːʃn]n. 部分;一份
sushi	['suːʃi]n. 寿司	miso	['miːsəʊ]n. 味噌
dessert	[dɪˈzɜːt]n. 甜点	mackerel	['mækrəl]n. 青花鱼
sea urchin	['siː ɜːtʃɪn]n. 海胆	sake	['saːki]n. 清酒

Task Three Sample Dialogues

1. Dialogue 1 Telephone Reservation for Company Party①

Staff: Good morning, Phoenix Restaurant. How may I assist you?

Guest: Yes, I'm interested in having a party to honor some of our retiring employees. Do you have a separate room for things like that?

Staff: May I have your name and company information, sir?

Guest: My name is Julian Mackey, ABC Consulting Company.

Staff: How many people will you have and when would you like to celebrate it,

扫码听听力

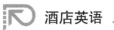

Mr. Mackey?

Guest: There will be about 16 people, and we'd like to attend on about the 16th of next month for dinner.

Staff: Let me check the reservation. Yes, we still have seats for that day. Could you please share more details about your event, so that we could arrange the most suitable room for you?

Guest: We want to have a cocktail hour first, and then dinner afterwards. Then we'll have some presentations and speeches after that. It'll probably last three to four hours.

Staff: That sounds great. So far, 2 options are available. We have a private room with a garden on the ground floor. Another option is on the second floor, private rooms are varied in different sizes with a long bar in the main hall. Which one do you prefer, Mr. Mackey?

Guest: The private room with a garden sounds nice.

Staff: Great, garden private room. We have a couple of different menu styles to choose from. Or you can work with our chef and design your own menu. And is it convenient for you to tell me your email address and telephone number, Mr. Mackey?

Guest: My phone number is 021-32039999, and my email address is julianmac@abcconsulting.com. I'm going to need some time to decide, but I'm sure we want one of the sit-down options.

Staff: Mr. Mackey, I would send related package information and price guidelines of these two kinds of private room to you through email. Please take it as a reference for your decision. If you have time, we will show you around the venue.

Guest: I'll look at your information and discuss it with my staff. We will get back to you. Thank you so much.

Staff: It'my pleasure. Thank you for your call, Mr. Mackey. Wish you a nice day!

> **Useful Expressions for Better Understanding of Dialogue 1**

(1) I'm interested in having a party to honor some of our retiring employees.
我想为我们即将退休的员工举办一个派对。

(2) How many people will you have and when would you like to celebrate it, Mr. Mackey?
麦基先生，你们的派对大概有多少人，你们想什么时间庆祝？

(3) Let me check the reservation. Yes, we still have seats for that day. Could you please share more details about your event, so that we could arrange the most suitable room for you?
我看一下我们的预订情况。是的，我们还有房间。您能否分享一下您的活动细节，以便我们为您安排合适的房间？

(4) We want to have a cocktail hour first, and then dinner afterwards. Then we'll

have some presentations and speeches after that. It'll probably last three to four hours.

我们想在吃饭前先开一个鸡尾酒会，接着是用餐，然后是致辞等，整个派对大概持续三至四个小时。

(5) So far, 2 options are available. We have a private room with a garden on the ground floor. Another option is on the second floor, private rooms are varied in different sizes with a long bar in the main hall.

目前房间有两种选择，一是您可以选择一楼的带花园的包间；二是您可以选择二楼的包间，包间的面积大小不一，大厅有可供喝酒的长吧台。

(6) We have a couple of different menu styles to choose from. Or you can work with our chef and design your own menu.

我们有不同种类的菜单可供您选择。或者您可以和我们的主厨讨论，设计自己的派对菜单。

(7) And is it convenient for you to tell me your email address and telephone number?

您是否方便告诉我您的邮箱地址和电话号码？

(8) I'm going to need some time to decide, but I'm sure we want one of the sit-down options.

我需要一些时间再做决定，可以肯定的是，我们想选择由服务生上菜的用餐方式。

(9) Mr. Mackey, I would send related package information and price guidelines of these two kinds of private room to you through email. Please take it as a reference for your decision. If you have time, we will show you around the venue.

麦基先生，我会将这两种包间的相关套餐信息和参考价格通过邮件发给您。您可以作为参考，如果您时间允许的话，我们也诚邀您来我们酒店看下场地。

2. **Dialogue 2   Taking Orders and Recommending Dishes in Italian Restaurant**②

扫码
听听力

Staff: Excuse me. Here are the menu and wine list, Ms. Alice. Can I get anything for you to drink while you are looking over the menu?

Guest: Water, please. Pizza is your specialty here. How long does it take to make a pizza?

Staff: Our pizzas are wood-fired and have a thin crust, so they don't take much time at all.

Guest: All right, you convinced me. What pizza would you recommend?

Staff: Sure, you can't go wrong with the Black Truffle Pizza with Bacon.

Guest: That sounds good. One portion, please. And I like seafood. Do you have any suggestions?

Staff: If you like seafood, you can choose crab, tuna, scallop, or prawn for appetizer. For soup, we have an abalone & mushroom or minestrone.

Guest: Great idea, we would like scallops for appetizers and minestrone.

Staff: Excellent choice. Pan-seared scallop and minestrone.

Guest: Main course, we would like to choose beef.

Staff: Our house specialty is Grilled Australian Wagyu Beef Ribeye with Black Pepper Sauce. And side dishes include Baked Tomatoes and Mashed Potatoes.

Guest: That sounds great. We will take that.

Staff: How would you like your steak done, rare, medium, or welldone③?

Guest: Medium.

Staff: And would you like desserts, Ms. Alice? We have a good selection of desserts.

Guest: We would like 2 Strawberry & Champagne Jelly.

Staff: Would you like some drinks to go with your meal?

Guest: Well, I think the Barolo Cabernet Sauvignon is a good choice, 1 bottle, please.

Staff: Thank you, Ms. Alice. Let me confirm your order.

➢ Useful Expressions for Better Understanding of Dialogue 2

(1) Excuse me. Here are the menu and wine list, Ms. Alice. Can I get anything for you to drink while you are looking over the menu?

打扰一下，爱丽丝女士，这是菜单和酒单。您看菜单的时候，需要喝点什么吗？

(2) Pizza is your specialty here. How long does it take to make a pizza?

披萨是你们的特色。需要等多长时间？

(3) Our pizzas are wood-fired and have a thin crust, so they don't take much time at all.

我们的披萨是用木头烤的，皮很薄，所以不会花太多时间。

(4) Sure, you can't go wrong with the Black Truffle Pizza with Bacon.

当然，黑松露意式培根披萨是个不错的选择。

(5) If you like seafood, you can choose crab, tuna, scallop, or prawn for appetizer.

如果您喜欢海鲜，开胃菜可以选择螃蟹、金枪鱼、扇贝、明虾。

(6) For soup, we have an abalone & mushroom or minestrone.

汤的话，我们有鲍鱼菌汤或意式蔬菜汤。

(7) Our house specialty is Grilled Australian Wagyu Beef Ribeye with Black Pepper Sauce. And side dishes include Baked Tomatoes and Mashed Potatoes.

我们的招牌菜是澳大利亚和牛肋眼配黑胡椒酱。配菜包括烤番茄和土豆泥。

(8) How would you like your steak done, rare, medium, or well done?

您的牛排要几成熟，一成、五成还是全熟？

(9) And would you like desserts, Ms. Alice? We have a good selection of desserts.

爱丽丝女士，你们要甜点吗？我们有很多甜点。

(10) Would you like some drinks to go with your meal?

您的餐需要搭配什么酒水呢?

3. Dialogue 3　Taking Orders and Table Service in a Japanese Restaurant①

Staff: Good evening, sir. Welcome to Ginza Onodera Restaurant. I'm Wendy. How can I address you?

Guest: Nice to meet you, Wendy. You can call me Larry.

Staff: Larry, our restaurant offers different styles of Japanese cooking. What would you like for your dinner, table d'hote or a la carte?

Guest: The "B" course looks good, and what kind of portions do you serve?

Staff: Would you prefer a light or a filling meal?

Guest: We're rather hungry.

Staff: Then I would recommend the "A" course. It consists of appetizer, sashimi, vegetable plate, cold dish, boiled food, sushi, egg, miso soup and dessert.

Guest: We will take the "A" course for two.

Staff: This set menu comes with 3 pieces of sashimi and 7 pieces of sushi, which do you prefer?

Guest: Sashimi we choose tuna, mackerel and scallop; sushi we prefer 2 supreme fatty tuna, 2 botan shrimp, 2 sea urchin, 1 spring onion fatty tuna roll.

Staff: For teppanyaki, you can try our house specialty, lobster or wagyu beef.

Guest: OK, lobster. What is tempura?

Staff: It is fish, prawns and assorted vegetables dipped in batter and then deep fried until crisp. It's very popular with guests.

Guest: We will take one portion.

Staff: What would you like to drink, Japanese sake or beer?

Guest: We would like to try Japanese sake.

Staff: Thank you, sir. Let me repeat your order.

➢ **Useful Expressions for Better Understanding of Dialogue 3**

(1) What would you like for your dinner, table d'hote or a la carte?

您晚餐想吃什么,套餐还是零点?

(2) The "B" course looks good, and what kind of portions do you serve?

B套餐看起来不错,它的份量大概多少?

(3) Would you prefer a light or a filling meal?

请问您想吃多一点还是少一点?

(4) Then I would recommend the "A" course. It consists of appetizer, sashimi, vegetable plate, cold dish, boiled food, sushi, egg, miso soup and dessert.

我建议您选A套餐,包括前菜、刺身、小菜拼盘、冷菜、熟食、寿司、玉子烧、味噌汤、甜品。

(5) Sashimi we choose tuna, mackerel and scallop; sushi we prefer 2 supreme fatty tuna, 2 botan shrimp, 2 sea urchin, 1 spring onion fatty tuna roll.

刺身，我们选择金枪鱼、青花鱼和扇贝；寿司，我们要 2 个大肥金枪鱼、2 个牡丹虾、2 个海胆、1 个葱花金枪鱼寿司卷。

(6) For teppanyaki, you can try our house specialty, lobster or wagyu beef.
至于铁板烧，您可以尝尝我们的招牌菜，龙虾或神户牛肉。

(7) It is fish, prawns and assorted vegetables dipped in batter and then deep fried until crisp. It's very popular with guests.
(天妇罗)是由鱼、明虾和多种蔬菜，混合蛋和面粉后再油炸做成的。这是一道非常流行的日本料理，很受客人的喜爱。

(8) What would you like to drink, Japanese sake or beer?
您想喝点什么，日本清酒还是啤酒？

4. Notes Related to Western Restaurant Service Dialogues

①餐厅的活动策划需要一定的技巧，举办的活动一定有目的、主题、参与活动的主要对象，也会有费用的限制。宾客与主办方的喜好有时也会纳入活动举办的考虑范围。分析要精准，多了解、多记录。对餐厅来说，活动的安排只是预订位置的一项增值服务，未来餐厅定制化的活动方案将会越来越完整和有创意。

②法餐和意餐在中国很受推崇。用餐的基本顺序：a. 品酒。要依据当天的状况搭配，有专门的餐前酒、佐餐酒、餐后酒。b. 开胃菜。多为冷盘或去油腻的料理。c. 汤。西餐中的汤一般可分为清汤和浓汤两大类。d. 主菜。通常是餐厅的特色菜，非常注意食材的选择和烹饪的艺术，以扒类和海鲜类居多，并配以特调的酱汁。e. 甜点。一道成功的甜点应该是一次聚会的压轴节目，甜品多见搭配佐酱，以增加甜味的层次感。f. 饮品。餐后饮料多为茶或咖啡，标志着整个宴席的结束。

③牛排熟度一般分为五个等级，分别是一成熟(rare)、三成熟(medium rare)、五成熟(medium)、七成熟(medium well)和全熟(well done)。

④日本料理中，最著名的莫过于刺身了，通常是蘸着酱油和芥末吃。寿司常使用海胆黄、鲍鱼、牡丹虾、扇贝、鲑鱼籽、鳕鱼鱼白、金枪鱼、三文鱼等海鲜切成片放在雪白香糯的饭团上。日式铁板烧是日本料理中最高级别的就餐形式，铁板烧是将食材直接放在热铁板上炙烤成熟，这些食材事先不能腌制加工，而是通过高热的铁板快速烹调成熟以保留其本身的营养和味道。常见的食材有牛肉、银鳕鱼、带子、鹅肝等。在大型的宴会、酒吧或寻常百姓的餐桌上，清酒一直是日本人最常喝的饮料。

Task Four　Procedure, Functional Expressions and Service Culture Points of Western Restaurant

1. Fine Dining VS Casual Dining

There are several classifications for restaurants, generally based on food and style, serving, preparation methods, and pricing. The two most popular categories are casual dining and fine dining. Among the key differences between the two dinings is the atmosphere and ambience. Casual dining is friendlier and more informal, whereas fine dining exudes a more elegant and formal atmosphere. The food on offer differs, and pricing comes into play as well.

	Fine Dining	Casual Dining
Differences	High-class and elegant in design; Formal dress code; Luxurious & unique food; Superior service	Relaxed decor; Casual dress code; Saving your time and money
Similarities	Ambience	

2. Western Restaurant Service

The following are the procedures and functional expressions for taking orders and table service for Western restaurants:

Procedure	Functional Expressions
Taking orders	①Ask guests if they want to order ②Suggestive selling What would you like for your dinner, table d'hote or a la carte? Excuse me, Mr. ××/Ms. ××/Sir/Madam, would you like to have an appetizer to start with, may I suggest …? For appetizer/soup/entrée/dessert, I would recommend … How would you like your steak done, rare, medium, welldone? What would you like to drink with your meal? Let me repeat your order.
Serve dishes and refill glasses	Here is your Grilled Beefsteak, medium with black pepper sauce. Hope you will like it. Would you like me to refill/collect your wine glass? Do you enjoy your Pan-seared Turbot Fillet? Next is your dessert. Would you like some tea or coffee?

3. Culture Points

Craftsman's Spirit

The craftsman's spirit is defined by the encyclopedia as one who is devoted to making things with perfection, precision, concentration, patience and persistence.

At 91, Japanese chef Jiro Ono is considered by many to be the greatest sushi chef in the world. What defines deliciousness in his Michelin three-star Tokyo restaurant is that it takes awe-inspiring steps of food preparation. Tuna is slowly cut in thin morsels, the world's finest rice is cooked and shaken with care, and nigiri sushi is brushed with soy sauce. "You must dedicate your life to mastering this skill," Ono says in the film. "This is the key to success." Jiro Ono, known as the master of sushi, believes in the spirit of the craftsman, or professional spirit, which makes his sushi restaurant the best in Japan. Octopus in Jiro's restaurant is required to have 40 to 50 minutes of massage to become softer and more aromatic. An apprentice of his once spent 10 years before meeting his standard to make the perfect omelet.

Task Five   Listening Ability Enhancement

1. Listen to five short dialogues and mark (√) which food category is mentioned in each dialogue

	Starter	Soup	Entrée	Dessert	Drinks
Dialogue 1					
Dialogue 2					
Dialogue 3					
Dialogue 4					
Dialogue 5					

2. Listen to the dialogue of dessert order and bill checking and fill in the bill checking form.

HOTEL SACHER			
Restaurant Rose			Bill No. 812034
Date	Table No.	Cover	Staff No.
01SEP21	1	2	Jess 1
Type	Amount	Order	Price
Appetizer	1	Grilled ___(3)___	128.00
Soup	1	Sweet Pepper ___(4)___ Soup	118.00
Entree	1	___(5)___ Fillet of Wolffish	308.00
Entree	1	Fried ___(6)___ of Roast Beef	318.00
Dessert	2	Strawberry-chocolate ___(1)___	178.00
Drink	2	___(2)___	132.00
Wine	1 ___(7)___	___(8)___ La Cuvee Brut	1280.00
Sub total		2462.00	
Room No.			
Name			
Way of Payment		___(9)___	
Total Paid		RMB ___(10)___	
Sign			

Unit 9 Western Restaurant Service

3. Listen to the passage of left or right service and fill in the blanks

Food service literature suggests that there is little ___(1)___ on the correct sides from which food should be served. One main rule serves can follow is that women are generally waited on before men. Use the following serving ___(2)___ as a guide:

Appetizers and salads. Appetizers and salads should be served from the right with the right hand. The ___(3)___ for appetizers and salads is usually already on the table.

Soups. If soup is being served, make sure the ___(4)___ is on the plate. Add a nice touch, with ___(5)___ underneath the bowl. Soup spoons should be set to the right of the bowl and soup served from the right.

Entrée. Entrée is also served from the right. It should be placed so the main element of the plate faces the guest. Flatware for the entrée should be placed on the table before the entrée arrives. Be sure the servers only touch the flatware by the handle and plates by the ___(6)___. If side dishes are served on separate plates, they should be served from the left.

Dessert. When serving dessert, the waitperson should place the ___(7)___ to the guest's left and serve the dessert from the right.

___(8)___. Drinks are served from the right and coffee is poured from the right.

Clearing. In ___(9)___, all plates and other dishes should be cleared from the right.

Signs that a guest is done. These signals include placing a ___(10)___ on top of the plate, pushing the plate to the side and turning the fork upside down across the plate, or both the knife and fork placed together, at an angle on the plate. However, even if your server sees these signals at a table, he or she should first ask the guests before they clear.

扫码
听听力

Task Six Interpretation

(1) Excuse me. Here are the menu and wine list. Can I get anything for you to drink while you are looking over the menu?

(2) How can I address you, madam? And is it convenient for you to tell me your telephone number and email address?

(3) If you like seafood, you can choose crab, tuna, scallop, prawn or octopus as an appetizer.

(4) How would you like your steak done, rare, medium, welldone?

(5) What would you like for your dinner, table d'hote or a la carte?

(6) 您想喝点什么，日本清酒还是啤酒？

(7) 我想为我们新进员工举办一个派对。

(8) 您的餐需要搭配酒水喝？

(9) 我看一下日历。那天餐厅还可以预订。您需要什么样的房间？

(10) 女士们，你们要甜点吗？我们有很多种甜点。

Task Seven Role Play

1. Make a situational conversation about the telephone reservation with Western restaurant

Paul Simon would like to prepare a big party for his wife's birthday. Service staff should check if guests need a designed menu or party decorations. Ask Paul Simon's personal information for further discussion.

2. Make a situational conversation about asking guest preference

A server is making suggestions for a guest. Firstly, please make sure which menu is suitable for the guest, a la carte or table d'hote? When recommending dishes, please confirm the guest's favorite food ingredient, ways of cooking, flavors and anything who doesn't like.

3. Make a situational conversation about taking an order in a Western restaurant

Sally Welt, a food blogger, walks into Panorama Restaurant, which offers French cuisine. Panorama Restaurant incorporates Chinese sensibilities into French chef's dishes. The 'White Asparagus Trio' is the house specialty. You may introduce your signature menu to her, including aperitif, appetizer, soup, entree, dessert and wine.

4. Make a situational conversation about serving dishes and recommending desserts and after-dinner drinks

You are a waiter/waitress, who is in charge of Table 6. Guests have started to eat beef steak. During your service, you should check the taste of the entree and refill the glasses. After guests finish the entree, you would recommend the desserts and make sure guests would like to finish the meal with a coffee, tea or after-dinner drinks.

Task Eight Extended Professional Knowledge Reading

Different Types of Food and Beverage Services in Hotels and Restaurants

There are many different Food and Beverage service types or procedures. This may range from full silver service in a fine dining restaurant to a self-service cafeteria where guests collect their own food from the counter. Here's the list of several styles of food service in hotel industry.

1. English Service/Family Style F&B Service

(1) English service requires the food to be placed on large platters or in large bowls.

(2) These food portions are then delivered to the guest's table by waiters/servers.

(3) Once the host checks and approves the food, the same is placed on the table.

(4) The guests then pass the food around the table and serve themselves.

(5) In some cases, the host may also ask the waiter to serve the food.

(6) This is a common type of F&B service style as the ease of service and waiters shouldn't be highly skilled.

(7) The Family style F&B service is easy to implement.

(8) The servers or waiters shouldn't be that skilled.

(9) This type of service also requires little dining area or space. There is a higher or rapid table turnover rate with this type of service.

(10) One of the major disadvantages of the family style service is the difficulty to control the portion sizes.

(11) This is because the last guest who gets served may not get enough items if other guests have taken more.

2. French Service

(1) French Service is a very detailed and highly skilled type of service.

(2) It is a very elaborate and expensive type of service.

(3) The chefs demonstrate culinary skill, by preparing meals in front of the guests.

(4) Normally all fine dining restaurants follow this type of service.

(5) VIPs and VVIPs are also given this kind of service style.

(6) Plated entrees are served from the right, all other courses from the left.

(7) Beverages are served from the right.

(8) French Service style is very expensive because it involves professional waiters to the server properly and slowly.

(9) The ambience and decor of the restaurant are always in high luxury.

(10) All diners are given individual attention and they enjoy it.

3. American Service/Pre-plated service

(1) One of the most common and widely accepted kinds of food and beverage service.

(2) The servers take guests' orders in the dining area.

(3) The order is sent to kitchen staff via KOT (Kitchen Order Ticket).

(4) Food is prepared and pre-plated in the kitchen itself by the chef.

(5) The server or bus person brings the food to the restaurant and place it on side stands.

(6) Pre-plated food is then served to the guests by the server.

4. Russian Service

(1) Similar to the French Service but faster and less expensive.

(2) Display and presentation are a major part of this service.

(3) Whole joints, poultry, game, fish etc. are elaborately garnished and dressed.

(4) After presenting to the guest the server or waiter portions or carve them and serve to the guests.

(5) Normally, only one server is required per table.

(6) No extra space is required for the equipment like the French F&B service type.

(7) Ideally suited for banquet service with a fixed menu.

Fill in the blanks based on text reading

4 Types of F&B Service	Highlights
English Service	
French Service	
American Service	
Russian Service	

Unit 9
练习答案

Unit 10
Room Service

Unit Objectives

After studying this unit, you should be able to do the following:
Knowledge & Ability Objectives
1. grasp the room meal delivery process and the service steps of the meal delivery robot;
2. be familiar with the terminology and sentence patterns of room service;
3. know the room service with an accurate English sentence pattern;
4. know the meal delivery service in English;
5. deal with the delivery needs of different customers.

Quality Objectives
1. understand the basic responsibilities of room service;
2. have the language and professional ability to accurately complete the room delivery related services in English.

 Task One Lead-in

1. Brainstorming

Look at the picture, a room service attendant is delivering a meal to the guest. What should he/she say to the guest? What should the service steps be like? Please discuss with your team members and write down the sentences they might say.

Room Attendant: _____

Guest: _____

2. Sequencing

The following statements describe the job procedure of a room service by an attendant. Discuss with your partner and put them in the correct order.

(Note: the picture is quoted from the following website
https://image.baidu.com/search/index? tn＝baiduimage&ct＝201326
592&lm＝-1&cl＝2&ie＝gb18030&word＝％BF％CD％B7％BF％CB％CD％
B2％CD％B7％FE％CE％F1％CD％BC％C6％AC&fr＝ala&ala＝1&alatpl＝normal
&pos＝0&dyTabStr＝MCwzLDUsMSw2LDQsNyw4LDIsOQ％3D％3D.)

A. Enquire;

B. Confirm the order;

C. Greet the guest;

D. Explain the choice;

E. Get further information;

Correct order: _____

Task Two Words and Expressions

service	['sɜːvɪs] n. 服务	deliver	[dɪ'lɪvə(r)] v. 传送;交付
spaghetti	[spə'geti] n. 意大利面	facility	[fə'sɪləti] n. 设施;设备
toast	[təʊst] n. 吐司	avoid	[ə'vɔɪd] vt. 避免;防止
champagne	[ʃæm'peɪn] n. 香槟	contact	['kɒntækt] vt. 联系
candle	['kændl] n. 蜡烛	prepare	[prɪ'peə(r)] v. 准备
latte	['lateɪ] n. 拿铁咖啡	delay	[dɪ'leɪ] v. 延迟;推迟
bunch	[bʌntʃ] n. 串;束;扎	order	['ɔːdə(r)] v. 点餐;订购
continental breakfast	n. 欧式早餐	croissant	[krwɑː'sɒŋ] n. 羊角面包

Task Three Sample Dialogues

1. Dialogue 1 Ordering Lunch by Phone①

Staff: Good afternoon. This is Tina speaking. How can I help you?

Guest: Good afternoon. This is room 521. I'd like to have lunch in my room, please?

Staff: Certainly, ma'am. We serve lunch until 14:00. What would you like to have?

Guest: What kind of noodles do you have?

Staff: We have Beijing noodles with sauce and traditional beef noodles.

Guest: I'd like a bowl of Beijing noodles with sauce.

Staff: Please wait a minute. Anything else, ma'am?

Guest: No, thanks, that's all.

Staff: So one of Beijing noodles with sauce will be delivered to Room 521.

Guest: Right.

Staff: Thank you for your calling, ma'am. Your order will be delivered in 15 minutes.

(A few minutes later)

Staff: Room service, may I come in?

Guest: Come in please.

Staff: Good afternoon, ma'am. Here are your noodles. Enjoy your meal.

Guest: Thank you so much.

> **Useful Expressions for Better Understanding of Dialogue 1**

(1) Good afternoon, ma'am. This is Tina speaking. How can I help you?

下午好，女士。我是蒂娜，请问有什么能帮到您？

(2) Can I have lunch in my room, please?

请问可以送午餐到我房间吗？

(3) We serve lunch until 14:00. What would you like to have?

我们午餐供应时间到14点，您需要点什么呢？

(4) I'd like a bowl of Beijing noodles with sauce.

一碗北京炸酱面，谢谢。

2. Dialogue 2 Room Service Delay②

Guest: Good afternoon. This is room 602. I ordered spaghetti for lunch at 13:00, but it hasn't arrived yet.

Staff: I'm sorry for that, let me check. Yes, your spaghetti has been prepared and sent to your room. I'll call to ask what happened. We are so sorry, sir. Because of the

COVID-19, there are more customers ordering meals today, and the hotel staff are not enough, so the delivery time will be longer, sorry for the inconvenience.

Guest: OK. Can I order other food? I'm hungry.

Staff: Sure, sir. What would you like to have, sir?

Guest: What kinds of coffee do you have?

Staff: We have Latte, Cappuccino, American coffee and Espresso.

Guest: A cup of Latte, please. And what kind of juice do you have?

Staff: We have mango, apple, orange, and pear juice. They are seasonal fruits.

Guest: A glass of mango juice, please.

Staff: No, problem. We will send your order immediately.

➢ **Useful Expressions for better understanding of Dialogue 2**

(1) I ordered spaghetti for lunch for 13:00, but it hasn't arrived yet.

我点的意大利面要求下午1点送到房间,但是现在还没有送到。

(2) I'm sorry for that, let me check. Yes, your spaghetti has been prepared and sent to your room. I'll call to ask what's happened. We are so sorry, sir. Because of the COVID-19, there are more customers ordering meals today, and the hotel staffs are not enough, so the delivery time will be longer, sorry for the inconvenience.

非常抱歉,我帮您查询一下。抱歉先生,您的餐点已经准备好,但是受新冠肺炎疫情的影响,现正处于送餐高峰期,送餐部人手不够,所以导致您的餐食等待时间过长,我会尽快为您安排送餐,很抱歉给您带来不便。

(3) OK. Can I order other food? I'm hungry.

好的,我还可以加餐吗?我现在很饿。

(4) They are seasonal fruits.

这些都是应季的水果。

(5) No, problem. We will send your order immediately.

没问题,我们立即为您下单。

3. Dialogue 3   Telephone order for American breakfast③

Staff: Good morning. Room Service. May I help you?

Guest: Yes. Can you tell me what you have for breakfast, please?

Staff: We serve Chinese, continental, American, and British breakfasts.

Guest: I'd prefer to have breakfast in my room. Could you send it to me now?

Staff: Certainly, sir. Would you please tell me your name and room number?

Guest: Jason Lowe. Room 1908.

Staff: Room 1908. What would you like to order, Mr. Lowe?

Guest: I'll have an American breakfast for two people.

Staff: OK. American breakfast for two people. What kind of juice would you like, mango, pineapple, tomato, kiwi fruit, orange or watermelon juice?

Guest: Orange juice sounds nice.

扫码
听听力

Staff: Yes, 2 glasses of orange juice. Would you like some cereals, Mr. Lowe?

Guest: 2 cornflakes with yogurt.

Staff: Yes, how would you like your eggs: boiled, poached, scrambled, fried or omelet?

Guest: 1 sausage with eggs, over easy; 1 cheese omelet, please.

Staff: Yes, what kind of bread would you like? We have toasts, rolls, croissants, muffins, doughnuts, and Danish pastry. With jam or butter?

Guest: 2 toasts with butter and marmalade.

Staff: Tea or coffee?

Guest: 1 American coffee and 1 Latte.

Staff: Thank you, Mr. Lowe. So you have ordered an American breakfast for two people, including 2 glasses of orange juice; 2 cornflakes with yogurt; 1 sausage with eggs and over easy, 1 cheese omelet; 2 toasts with butter and marmalade; 1 American coffee and 1 Latte. Am I correct? Would you like anything else?

Guest: Exactly. That's all.

Staff: Thank you, Mr. Lowe. Your breakfast will be sent to your room in 30 minutes.

➢ Useful Expressions for Better Understanding of Dialogue 3

(1) Good morning. Room Service. May I help you?

早上好，送餐部，请问有什么可以为您效劳的？

(2) We serve Chinese, continental, American, and British breakfasts.

我们供应的有中式、欧式、美式和英式早餐。

(3) What kind of juice would you like, mango, pineapple, tomato, kiwi fruit, orange or watermelon juice?

您想喝什么果汁，芒果、菠萝、番茄、猕猴桃、橙汁、西瓜汁？

(4) Would you like some cereals, Mr. Lowe?

麦片需要吗？罗伊先生。

(5) 2 cornflakes with yogurt.

2杯酸奶玉米片。

(6) How would you like your eggs: boiled, poached, scrambled, fried or omelet?

鸡蛋您想怎么做：水煮、荷包蛋、炒鸡蛋、煎鸡蛋、蛋卷？

(7) 1 sausage with eggs, over easy; 1 cheese omelet, please.

1份香肠煎蛋，鸡蛋双面煎；1份奶酪煎蛋卷。

(8) We have toasts, rolls, croissants, muffins, doughnuts, and Danish pastry. With jam or butter?

我们有吐司面包、面包卷、牛角包、松饼、甜甜圈、丹麦酥皮饼，需要果酱或黄油吗？

(9) 2 toasts with butter and marmalade.

2份吐司面包加黄油和橘子酱。

(10) 1 American coffee and 1 Latte.

1杯美式咖啡，一杯拿铁。

(11) Your breakfast will be sent to your room in 30 minutes

您的早餐将会在30分钟后送往您的房间。

4. Dialogue 4　　An Anniversary Service①

Staff：Good afternoon，Mr. James. How can I help you?

Guest：Good afternoon，I realized that my anniversary is coming soon. I want to give my wife a surprise.

Staff：Congratulations! Mr. James. What do you have in mind?

Guest：I am thinking if you could arrange to have a small cake with our names on it，and a bunch of roses. Oh，it would be better with some champagne.

Staff：Sure，no problem. Could you tell me you and your wife's names? We'll even put a few candles on it for you.

Guest：My name is James，and my wife's name is Lillian.

Staff：OK. Could you tell me how long have you been married? We can write blessings on the cake.

Guest：It has been 2 years. Do you have any small cards? Can I write something on it to my wife?

Staff：I'm sure we could，because you are our hotel's member，so these cards are gifts free to you.

Guest：Great!

Staff：What kind of champagne would you like，Mr. James? Dry or sweet?

Guest：How much are they?

Staff：Both are 233 yuan. And the birthday cake is 88 yuan.

Guest：OK，I want a bottle of dry champagne. We will return to the hotel at 15：00. Please prepare it for me in advance.

Staff：No problem，Mr. Green. We'll send them up as soon as possible. Your order will be included in your bills. Have a nice day!

> **Useful Expressions for Better Understanding of Dialogue 4**

(1) I realized that my anniversary is coming soon. I want to give my wife a surprise.

我意识到我的结婚纪念日到了，我想给我妻子一个惊喜。

(2) What do you have in mind?

您有什么想法呢?

(3) I am thinking if you could arrange to have a small cake with our name on it，and a bunch of roses. Oh，it would be better with some champagne.

我想准备一个印有名字的蛋糕和一束玫瑰花，再配上香槟。

(4) We'll even put a few candles on it for you.

我们还会配送蜡烛给您。

(5) Do you have any small card? Can I write something on it to my wife?

你们有贺卡吗？我能写些祝福给我妻子吗？

(6) What kind of champagne would you like, Mr. James? Dry or sweet?

您想要什么类型的香槟呢？是干香槟还是甜香槟？

(7) We will return to the hotel at 15:00 this afternoon. Please prepare it for me in advance.

我们大概下午3点返回酒店，麻烦你们提前帮我准备好。

(8) We'll send them up as soon as possible.

我们会及时送到。

5. Dialogue 5 Robot Meal Delivery service⑤

Staff: Good afternoon, Sir. How may I help you?

Guest: Good afternoon, I want takeout into the room. But I have a cold and can't go downstairs to pick up my takeout. Could you deliver it to my room?

Staff: I'm sorry, sir. I'm afraid not. In order to avoid the COVID-19 and reduce personnel exposure, we have pushed out a robot meal delivery service, which allows delivery man to take your order food on the robot and enter your room number to deliver it to your room.

Guest: Oh, your hotel's facilities are very advanced.

Staff: Thank you, sir. What time will your takeout arrive? Please call the front desk when your takeout arrives. The front desk staff will teach the delivery man how to operate. Besides, our robot meal delivery is charged by hour, 10 yuan per hour, which will be credited to your bill.

Guest: OK.

Staff: Thank you for calling, Sir.

Guest: OK, I'll book your hotel next time.

Staff: Thank you, sir. If the robot has any problems, please contact the front desk any time.

Guest: Thank you.

扫码
听听力

➤ Useful Expressions for Better Understanding of Dialogue 5

(1) I want takeout into the room. But I have a cold and can't go downstairs to pick up my takeout. Could you deliver it to my room?

我想点外卖到我的房间，但是我有些感冒不方便下楼取，你能帮我送到房间吗？

(2) In order to avoid the COVID-19 and reduce personnel exposure, we have push out a robot meal delivery service, which allows delivery man to take your order food on the robot and enter your room number to deliver it to your room.

为了避免新冠肺炎疫情患病人数增加，为了减少人员接触，我们酒店推出了机器人送餐服务，您可以让外卖员把您的餐点放在送餐机器人里面并输入您的房间号，送餐机器人就能送到您的房间。

（3）Your hotel's facilities are very advanced.

你们酒店的设施设备很先进。

（4）What time will your takeout arrive? Please call the front desk when your takeout arrives. The front desk staff will teach the delivery man how to operate. Besides, our robot meal delivery is charged by hour, 10 yuan per hour, which will be credited to your bill.

您的外卖大概什么时候到呢？快到的时候您可以致电前台，前台工作人员会教外卖员如何操作送餐机器人。同时，我们的送餐机器人是收费的，每小时10元，将会计入您的酒店账单中。

（5）I'll book your hotel next time.

我下次还会预订你们的酒店。

（6）If the robot has any problems, please contact the front desk any time.

如果在机器人使用过程中有任何问题，请您致电前台。

6. Notes Related to Check in Dialogues

①对话中叫 room service 是电话点餐，基本上每位客人入住的客房里都会有相应的菜单（包含中西餐、酒水等），上面标注相应的菜品及价格，客人可根据自己的需求拨打酒店前台或菜单上的订餐电话进行电话点餐，之后会有相应的送餐员送到相应房间。点餐的费用会在退房时一起结算，一般会额外收取10%—15%服务费。

②如果你是一位客房部送餐员，送餐过程中如遇到客人投诉送餐过慢，应立即向客人表示抱歉，并向客人耐心解释。送餐慢可能会导致客人对酒店的印象减分，因此送餐员应尽量减少此类问题发生，同时也应尽最大努力满足客人的需求。

③星级酒店中的"欧式早餐"也叫"简单早餐"，而美式早餐相对项目繁多，因此也被称为"复杂式早餐"和"全早餐"。在酒店服务中，客人通过送餐服务来点美式早餐的居多。点单时要和客人们确定以下五种类型的餐饮：水果或果汁、谷类、蛋类、面包、饮品。

④作为一名送餐服务员，日常也需要为客人处理一些特殊要求。要及时与前厅对接入住客人的特殊要求，了解客人喜好，随机应变。

⑤Robot meal delivery service 是现在新型酒店智能数字化产物，特别是在新冠肺炎疫情的影响下，机器人送餐服务在各大酒店使用率上升，一方面缓解酒店员工人手不足的问题，另一方面提升酒店智能数字化设施设备能力。酒店设施设备智能数字化提升也是将来酒店业硬件设施应具备的重要条件之一。

Task Four　Procedure, Functional Expressions and Service Culture Points of Room service

1. Ordering by Phone Information

（1）Greet the guests.

Good morning/afternoon/evening, sir/madam!

(2) Enquire the guests.

How can I help you?

(3) Explain the choice.

What kind of breakfast/lunch/dinner/drinks do you want to order?

(4) Confirm the order.

OK, Sir/Madam. Your order is ×××. Is that right?

(5) Get further information.

Do you have anything else? Thank you for your call.

2. Culture Points

(1) Professional ethics.

Good professional skills will help employees love their job, enhance their learning and working attitude, improve their service skills and provide high-quality services for guests.

(2) Hotel service awareness.

To be a room attendant, you should be warm, thoughtful, and active awareness and behavior of hotel employees can provide good service for guests. It is the key to improve the service quality of the hotel. Establishing service awareness is not only the premise of hotel employees, but also one of the most basic professional qualities of employees.

(3) Communication skills.

We should have good communication skills and ability, resolve misunderstandings and contradictions in interpersonal relations, and listen to different opinions and suggestions. Some problems in the service process also require employees to actively communicate and coordinate in appropriate ways and methods, so as to establish good interpersonal relations in complex and changeable social communication, work effectively and achieve career success.

Task Five Listening Ability Enhancement

1. Listen to the dialogue of group check in and fill in the blanks

Staff: Good evening, __(1)__, how can I help you?

Guest: This is Tina in Room 361. I would like to order room service for our __(2)__.

Staff: Yes, madam. What would you like to __(3)__?

Guest: I have no idea. What would you __(4)__?

Staff: Would you please take a look at the room service __(5)__ on your desk?

扫码
听听力

酒店英语

扫码
听听力

Guest: Oh, I see. I'll look it over and call you back.

Staff: We're looking forward to ___(6)___ you, madam.

2. Listen to the conversations and fill in the form

	Conversation 1	Conversation 2
Guest Name		
Room Number		
Sort of Breakfast		
Coffee/Tea		
Kind of Juice		

Task Six　　Interpretation

(1) May I have your name and room number, please?

(2) What would you like to order?

(3) Room service. How may I help you?

(4) Would you like anything else?

(5) We will provide you with the best service.

(6) It will be brought up right away.

(7) 机器人送餐服务是现代酒店新型送餐的一种方式。

(8) 你好，我想点一杯苹果汁送到我房间。

(9) 您除了可以拨打电话订餐，还可以在电视菜单上点餐。

(10) 祝您入住愉快。

(11) 我想点一份中式早餐，明早8点钟送到我的房间。

(12) 我们的客户服务是24小时在线。

Task Seven　　Role Play

1. Make a situational conversation about the ordering breakfast by phone

Student A: You are a hotel guest and call room service to order American breakfast.

Student B: You are a hotel room service attendant. Answer the call and take the order.

Roll of fruit juice: Orange/Apple/Mango/Tomato.

Choice of Bread: Bread roll/White Toast.

Beverages: Coffee/Milk/English Tea/Chinese Tea.

2. Make a situational conversation about the room service delay

Student A: You are a hotel guest and call room service to ask why your breakfast hasn't been sent up yet.

Student B: You are a hotel room service attendant. Answer the call and apologize. Promise to send the guest another breakfast.

3. Make a situational conversation about a birthday party

Student A: Your son is going to have a birthday party. You call room service to order a birthday cake for him. It is a chocolate cake with the words written "Happy Birthday, James". You also want four candles and some food and drinks.

Student B: You are a hotel room service attendant. Answer the call and make clear guest's requests. Recommend food and drinks.

Task Eight Extended Professional Knowledge Reading

Hotel Room Service Specification

Booking: (1) When accepting a room meal reservation, the operator should answer the phone within three rings and say hello to the guest politely. (2) Ask the guest's name, room number, ordering content, delivery time and special requirements, and recommend them to the guest in due time. (3) Repeat the specific requirements and ordering contents of the guest. After being confirmed by the guest, tell the waiting time and thank the guest.

Preparing: (1) Send the order to the kitchen in time after receiving the order. (2) Prepare paper napkins, knives and forks and other tableware according to the ordering contents. (3) Check whether the dishes accord with the requirements.

Delivering: (1) After confirming that the guest's room number is correct, knock on the door politely and say "Room service". (2) After the guest opens the door, say hello to the guest and put the food in the designated position with the consent of the guest. (3) Ask the guest if there is any service and tell the guest to enjoy it slowly and close the door gently.

Recycling: (1) Call the guest and ask whether the meal is finished and tell the room service attendant to recycle the tableware in the room. (2) If the guest is not in the room, ask the room service attendant to open the door, take out the tableware and clean it on time.

Question discussion based on the reading.

① How many steps are there in the room service process?

② What do you think is the most important step and why?

Hotel Online Check in

In the catering industry, with the wide application of artificial intelligence, the "smart restaurant" is becoming more and more common.

For enterprises, the rental price of robots is only half that of waiters. If they are used for a long time, the service life of 5-8 years can be recovered in about one year. Restaurants basically invest little in service.

The delivery robot is safer than traditional food delivery. The delivery robot can effectively meet different transportation needs, such as the room service attendant or cashier, and support screen click or watch remote control; machine control is more convenient. Delivery robots help to improve service efficiency and reduce labor costs.

Question: What benefits do you think delivery robot service can bring to the hotel industry? Why?

_____

Unit 11
Banquet and Beverage Service

After studying this unit, you should be able to do the following:

Knowledge & Ability Objectives

1. grasp the service steps of the banquet service and beverage service;

2. be able to understand banquet service phrases and sentence patterns;

3. be able to make a banquet service plan for customers in English;

4. know the beverage culture and types.

Quality Objectives

1. understand the basic responsibilities of banquet service and beverage service;

2. have the language and professional ability to accurately complete the banquet service in English.

Task One   Lead-in

Brainstorming

Look at the picture, the host is reserving to the guest. What should he say to the guest? What should the service steps be like? Please discuss with your team members and write down the sentences they might say.

Staff: _____

Guest: _____

酒店英语

(Note: the picture is quoted from the following website https://image.baidu.com.)

Task Two　Words and Expressions

host	[həʊst]n. 餐厅男领位员	menu	['menju:]n. 菜单
hostess	[həʊstəs]n. 餐厅女领位员	beer	[bɪə(r)]n. 啤酒
head waiter	餐厅领班	alcoholic	[ˌælkə'hɒlɪk]adj. 含酒精的
waiter	['weɪtə(r)]n. 男服务员	Cappuccino	[ˌkæpu'tʃi:nəʊ]n. 卡布奇诺咖啡
waitress	['weɪtrəs]n. 女服务员	on the rocks	加冰块
banquet	['bæŋkwɪt]n. 宴会	snack	[snæk]n. 小吃
private room	包房	double	['dʌbl]adj. 双份(浓度)的
cocktail	['kɒkteɪl]n. 鸡尾酒	aperitif	[əˌperə'ti:f]n.(餐前)开胃酒

Task Three　Sample Dialogues

1. Dialogue 1　Banquet Reservation①

Staff: Good afternoon. Sheraton Hotel Banquet Service. I'm today's hostess. How may I help you?
Guest: We want to have a banquet in your hotel. Can you arrange it for us?
Staff: Certainly, ma'am. When would you like your banquet?
Guest: On April 5th.
Staff: How many people?

Guest: About 100 people.

Staff: How many tables would you like?

Guest: Ten tables.

Staff: I recommend our Crystal Hall. It can seat 100-120 people comfortably. How much would you like to spend for each table?

Guest: 1000 yuan.

Staff: Are there any special demands for the banquet menu?

Guest: No, thanks.

Staff: OK. Thank you for your call. We look forward to meeting you soon.

➢ Useful Expressions for Better Understanding of Dialogue 1

(1) Good afternoon. Sheraton Hotel Banquet Service.... How may I help you?

下午好。希尔顿酒店宴会服务中心。……请问有什么能帮到您？

(2) We want to have a banquet in your hotel. Can you arrange it for us?

我们想在贵酒店举办一场宴会，可以为我们安排一下吗？

(3) When would you like your banquet?

您的宴会打算什么时间举办呢？

(4) I recommend our Crystal Hall. It can seat 100-120 people comfortably. How much would you like to spend for each table?

我推荐您预订水晶厅，可以容纳100—120人。您打算每桌的预算是多少呢？

(5) Thank you for your call. We look forward to meeting you soon.

感谢您的来电，我们期待与您会面。

2. Dialogue 2   Seating Guests② and Aperitif Service③

Staff: Good evening. Welcome to our restaurant. I'm today's host. Do you have a reservation?

Guest: Yes, it's Tom.

Staff: Let me check the list. Yes, you booked a table for five. Would you like a table near the window?

Guest: If you have, I want it.

Staff: There is a table by the window. This way, please. Here is the menu. The waiter will help you to take your order. Please wait a moment.

Guest: Thank you.

Staff: My pleasure. Please enjoy your meal.

Staff: Good evening. Here is the menu. Would you like something to drink before dinner?

Guest: What kind of aperitif do you have? Can you recommend something for us? I want some local wine.

Staff: How about Dry Sherry? It tastes fresh with vanilla flavor. It's a good choice as an aperitif.

扫码

听听力

Guest: Nice choice. Do you recommend something for the main course?
Staff: How about Pan-fried salmon? Seafood with white wine, it tastes light.
Guest: OK. Two glasses of Dry Sherry, and double Pan-fried salmon.
Staff: Sure. I will deliver your order right away.

➢ **Useful Expressions for Better Understanding of Dialogue 2**

(1) Good evening. Welcome to our restaurant.... Do you have a reservation?
晚上好，欢迎光临。……请问您有预订吗？

(2) Let me check the list. Yes, you booked a table for five. Would you like a table near the window?
我查看一下记录，您预订的是五人桌，您想座位靠窗边吗？

(3) There is a table by the window. This way, please. Here is the menu. The waiter will help you to take your order. Please wait a moment.
正好现在有一桌靠窗的桌位，这边请。这是菜单您看一下，服务员将会为您点餐，请稍等。

(4) My pleasure. Please enjoy your meal.
这是我的荣幸，祝您用餐愉快。

(5) Would you like something to drink before dinner?
您想要餐前喝点什么吗？

(6) What kind of aperitif do you have? Can you recommend something for us? I want some local wine.
餐厅有什么类型的餐前酒呢？你能推荐一些给我们吗？我想尝试本地的葡萄酒。

(7) How about Dry Sherry? It tastes fresh with vanilla flavor. It's a good choice as an aperitif.
干型雪莉酒如何？口感清新伴有香草味道，是作为餐前酒的不错选择。

(8) Do you recommend something for the main course?
有什么主菜推荐吗？

(9) How about Pan-fried salmon? Seafood with white wine, it tastes light.
香煎三文鱼如何？海鲜搭配白葡萄酒，口感清爽。

3. Dialogue 3   Recommend a Cup of Coffee

Staff: Good morning, Sir. Welcome to our lobby bar.
Guest: Good morning, I like coffee. Do you have any recommendations?
Staff: Sure, here is our menu. How about a Cappuccino?
Guest: I'd like a cup of Cappuccino.
Staff: Sure. Would you like a single or double?④
Guest: Double will be better.
Staff: Sure, a double Cappuccino is coming soon. Would you like anything else?
Guest: No, thanks.
Staff: OK. It will just take a few minutes.

扫码
听听力

➢ **Useful Expressions for Better Understanding of Dialogue 3**

(1) Good morning, Sir. Welcome to our lobby bar.

早上好,先生。欢迎来到我们大堂吧。

(2) Good morning, I like coffee. Do you have any recommendations?

早上好,我平时喜欢喝咖啡。你有什么好的推荐吗?

(3) I'd like a cup of Cappuccino.

我想要一杯卡布奇诺咖啡。

(4) Would you like a single or double?

您想要单份(浓度)的还是双份(浓度)的?

(5) Double will be better.

双份(浓度)的会好一些。

4. Dialogue 4   Trying Local Beer

Staff: Good evening, Sir. How may I help you?

Guest: Good evening, I'd like some drinks. Can you recommend something?

Staff: Our local Tsingtao beer is more popular, and our Whisky is also good. You can try it.

Guest: OK. One bottle of beer and a Whisky on the rocks, please.

Staff: No problem. Would you like some snacks to go with your drinks?

Guest: Well, a plate of peanuts.

Staff: I will be right back with your orders.

➢ **Useful Expressions for Better Understanding of Dialogue 4**

(1) Good evening, I'd like some drinks. Can you recommend something?

晚上好,我想喝点酒,有什么推荐吗?

(2) Our local Tsingtao beer is more popular, and our Whisky is also good. You can try it.

我们当地的青岛啤酒和威士忌不错,您可以试一试。

(3) One bottle of beer and a Whisky on the rocks.

一瓶啤酒,一杯威士忌加冰。

(4) a plate of peanuts.

一盘花生。

(5) I will be right back with your orders.

马上为您上。

5. Dialogue 5   Cocktail Service[⑤]

Staff: Good evening. How may I help you? This is our wine list.

Guest: OK.

Staff: Do you have any preference? Alcoholic or non-alcoholic?

Guest: I prefer alcoholic. Can you recommend some cocktails for us?

Staff: How about dry Martini? It not only retains its taste, but also makes you feel smooth.

Guest: Sounds great. Get one, please.

Staff: Would you like it straight up or on the rocks?

Guest: On the rocks.

Staff: Do you want to try our special cocktail? Margarita.

Guest: One more, please. Also on the rocks. My friend wants a Brandy.

Staff: Sure, no problem. One dry Martini and one Margarita, and one Brandy, is that right?

Guest: Yes.

Staff: Thank you very much. Prepare for you right away.

➤ Useful Expressions for Better Understanding of Dialogue 5

(1) Good evening. How may I help you? This is our wine list.
晚上好，请问有什么可以帮您？这是我们的酒水单。

(2) Alcoholic or non-alcoholic?
有酒精还是无酒精饮料？

(3) Can you recommend some cocktails for us?
关于鸡尾酒你有什么好的推荐吗？

(4) How about dry Martini? It not only retains its taste, but also makes you feel smooth.
您可以尝试干马提尼，它不仅保留了马提尼原始的味道，口感也很顺滑。

(5) Straight up or on the rocks?
直饮还是加冰块？

(6) Do you want to try our special cocktail? Margarita.
想尝尝我们特制的鸡尾酒，玛格丽特吗？

(7) My friend wants a Brandy.
我朋友想要一杯白兰地。

6. Notes Related to Check in Dialogues

①作为一个宴会预订人员，当顾客询问宴会预订时应与顾客确认相关基本信息，如时间、人数、特殊偏好等。根据客人不同的需求为其制定不同的方案和准备宴会厅。

②作为一位餐厅领位员，引导顾客就座时应询问其是否有预订，同时询问顾客有无特殊要求，如：喜欢靠窗还是不靠窗，是在吸烟区还是非吸烟区就餐等。

③餐前酒：可以刺激食欲的酒都可以称为餐前酒或开胃酒。一般来说，餐前酒推荐干型的白葡萄酒或红葡萄酒，口感清新不浓郁且有助于开胃。

④点咖啡时，应询问顾客需要单份（浓度）还是双份（浓度）。

⑤鸡尾酒（Cocktail）是一种混合饮品。通常以朗姆酒、金酒、龙舌兰、伏特加、威士忌、白兰地等烈酒或葡萄酒作为基酒，再配以果汁、蛋清、苦精、牛奶、咖啡、糖等其他辅助材料，加以搅拌或摇晃而成，最后还可用柠檬片、水果或薄荷叶作为装饰物。

Task Four Procedure, Functional Expressions and Service Culture Points of Reservation

1. Reservation as a Restaurant Host

(1) Greet the guests.

Good morning/afternoon/evening sir/madam! How may I help you?

(2) Ask guests for reservation information.

Date/Time/Number of people at dinner/Smoking or Non-smoking/Special requests.

(3) Get the information from guests.

Time of arrival/name/phone number.

(4) Confirm reservation.

(5) Thank guests.

Thank you for your call/Thank you for making a reservation.

2. Reservation as a Bartender

(1) Greet the guests.

Good morning/afternoon/evening sir/madam! How can I help you?

(2) Take orders.

Repeat orders/Written down guest's special requests/Ask about guest's like

(3) Confirm the orders.

(4) Serving for guests.

(5) Settle the bill.

(6) Thank you to the guests.

3. Culture Points

How to be an excellent waiter/waitress?

(1) Perfect intention, satisfaction and surprise.

Care about the guests all the time when they need some help.

(2) Observe carefully and keep organized.

Always at your service heart.

(3) Keep in good condition.

(4) Learn to communicate and be good at summarizing.

(5) Focusing.

(6) Focus on customer experience.

Learning, listening and analyzing customer needs.

(7) Keep looking for better ways to solve the problems.

(8) Always be confident.

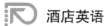

Task Five Listening Ability Enhancement

1. Listen to the conversation and decide if the following statements are true (T) or false (F)

（1）The reservation was made on the phone.
（2）Mr. Smith would like a table in the open.
（3）Mr. Smith wanted to book two tables.
（4）The reservation was for four people.
（5）Mr. Smith booked Room 888 for dinner on Sunday.
（6）The restaurant is a Japanese restaurant.

2. Listen to the four questions and choose the right answers

（1）A. A table for two, please.   B. A cup of coffee, please.   C. I have a reservation.
（2）A. Here is our menu.   B. Wait a minute, please.   C. Sure, sir.
（3）A. What kind of tea would you like?   B. I don't care.   C. Sorry, we don't have.
（4）A. On the rocks?   B. No, we don't have.   C. What about Beijing beer?

Task Six Interpretation

（1）What time do you want to reserve the table?
（2）Would you give me your name and phone number?
（3）Thank you for making the reservation with us.
（4）Non-smoking, please.
（5）The restaurant is full now.
（6）Do you mind sharing the table with others?
（7）本地啤酒非常受欢迎。
（8）你好，我想要一杯鲜橙汁。
（9）您想要什么类型的甜点？
（10）您是要白葡萄酒还是红葡萄酒呢？
（11）我想要一杯无酒精饮料。
（12）抱歉先生，我们目前只有应季水果果汁。

Task Seven Role Play

1. Make a situational conversation about the banquet reservation

Student A: You want to reserve a banquet for 100 people in the Hilton Hotel in

May, and you will need 9 tables.

Student B: You are the banquet manager, answer the guest's request and details.

2. Make a situational conversation about recommending coffee

Student A: You want to order some drinks from the list.

Student B: You are a lobby bar staff, take down the guest's request.

> Black coffee 黑咖啡　　　　Latte 拿铁
> Cappuccino 卡布奇诺　Espresso 意式浓缩咖啡

Task Eight　Extended Professional Knowledge Reading

1. Chinese Banquet Etiquette Precautions

(1) Understanding seating etiquette;

(2) Be consistent with dining etiquette;

(3) Pay attention to table taboos;

(4) Pay attention to eating;

(5) Pay attention to the allocation of seats.

Question: What else do you think should be paid attention to in Chinese food etiquette?

2. How to Match Cuisine and Wine

You can choose prepared wine and aperitif before meals, while cold dishes and seafood are used for white wine, meat is used for red wine, and sweet wine or sparkling wine should be used for dessert. It is best to choose wine from the same country and region as the banquet wine.

White wine is suitable for appetizers or seafood and other dishes. Beef and other delicious meat dishes with red wine. Fried meat with light red wine. We should know how to identify the wine label. Look at the label of the wine and check whether it is the wine you want. Such as the harvest age of the grape, the name of the wine and the origin of the wine. When the wine bottle is opened, you can change the wine except for obvious deterioration problems. Generally, you are not allowed to return it.

Question: What knowledge of wine have you learned through reading?

Unit 12
Telephone Service

Unit Objectives

After studying this unit, you should be able to do the following:

Knowledge & Ability Objectives

1. knowing the telephone courtesy standard;

2. making a wake-up call;

3. handling incoming calls;

4. dealing with other needs which include guest message, emergency situations and so on;

5. grasping words, phases, sentences related to telephone service.

Quality Objectives

1. to listen and communicate with guests professionally;

2. become an excellent operator with responsibility, cross cultural ability.

Task One Lead-in

1. Topic Discussion

Every luxury hotel provides telephone service, which has a huge influence on guest impressions. In your opinion, which is the most important skill to satisfy the guest, the professional language, tone of voice or the attitude?

2. Matching These English Phrases up with Chinese Phrases

①Telephone Etiquette　　　　　A. 客人留言

②Handling Incoming Calls　　　B. 房间工程

③Wake-up Calls　　　　　　　C. 叫醒电话

④Emergency Situation　　　　　D. 接听电话

⑤Engineering Service　　　　　E. 紧急情况

⑥Guest Messages   F. 电话礼仪

Task Two   Words and Expressions

operator	[ˈɒpəreɪtə(r)]n. 接线员	wake-up call	n. 叫醒服务
specific	[spəˈsɪfɪk]adj. 具体的	Human Resource Department	人事部
Reservation Department	预订部	Sales Department	销售部
phoenix	[ˈfiːnɪks]n. 凤凰	recruit	[rɪˈkruːt]n. 新成员 v. 招募
advertisement	[ədˈvɜːtɪsmənt]n. 广告	interview	[ˈɪntəvjuː]n. 面试 v. 采访
consult	[kənˈsʌlt]v. 咨询	engage	[ɪnˈɡeɪdʒ]v. 占用
extend	[ɪkˈstend]v. 转接	banquet	[ˈbæŋkwɪt]n. 宴会
room rate	房价	reservation	[ˌrezəˈveɪʃn]n. 预订
beverage	[ˈbevərɪdʒ]n.（酒精）饮料	standard room	标准间
gourmet	[ˈɡʊəmeɪ]n. 美食家	projection TV	投影电视
nursing-bottle warmer	温奶器	business hour	营业时间

Task Three   Sample Dialogues

1. Dialogue 1   Wake-up Call①

Staff: Good evening, Service Center. I'm Kobe. How may I help you?

Guest: Good evening, I need a wake-up call early tomorrow morning.

Staff: No problem. May I have your name? And could you tell me the specific time?

Guest: Alexander Collin, and I need a wake-up call at 5:15 a.m..

Staff: May I have your room number?

Guest: Room 1210.

Staff: OK, Mr. Collin, may I repeat it? 5:15, tomorrow morning, which is October 5th, Room 1210, is that right?

Guest: Yes, thanks.

Staff: My pleasure. Is there anything else I can help you with?

Guest: No, thank you.

Staff: Always at your service. Have a nice evening.

(Next morning)

Staff: Good morning, Mr. Collin, this is your wake-up call service. Now it's 5:15 a.m., the weather is sunny, and the temperature is 26 degrees centigrade. We hope you have a nice day!

Guest: Thank you very much.

➤ Useful Expressions for Better Understanding of Dialogue 1

(1) How may I help you?

请问您有什么需要吗？/请问有什么可以帮您的吗？

(2) May I have your name?

请问您叫什么？

(3) And could you tell me the specific time?

能告诉我具体的时间吗？

(4) May I have your room number?

请问您的房号是多少？

(5) Is there anything else I can help you with?

还有其他需要我帮忙的吗？

(6) Always at your service.

随时为您效劳。

(7) Have a nice evening.

祝您有个愉快的晚上。

2. Dialogue 2   Answering Outside Line[②]

(Scene 1: Transfer call to Human Resource Department)

Staff: Good morning, thank you for calling Country Garden Phoenix Hotel. How may I assist you?

Guest: I saw a hotel recruit advertisement on the website, and I want to take this interview, but I want to know some details. The line is engaged. Can you put me through to the HR Department, please?

Staff: Certainly, I'm going to extend your call to the Recruitment Supervisor's office.

Guest: Thank you.

Staff: You're welcome

(Scene 2: Transfer call to Reservation Department)

Staff: Good evening, thank you for calling Country Garden Phoenix Hotel. What can I do for you?

Guest: Can you put me through to the Sales Department or Reservation

Department? I'd like to consult the price for a banquet, and room rate for a group reservation.

Staff: I am sorry, Sir. They are not available. Are you inquiring about a reservation? How may I assist you with your reservation?

Guest: Sure, what's the price of a 50 people banquet for 1 day, and the room rate of 15 standard rooms for 1 night?

Staff: Our price of a banquet for 1 day with 50 people is 80000 yuan, which includes soft drinks, and free parking during that day. As for the rate of standard room, it is 800 yuan per day for a group which includes breakfast.

Guest: I'd like to reserve a banquet with 50 people and 15 standard rooms the day after tomorrow.

Staff: OK, may I know the time for the banquet? And your name, contact phone, please?

Guest: 6:30 p.m., my name is George Bush, and my phone number is 135×××× 8694.

Staff: OK, Mr. Bush, you booked a banquet at 6:30 p.m. with 50 people and 15 standard rooms the day after tomorrow, which is November 29th. Is that correct?

Guest: Right, thank you.

Staff: It's my pleasure, is there anything else I can help you with?

Guest: No, thanks.

Staff: I'm always at your service. Have a nice evening.

(Scene 3: Leave message)

Staff: Good morning, Sheraton Wuhan Hankou Hotel. How may I assist you?

Guest: Good morning, can you extend my call to Room 2016? The guest is my friend and her name is Zoey Brown. I tried several times, but the line is still busy, and I couldn't contact her.

Staff: Sure, please hold on. (A few minutes later) I am sorry, the line of Room 2016 is not available. Would you like to wait?

Guest: I'm afraid not. I've booked a spa 15 minutes later. Can I leave a message for her? Just tell her I've reserved dinner for us in Feast at 6:30 p.m. today, and don't be late. That's all. Thank you.

Staff: May I know your name and contact number?

Guest: Fiona, 138××××3868.

Staff: Please allow me to confirm: Ms. Fiona, you've booked 6:30 p.m. in Feast today for you and Ms. Zoey, she is our guest in Room 2016. Is that right?

Guest: Yes, thanks.

Staff: You're welcome. Is there anything else I can help you with?

Guest: No, bye.

Staff:Goodbye, have a wonderful day.

> **Useful Expressions for Better Understanding of Dialogue 2**

(1)Thank you for calling Country Garden Phoenix Hotel.

谢谢您致电凤凰花园酒店。

(2)How may I assist you?

有什么可以帮您的吗?

(3)The line is engaged.

电话占线。

(4)Can you put me through to HR Department, please?

您能把我的电话转到人事部吗?

(5)I'm going to extend your call to Recruitment Supervisor's office.

我马上帮您把电话转到招聘主管办公室。

(6)What can I do for you?

有什么可以帮您的吗?

(7)I'd like to consult price for banquet, and the room rate for group reservation.

我想咨询下预订宴会的费用和团队预订的房价。

(8)Our price of banquet for 1 day with 50 people is 80000 yuan which includes soft drinks, and free parking during that day.

50人参加的宴会一天的费用是80000元,含软饮,同时那天停车免费。

(9)As for the rate of standard room, it is 800 yuan per day for group which includes breakfast.

团队预订的房价是每天800元,含早餐。

(10)May I know the time for the banquet?

请问宴会具体的时间是几点?

(11)Can you extend my call to Room 2016?

你能帮我转接到2016房吗?

(12)The line of Room 2016 is not available. Would you like to wait?

2016房打不通。您可以稍等下吗?

(13)Have a wonderful day.

祝您有个精彩的一天。

3. Dialogue 3   Handing Internal Calls[③]

Staff:Good afternoon, Guest Service Center, what can I do for you?

Guest:The air-conditioner doesn't work. Can you please send someone to fix it?

Staff:Certainly. I'll send an air-conditioning attendant as soon as possible. Is there anything else I can help you with?

Guest:Is it a projection TV in my room? How can I use it? Should I install a screen projection App? It differs from the normal one.

Staff:Don't worry, the staff will help you in a minute.

Guest: OK, thanks. Almost forgot, where can I borrow a warmer for a nursing-bottle?

Staff: What type of nursing-bottle warmer would you like?

Guest: All is fine.

Staff: Please wait a moment, our room attendant will bring it for you.

Guest: Sorry to disturb you for so long. The last one, can you recommend some dishes in your hotel? We're new here and want to try local food.

Staff: Welcome and you won't miss Steamed Wuchang Fish in our restaurant. The taste is gorgeous, fleshy, and tender. This dish is known for being delicious and healthy.

Guest: I can hardly wait. Which restaurant serves it in your hotel? And when does it open?

Staff: Our Chinese restaurant serves this dish. The business hour is from 11:30 a.m. to 2:00 p.m., and another one is from 5:00 p.m. to 8:00 p.m.. Just in case, you may book a table before you go. Many people go there and have meals.

Guest: Thank you for your kindly advice.

Staff: It's my pleasure. Is there anything else?

Guest: No, thank you so much. Bye.

Staff: Don't mention it, I'm always at your service. Goodbye.

> Useful Expressions for Better Understanding of Dialogue 3

(1) I'll send air-conditioning attendant as soon as possible.
我马上派一位空调维修工去修理。
(2) Should I install a screen projection App? It differs from the normal one.
我应该安装一个投影的应用小程序吗？这个跟一般的有点不一样
(3) The taste is gorgeous, fleshy, and tender. This dish is known for being delicious and healthy.
它的味道棒极了，口感鲜嫩。这道菜以好吃和健康出名。
(4) What type of nursing-bottle warmer would you like?
您想要什么型号的温奶器？
(5) I can hardly wait. Which restaurant serves it in your hotel?
我迫不及待想去吃了。你们酒店哪一家餐厅有这道菜？
(6) Just in case, you may book a table before you go.
为了以防万一，您可以去之前先预订位子。

4. Notes Related to Telephone Service Dialogues

①Wake-up call

有的酒店使用电话进行人工叫醒，有的酒店使用电话进行机器叫醒。有的酒店视客人接听电话为成功叫醒的标志，有的酒店视客人应答叫醒服务为成功叫醒的标志。
不管是何种叫醒方式，成功叫醒的标志是什么，叫醒服务都必须包括以下内容：

早上/下午/晚上好，××先生/女士，现在的时间是×××，这是您的叫醒服务。

有的酒店叫醒服务的内容还会涉及当天的天气、温度，以及其他提醒事项，比如下雨可以提醒客人外出带伞，气温骤降可以提醒客人加衣等。

②Outside line

酒店总机最常接到的外线电话的种类有：咨询招聘信息、预订，除此之外，还有部分是需要帮助非住店客人转接电话给住店客人，或者给住店客人留言的。

有的酒店预订部归属于总机，有的则属于销售部。预订部的员工下班后，24小时都有人上班的总机部则需承担晚间预订的工作。

记录留言时，总机的工作人员必须特别小心，反复跟客人确认日期。美式英语表达日期的格式为：月，日，年；英式英语表达日期的格式为：日，月，年。

③Internal calls

总机最常接到的住店客人的电话类型分别是：房间的工程维修、房间设备的使用、酒店娱乐和餐厅等部门的营业时间。

因此在总机工作的员工要经常跟各部门保持良好的沟通状态，尤其是工程部；此外还要熟悉各类酒店产品，了解它们的特点、价格和营业时间，以便给客人推荐。

由于信息技术的发展，大家可以通过手机或者电脑进行跨市、跨省、跨国联系，多年前需要总机转接国内或国际长途电话的情况几乎已经不存在了。

Task Four Procedure, Functional Expressions and Culture Points of Telephone Service

1. Observe the Rules on Telephone Etiquette

(1) Answer the call within 3 rings. (If you cannot answer in time, please make an apology to the guest.)

(2) Be friendly and helpful.

(3) Use the correct standard greeting.

2. Answering Calls

(1) Outside line.

Good morning/afternoon/evening, thanks for calling ×× Hotel. How may I assist you?

(2) Internal calls.

Good morning/afternoon/evening, Service Center. This is Susan. How may I assist you?

3. Guest Calls

Good morning, (guest's name/Mr./Mrs./Miss...). Services Center, this is Susan. How may I assist you?

4. Extending Calls

(1) Certainly, may I extend your call to (person's name)'s office?

(2) Certainly, may I extend your call to (guest's name)'s room?

5. Calls Returned (no response)

(1) Outside line.

①I am sorry, (guest's name/Mr./Mrs./Miss....). There was no response from (guest's name). Would you like to leave him/her a message?

②I am sorry, (guest's name/Mr./Mrs./Miss...). There was no response. How may I assist you, (guest's name/Mr./Mrs./Miss...)?

(2) Internal line.

①I am sorry, (caller's name/Mr./Mrs./Miss/Ms.....).

②There was no response in (person's name)'s office.

③How may I assist you, (guest's name/Mr./Mrs./Miss/Ms.....)?

6. Line is Busy

(1) I am sorry, (guest's name/Mr./Mrs./Miss/Ms.....).

(2) The line is not available.

(3) Would you like to wait, (guest's name/Mr./Mrs./Miss/Ms.....)?

7. If Caller Would Like to Leave a Message

(1) Take messages by legibly writing.

(2) Caller's last name, first name.

(3) Caller's phone number.

(4) Person requested.

(5) Messages.

(6) Suggested time to call back.

(7) Repeat all information to the caller for verification and double check the spelling of names.

8. Culture Points

Most people believed that the operator's voice should be sweet. If their voice sounds good, they can be an excellent operator in the hotel. However, caring for guest is the most important thing. Furthermore, operators should be good at exploring and finding guest individual needs when a guest makes a phone call. For instance, if a guest makes a call for a nursing bottle warmer, staff can send one to her room. Besides, we could think about what kind of guest she is. Obviously, she is a guest who has a baby in our hotel. If we do care for the guest, we may send a nursing bottle warmer, and baby toys such as Jellycat, Fisher-price to her room. Also, we can recommend our entertainment facilities for the baby. These actions are really "caring guests".

Task Five Listening Ability Enhancement

1. Listen to the dialogue of telephone service, and fill in the blanks

Staff: Beijing Hotel, how can I help you?

Guest: Yes, can you ___(1)___ to Mr. Brown in room 508, please?

Staff: Certainly, sir. Could you ___(2)___ while I put you through?

(One minute later)

Staff: Hello, Sir. I'm afraid there is no ___(3)___. Would you like to ___(4)___ for him?

Guest: Thank you. Just tell him I'm going to call him this evening ___(5)___ 8:30.

Staff: May I have your name?

Guest: Yes, it's George Gail.

Staff: Would you like to give me your telephone number, so he can ___(6)___ if necessary?

Guest: Yes, good idea. My number is 13871178834.

Staff: 13871178834, thank you. I'll ___(7)___ he gets the message.

Guest: Thank you, goodbye.

Staff: Bye.

2. Listen to the dialogue of telephone service

(1) Fill in the "Guest Told Me" form.

Example:

				Guest Told Me			
Time	Guest Name	Room No.	SPG/VIP Level	Company	Guest Comments	F/U	Record
GSC宾客服务中心							

(2) Choose the right answer according to the dialogue.

①What kind of problem confused the guest? (   )

A. The air-conditioner doesn't work.

B. The curtain is dirty.

C. The minibar is empty.

D. The humidifier doesn't work.

②Who will help the guest to maintain the equipment?（　　）

A. Room attendant

B. Repairman

C. Receptionist

D. Operator

Task Six　Interpretation

(1) Just in case, you may book a table before you go.

(2) The business hour is from 11:30 a.m. to 2:00 p.m., and another one is from 5:00 p.m. to 8:00 p.m..

(3) Please wait a moment, our room attendant will bring it for you.

(4) I'm going to extend your call to Recruitment Supervisor's office.

(5) Thank you for calling Country Garden Phoenix Hotel.

(6) Are you inquiring about reservation?

(7) 有什么可以帮您的吗？

(8) 不好意思，电话现在无法接通。

(9) 你能帮我把电话转接到1105房吗？

(10) 207房的电话占线，您可以稍等下吗？

(11) 祝您有个精彩的一天。

(12) 随时为您效劳。

Task Seven　Role Play

1. Make a situational conversation about the wake-up call

Information：

Joe is an operator in Tianyu Lake Hotel.

Linda is a guest in Room 116. She makes a wake-up call on July 6, at 4:30 a.m..

2. Make a situational conversation about answering outside line

Eva is an operator in Country Garden Phoenix Hotel.

Paul is a guest. He wants to consult the banquet package for over 100 people.

3. Make a situational conversation about handing internal calls

Kevin is an operator at Sheraton Wuhan Hankou Hotel.

Catherine is a guest in Room 1780. She is complaining about the noise in the next room. She would like to change rooms.

Task Eight   Extended Professional Knowledge Reading

Soft Skill on the Telephone Service

There are some different names for the telephone service, such as "Royal Service" "Guest Service Center" and "Service Center".

However, the service is more important than the name. How to provide the satisfied service as an operator? Normally, people believed that voice affected hotel experience. As a matter of fact, soft skills play a significant role in the telephone service.

Soft skill includes many factors, which are emotional quotients, communication, understanding, analyzing and solving issues. Only if we have the soft skill, can we meet the needs and provide outstanding service to our guests.

Questions discussion based on the reading.

①What means "soft skill"?

②Which one is more important, the name or the service?

③How can an operator be a good staff member in the guest service?

The System on Telephone Service

With the rapid development of information technology, there are many systems in the hotel to help our staff. As for telephone service, there are some different systems due to different management companies.

For instance, lots of local hotels use "Green Cloud" "CSHIS Professional" and "SHIJI-XR" to help the operators in their work.

For international hotel management companies, these systems are used to assist telephone service:

Alcatel. It is a kind of telephone switchboard.

Opera. It can help operators note down guest individual needs.

VMS. It is a charging and wake-up system for guests.

MGS-GXP. It is called Guest Experience Platform as well, which is developed by Marriott independently. Guest can communicate with hotel staff, and talk about their needs. It is like QQ or Wechat in Marriott hotel.

Hot-SOS. It is developed by Hyatt independently. Operators use it to check the room situation, which helps them to make reservations.

Reserve. It assists operators to make a reservation for guests.

Jds. It is another wake-up system.

Royal Service Manager. It is developed by Fairmont independently, which lists all

Unit 12　Telephone Service

telephone demands or complaints during guests' stay, so that the hotel can find the problems and meet guests' needs.

Avaya. It is another kind of telephone switchboard.

Infrasys. It helps operators to order food for guests.

(1) Read the passage and write down the system on telephone service in local hotel

_____
_____
_____
_____
_____

(2) Decide if the following statements are true(T) or false(F), according to the passage

(　　)①Infrasys is a switchboard.

(　　)②MGS-GXP only can be used in Hyatt.

(　　)③Only receptionist can use Opera.

(　　)④VMS can make a wake-up call.

Unit 12
练习答案

Unit 13
Business Center

Unit Objectives

After studying this unit, you should be able to do the following:

Knowledge & Ability Objectives

1. dealing with normal secretarial tasks: printing, copying, canning and so on;

2. sending fax;

3. to provide personal services: typing, booking tickets and so on;

4. grasping words, phases, sentences related to business center.

Quality Objectives

1. do secretarial service professionally;

2. to be an outstanding hotel staff with responsibility and caring.

Task One Lead-in

1. Topic Discussion

In recent years, some hotels canceled the Business Center, especially in vocational hotels. In your opinion, should the Business Center be canceled?

2. Matching These Pictures with Words

(1)    A. Printing

Unit 13 Business Center

(2)  B. Fax

(3)  C. Typing

Task Two Words and Expressions

Business Center	商务中心	Secretarial Service	文秘服务
single-sided	单面	double-sided	双面
print	[prɪnt] v. n. 打印	discount	[dɪsˈkaʊnt] v. 打折 [ˈdɪskaʊnt] n. 折扣
insert	[ɪnˈsɜːt] v. 插入	margin	[ˈmɑːdʒɪn] n. 边缘；页边空白
document	[ˈdɒkjumənt] v. 记录 n. 文件	file	[faɪl] v. 归档 n. 文件
charge	[tʃɑːdʒ] v. 收费 n. 费用	flash disk	硬盘
facsimile	[fækˈsɪməli] n. 传真	Macao	n. 澳门（中国地名）
scanning	[ˈskænɪŋ] n. 扫描	automatically	[ˌɔːtəˈmætɪkli] adv. 自动地
original files	原件	audio	[ˈɔːdiəʊ] n. 录音
written material	书面材料	typing service	打字服务
xerophthalmia	干眼症	have/take a rest	休息

Task Three Sample Dialogues

1. Dialogue 1 Secretarial Service[1]

Staff: Good morning. Welcome to the Business Center. How may I assist you?

Guest: Good afternoon. Can you help me print a document?

Staff: Certainly.

Guest: How much do you charge?

Staff: There is a little difference between A4 and A3.

Guest: A4 please.

Staff: The price list is on the wall. According to the price list, 2 yuan per single sided piece, 4 yuan per double-sided for copying, and 4.5 yuan per single-sided and 6.5 yuan per double-sided for printing in color.

Guest: Can I get a discount?

Staff: 20% discount is allowed for over 10 pieces for each item. How many pieces would you like to have?

Guest: I'd like to print 30 copies for this document.

Staff: Single or double-sided pieces do you need?

Guest: Double-sided. I'm in a rush. Can you finish it as soon as possible?

Staff: No problem. Double-sided for the printing with 30 copies, as soon as I can, is that right?

Guest: Yes, that's right.

Staff: Where is the file?

Guest: In my flash disk. Here you are.

Staff: Do you have any other requirements?

Guest: Will you page the file up for me in the upper right hand corner, and adjust the margin from 1cm to 2.5cm.

Staff: The page number is inserted in the upper right hand corner. And the margin is adjusted from 1cm to 2.5cm, right?

Guest: Yes.

Staff: Done. Here we go.

Jones: Good, thanks.

Staff: You're welcome. Always at your service.

> Useful Expressions for Better Understanding of Dialogue 1

(1) Welcome to the Business Center. How may I assist you?
欢迎光临商务中心，有什么可以帮您的吗？

(2) Can you help me print a document?

能不能帮我打印下文件?

(3) How much do you charge?

怎么收费的啊?

(4) According to the price list, 2 yuan per single-sided piece, 4 yuan per double-sided for copying, and 4.5 yuan per single-sided and 6.5 yuan per double-sided for printing in color.

根据价目表,单面复印一张1元,双面复印一张4元;单面彩印一张4.5元,双面彩印一张6.5元。

(5) Can I get a discount?

有没有折扣啊?

(6) The page number is inserted in the upper right hand corner. And the margin is adjusted from 1cm to 2.5cm, right?

页码已经插入到右上角,页边距从1厘米调整到2.5厘米,对吗?

2. Dialogue 2　Sending fax②

Staff: Good afternoon. Welcome to the Business Center. How may I help you?

Guest: Good afternoon. Would you like to send a facsimile to me?

Staff: Sure. When would you like to send it?

Guest: At 7:20 a.m. tomorrow.

Staff: Are the files all here?

Guest: Yes.

Staff: You are going to fax these documents in order at 7:20 a.m., is that right?

Guest: Yes, that's right.

Staff: May I know the fax number?

Guest: The facsimile number is 0085-66778

Staff: Where would you like to send it?

Guest: Macao.

Staff: Have a seat, please. Would you like to wait for the scanning?

Guest: OK.

Staff: The scanning is completed. The facsimile will be sent automatically at 7:30 a.m., and we'll contact you and give you the sending report as soon as it has been successfully sent. Here are your original files.

Guest: Thank you. How much does the fax cost?

Staff: It is 15 yuan per page when sending a fax to Macao. It comes to 150 yuan. How could you make your payment?

Guest: By credit card. If there is any fax back to me, please send it to my room.

Staff: Roger that. I'll have it sent to your room as soon as possible.

Guest: Thank you so much!

Staff: Don't mention that, with my pleasure.

扫码
听听力

Useful Expressions for Better Understanding of Dialogue 2

(1) Would you like to send a facsimile to me?

你能帮我发个传真吗?

(2) You are going to fax these document in order, at 7:20 a.m., is that right?

您想明天早上 7:20 按文件的这个顺序发传真,对吗?

(3) May I know the fax number?

请问传真的号码是多少啊?

(4) Would you like to wait for the scanning?

您想在这里等扫描吗?

(5) How much does the fax cost?

传真多少钱呀?

(6) It is 15 yuan per page when sending a fax to Macao.

发到澳门的传真 15 元一页。

(7) It comes to 150 yuan.

一共 150 元。

(8) How could you make your payment?

您准备以什么方式付款呢?

3. Dialogue 3　Personal Service③

扫码
听听力

Staff: Good morning, Sir. Welcome to the Business Center. What can I do for you?

Guest: Yes, can you help me to transfer this audio resource to written material? I really need the typing service because my xerophthalmia is getting worse. The doctor said I couldn't use the computer in a few days.

Staff: Sure, I'd love to help you. Don't worry. By the way, how long does the audio last?

Guest: About half an hour.

Staff: I can finish it in one hour. Would you mind having a seat here, or having a rest in your room?

Guest: I'm going to step out. I'll come back in 2 hours.

Staff: Why not take a rest? Anything I can help you?

Guest: A customer super loves Fun Factory'talk show, I heard there will be an open mic, so I plan to buy a ticket for her as a present.

Staff: Me too! Have a seat, please, I'll book a ticket online and she will love this gift. By the way, who is her favorite?

Guest: Yang Li, Zhao Xiaohui …

Staff: Incredible, me too. So I'm going to book a ticket, and then do the typing thing. I'll handle these properly.

Guest: Thank you so much!

Note

Staff: You're welcome! I'm always at your service.

➤ **Useful Expressions for Better Understanding of Dialogue 3**

(1) Can you help me to transfer this audio resource to written material?
你能帮我把这段录音转成文字吗?
(2) How long does the audio last?
这段录音有多长?
(3) I plan to buy a ticket for her as a present.
我计划买张票作为礼物给她。
(4) I'll handle these properly.
我能处理好这些事情。

4. Notes Related to Business Center Dialogues

① Secretarial Service

打印文稿要进行内容检查(无违法犯罪);同时要准确记录客人的姓名、房号、打印格式、字型、时间等要求;要求打字员电脑打字技术熟练,校对准确,打字每分钟不少于150字,错字不少于2‰。若客人自带U盘打印文件,要先杀毒。

复印文件也要检查清楚内容;同时要准确记录客人姓名、房号、复印张数、纸型、规格等,要求复印操作技术熟练,复印效果良好;能够按客人要求装订,装订效果美观整齐。

② Sending Fax

随着社会的发展,我们已经进入了信息化时代,智能手机和电脑已普及,越来越多的商旅客人可以通过微信发送电子文件。但是考虑到文件的法律有效性,尤其是需要盖单位公章的情况,以及传送的时效性等因素,正式公文仍采用发传真形式,而不通过邮件和微信发送。

收发传真时,要正确记录客人姓名、房号、发送国家、地区及文稿内容,要求发送呼号、线路沟通快速,操作技术熟练。发送时间一般不超过10分钟。接受电传或传真时,应遵守规定规程,收件内容、收件人、收件时间要登记清楚。交稿转交客人送出时间或通知客人取的时间一般不超过10分钟。

③ Personal Service

很多酒店的商务中心已经不提供订票和租借会议室服务。很多酒店也不再作为中介,给参加会议的客人或者主办单位安排会议翻译的服务。但是本着用心服务客人、让客人满意的服务宗旨,酒店采取特殊情况特殊对待的原则。如果真的有客人因为各种原因需要打字或者其他服务,商务中心员工依然要尽力提供相关服务。比如"瑞吉"这个品牌的酒店,一直秉持着提供无可比拟的个性化定制、周到先行服务的理念。

Task Four Procedure, Functional Expressions and Culture Points of Business Center

1. Daily Task List
(1) Read Log Book.

(2) Start a computer.

(3) All fax machines worked and had enough fax paper.

(4) All types of paper are enough.

(5) Photocopy machine functioned.

(6) Fax in or out.

(7) Register B/C photocopying control sheet.

(8) Register B/C in coming fax control report.

(9) All fax to guests have been delivered and recorded.

(10) All fax not received have been recorded.

(11) Write down the log book.

2. Incoming Fax

(1) Recording the information on the Business Center Control Sheet.

(2) Providing a Business Center Accounting Voucher and charge the guest according to the incoming fax/email charges.

(3) Preparing the envelope, write down the guest name and room number on the envelope.

(4) Contacting the Concierge to deliver the Incoming Fax immediately.

(5) Asking the Bellman to acknowledge for pick-up of the fax.

(6) Posting the charges to the guest account and distributing the voucher.

3. Outgoing Fax

(1) To double check the fax number (also country and area code) with the guest.

(2) To provide a Business Center Accounting Voucher and fill it in completely.

(3) To fill in the Business Center Control Sheet.

(4) To obtain the guest signature on the Business Center voucher. Verify guest name and room number with the computer system.

(5) To check if the guest would like to wait at the Business Center to collect the fax or prefer the fax to be sent to his room.

(6) To send the fax through without any delay.

(7) To obtain the duration of the fax used and attach the Send Report from the fax machine to the guest fax with a paper clip in order to ensure the guest that the fax has been sent.

4. Culture Points

Although the Business Center is a dazzling department, even some hotels cancel this department, but for business guests, it still plays an important role in their business trips due to multi-functional relative facilities and equipment. It makes the benefit of satisfied and surprising service for business men. Should we cancel it? The only standard of measurement is whether the guests need it or not? All in all, serving guests and meeting their needs are the aims of all hotels.

Unit 13 Business Center

Task Five Listening Ability Enhancement

1. Listen to the dialogue of secretarial service and fill in the blanks

Staff: Good morning, Mr. Jones. Welcome to the Business Center, __(1)__?

Guest: Can you help me to __(2)__ this photo?

Staff: My pleasure. Where would you like to __(3)__ it?

Guest: In this __(4)__.

Staff: It's done. How about this?

Guest: That's nice, thank you. Can you __(5)__ these pimples?

Staff: Of course.

Guest: Could you please __(6)__ to the luminance and the contrast?

Staff: How about now?

Guest: Great.

Staff: Is it OK for JPG?

Guest: Yes, thanks.

Staff: Do you need to print it?

Guest: Yes, I'd like to __(7)__ it in 8 inches of __(8)__ and __(9)__ it.

Staff: Done, here we go. Would that be all right?

Guest: Very nice. How much?

Staff: According to the __(10)__, it comes to 45 yuan. Would you like to pay by cash or charge it to your room bill?

Guest: By cash.

Staff: May I know your room number?

Guest: Sure, 1221

Staff: Would you please sign the bill?

Guest: Sure. Thank you.

Staff: You're welcome. I'm always at your service.

扫码听听力

2. Listen to the dialogue of sending fax and fill in the blanks

Guest: Good morning, I want to __(1)__.

Staff: Yes. __(2)__ which country, Sir?

Guest: To __(3)__.

Staff: May I know your __(4)__, please?

Guest: Yes, this is the fax number.

Staff: OK, please wait a moment.

Guest: How much for __(5)__?

Staff: __(6)__ yuan per page. How would you like to __(7)__?

Guest: By __(8)__.

扫码听听力

Staff: Can I have your ___(9)___ here?

Guest: Certainly, thanks.

Staff: You're welcome. My pleasure.

3. Listen to the dialogue of booking ticket and fill in the blanks

Staff: Good afternoon, madam. Welcome to the Business Center. How may I assist you?

Guest: Yes. I'd like to ___(1)___ for ___(2)___ meeting.

Staff: All right, may I know your name?

Guest: ___(3)___

Staff: Mrs. Ruth, we have 3 types of meeting rooms and ___(4)___ equipment. Would you mind telling me how many people will be there? And other information, like ___(5)___ and so on.

Guest: Our meeting will be held on ___(6)___, from ___(7)___, and there will be ___(8)___ people here.

Staff: I got it. What kind of equipment do you need?

Guest: Except for the tables and chairs, the LED screen, HD projector, computer, and stereo equipment should be needed.

Staff: The Moon banquet hall can meet your requirements, which can accommodate 50—60 people with advanced meeting facilities.

Guest: How much?

Staff: The rental fee is 10000 yuan per day, including a full set of meeting facilities and tea break services both in the morning and afternoon; furthermore, we provide free parking the whole day. Besides, we serve a buffet lunch which combines the Western and Chinese dishes.

Guest: OK, I'll take this package.

Staff: Would you mind paying ___(9)___ yuan as a ___(10)___?

Guest: Of course not. Here you are.

Staff: Thank you, madam. May I have your contact number, please?

Guest: Yes. My phone number is ___(11)___.

Staff: OK, Mrs. Ruth. May I repeat the information: you rent Moon banquet hall for a seasonal meeting on October 16th, from 9a. m. to 5p. m.. There will be 50 people. The 10000 yuan package includes ___(12)___ meeting equipment, tea break services in the morning and the afternoon, buffet lunch, and free parking during that day. Your phone number is 13612332199. You have paid a deposit of 2000 yuan. Is that correct?

Guest: Correct!

Staff: OK, here is the receipt of the deposit for you. Please keep it safe. Thank you for your coming. See you soon.

Guest: Bye.

Unit 13 Business Center

Task Six Interpretation

(1) Welcome to the Business Center. How may I assist you?

(2) The page number is inserted in the middle of the bottom. And the margin is adjusted from 1.5 cm to 2.5 cm.

(3) It is 15 yuan per page when sending fax to Macao.

(4) Would you like to wait for the scanning?

(5) Can you help me to transfer this audio resource to a written material?

(6) According to the price list, 1 yuan per single-sided piece, and 4.5 yuan per single-sided for printing in color.

(7) 能不能帮我打印下文件?

(8) 传真多少钱啊?

(9) 您选择什么方式付钱啊?

(10) 有没有优惠啊?

(11) 您能付 1000 元押金吗?

(12) 您的联系电话是多少?

Task Seven Role Play

1. Secretarial Service

Addison is a guest in Room 303 who will take part in the 2022 Avant-garde Art Exhibition. He wants to print a document with 57 pages, and color copying 10 "Avant-garde Art Exhibition Plan".

Blake is a Business Center staff in Marriott Executive Apartments

2. Sending Fax

Clare is a guest in Room 1801. She would like to send a fax to an overseas company.

Daniel is a Business Center staff member in Fairmont Wuhan.

3. Personal Service: typing, booking tickets

Joyce is a guest in Room 12301 who has dry eye syndrome (xerophthalmia). He needs help with typing. Besides, he wants to book a ticket of a talk show as well.

Edward is a Business Center staff in the St Regis Changsha.

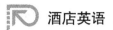 酒店英语

Task Eight Extended Professional Knowledge Reading

Item price in Business Center

Please read this form below carefully, and choose the right answer

Item	Price
Photocopying	
A3 Size	RMB 5.00/page
A4 Size	RMB 3.00/page
Printing	
A3 Laser Printing	RMB 6.00/page
A4 Laser Printing	RMB 4.00/page
A3 Color Printing	RMB 15.00/page
A4 Color Printing	RMB 10.00/page
Facsimile	
Outgoing Local	RMB 6.00/page
Outgoing Domestic	RMB 6.00/page
Outgoing HK/Macao/Taiwan	RMB 10.00/page
Outgoing International	RMB 16.00/page
In-coming Fax	RMB 5.00/page
Telephone and Internet Service	
Local Call	RMB 0.50/min
DDD	RMB 1.00/min
HK/Macao/Taiwan	RMB 2.00/min
IDD	RMB 8.00/min
Laminating	
Laminating A4	RMB 10.00/page
Laminating A5	RMB 15.00/page
Scanning Service	
Scanning A4	RMB 15.00/page

According to item price form, which service could be provided in the Business Center?

①Facsimile

②Laminating

③In-coming Fax

Services in Business Center

Traditionally, there are some services in Business Center, which include ticket booking, printing, copying, laminating, scanning, telephone, Internet, renting meeting room and other equipment, fax and express service.

At present, with the rapid development of society and information technology, some services have been assigned to other departments because of labor cost saving and increasing efficiency.

For instance, there is a small meeting room in most hotel lounges, and it can provide renting service to both VIP and non-member guests. Furthermore, with the increasing number of people using smart phones, guests prefer to use mobile App to book tickets, send or collect packages. These are more convenient than asking Business Center staff for help.

As for printing, copying, scanning and so on, other departments (the Front Office, Lounge) also provide secretarial service, though the Business Center is more professional in secretarial service due to advanced secretarial equipment.

To sum up, services and facilities are decided on targeting market needs. To compare with the traveler guests, business guests have more opportunities to use Business Center service.

(1) Which service has not been widely provided in the Business Center recently? (　　)

A. Laminating

B. Scanning

C. Local Call

(2) Decide if the following statement are true (T) or false (F), according to the passage.

(　　)① The service for renting a small meeting room is only for VIP guests.

(　　)② Some services of the Business Center Department have been assigned to other departments because of labor cost saving and increasing efficiency.

(　　)③ Guests choose printing, copying, scanning in the Business Center because it is more professional in secretarial service.

(　　)④ To compare with the business guests, traveler guests have more opportunities to use the Business Center service.

(　　)⑤ The Business Center provides lots of services such as ticket booking, printing, copying, laminating, scanning, telephone, Internet, renting meeting room and other equipment, fax and express service.

Unit 13
练习答案

Unit 14
Sales and Shopping Center Service

Unit Objectives

After studying this unit, you should be able to do the following:

Knowledge & Ability Objectives

1. understand the concept and content of hotel marketing;
2. provide the information of basic facilities and services of a hotel;
3. understand the processes of shopping center service;
4. introduce and recommend hotel services;
5. fill in a memo for sales appointments;
6. make a conversation about shopping at a hotel;
7. update oneself with the information of digital display devices at a hotel.

Quality Objectives

1. understand the basic responsibilities of sales service;
2. develop professional quality as a sales clerk;
3. cultivate the professional quality of cross-cultural communication skills.

 Task One Lead-in

1. Matching

Match the following pictures with the corresponding names of Chinese products given in the box

| tri-colored pottery | cloisonne | blue-and-white porcelain | herbal medicine |
| silk | batik | tea | embroidery |

Unit 14 Sales and Shopping Center Service

_____ _____ _____ _____

_____ _____ _____ _____

2. Sequencing

The following statements describe the job procedures of a receptionist. Discuss with your partner and put them in the correct order.

A. Explain the products to the guest (quality, color, size, feature, etc.)
B. Greet and welcome the guest
C. Show the sample
D. Pack the products
E. Offer caution
F. Accept the payment
G. Recommend the products

Correct order: _____

Task Two   Words and Expressions

pottery	['pɒtərɪ] n. 陶器	postage	['pəʊstɪdʒ] n. 邮资；邮费
porcelain	['pɔːsəlɪn] n. 瓷器	package	['pækɪdʒ] n. 包；包裹
paper-cutting	[peɪpə'kʌtɪŋ] n. 剪纸	receipt	[rɪ'siːt] n. 收到；收据
embroidery	[ɪm'brɔɪdərɪ] n. 刺绣	facility	[fə'sɪlətɪ] n. 设备
batik	[bə'tiːk] n. 蜡染	sauna	['sɔːnə] n. 桑拿浴
fragile	['frædʒəl] adj. 易碎的；脆的	craftsmanship	['krɑːftsmənʃɪp] n. 手艺；技艺
imperial	[ɪm'pɪərɪəl] adj. 帝国的	interactive	[ˌɪntə'æktɪv] adj. 合作的；互动的

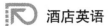

Continued

cloisonne	[klwa:'zɒŋ'neɪ] n. 景泰蓝	brochure	['brəʊʃə(r)] n. 手册；小册子
exquisite	[ɪks'kwɪzɪt] adj. 精致的；精美的	multimedia	['mʌltɪmiːdɪə] n. 多媒体
display	[dɪ'spleɪ] n. 陈列；展览	recreation	[ˌrekrɪ'eɪʃn] n. 娱乐（方式）；消遣
discount	['dɪskaʊnt] n. 折扣	Customs	['kʌstəmz] n. 海关
negotiable	[nɪ'gəʊʃɪəbl] adj. 可谈判的；可协商的；可商量的	commission	[kə'mɪʃn] n. 委员会；佣金
preferential	[ˌprefə'renʃl] adj. 优惠的；特惠的	existing customer	[ɪg'zɪstɪŋ kʌstəmə] n. 常惠客户

Task Three　Sample Dialogues

1. Dialogue 1　Shopping at a Hotel

Staff：Good morning. How can I help you?

Guest：I want to buy a porcelain vase made in Jingdezhen, Jiangxi Province.

Staff：Please come this way. We have a large collection of vases here. Which color and size would you prefer?

Guest：I'm looking for a medium-sized vase with traditional Chinese designs.

Staff：How about this one? It's decorated with a Chinese dragon flying in the clouds. In Chinese culture, dragons symbolize wealth and good fortune. Porcelain with this pattern usually belongs to the imperial family①.

Guest：I don't quite like its shape.

Staff：How about this one? It has a pale blue background with traditional Chinese flowers and bird designs.

Guest：It looks amazing. I like it. What's the price?

Staff：You have a good taste. It costs 800 yuan with the tax.

Guest：Can you give me a discount?

Staff：I'm afraid we can't. Our prices are non-negotiable. Our porcelain is exquisite handmade. This piece's quality is well worth its price.

Guest：Could you please pack the vase and ship it to London for me?

Staff：Yes, we can do that for you. But it requires an additional fee.

Guest：How much will that cost?

Staff：Around 260 yuan. A special wooden shipping box will cost an extra 50 yuan.

Guest: I've changed my mind. I'll just take it with me.

Staff: I'll package it with a lot of bubble wrap. The porcelain vase is fragile. Please handle it with care. Please go to the cashier to pay for it.

Guest: OK.

Staff: Thank you. Here is your change and receipt. Please check them out. Please also keep your receipt in case your antique is inspected at Customs.

➤ **Useful Expressions for Better Understanding of Dialogue 1**

(1) In Chinese culture, dragons symbolize wealth and good fortune. Porcelain with this pattern usually belongs to the imperial family.

在中国文化中，龙纹是富贵吉祥的象征。有龙纹的瓷器通常供皇室使用。

(2) You have a good taste.

你的品位颇佳。

(3) Can you give me a discount?

能给我打折么？

(4) Our prices are non-negotiable. Our porcelain is exquisite handmade. This piece's quality is well worth its price.

我们的价格是固定的。请考虑精细的手工做工。它们物有所值。

(5) The porcelain vase is fragile. Please handle it with care.

瓷花瓶易碎。请小心轻放。

(6) Please also keep your receipt in case your antique is inspected at Customs.

古董收据请妥善保管，以备海关查验。

2. Dialogue 2　Hotel Rooms Sales

Staff: Good morning! InterContinental Hotel-Sales Department. How can I help you?

Guest: Hello! This is Alex Lee from International Holiday Tours. May I speak to your sales manager?

Staff: Certainly, Mr. Lee, please stay on the line. I'll transfer your call to the manager's office.

Guest: Thank you.

(after a few seconds)

Staff: Hello! Sam Liu speaking.

Guest: Hello, Mr. Liu. This is Alex Lee from International Holiday Tours. I'm calling to discuss the reservations for our groups next year.

Staff: Thank you for choosing us, Mr. Lee. We are honored that you favor us with your business.

Guest: No problem. We need to make sure our VIP guests get high-quality accommodations. I'd like to know your group room rates for the coming year as well as your terms and conditions.

扫码
听听力

Staff: Sure. We have different rates for groups and fully independent travelers (FIT) throughout the year. You know, the peak, shoulder and the low seasons②.

Guest: OK. Would you be able to give us preferential rates?

Staff: Yes, of course. The prices for multiple groups and existing customers are always negotiable. We also offer a commission to travel agencies.

Guest: That sounds good to me. I think I'd like to pay a visit to your office to discuss the details. Is three o'clock tomorrow afternoon convenient for you?

Staff: Yes, I'll be available then. I plan to be in my office tomorrow afternoon.

> Useful Expressions for Better Understanding of Dialogue 2

(1) We are honored that you favor us with your business.

很荣幸您对我们的业务青睐有加。

(2) We have different rates for groups and fully independent travelers (FIT) throughout the year.

我们在一年中的不同时期为团体和散客提供不同的价格。

(3) The prices for multiple groups and existing customers are always negotiable.

对于团队和常惠客户，价格是可以协商的。

(4) We also pay a commission to travel agencies.

此外，我们向旅行社支付一笔佣金。

3. Dialogue 3　Conference Room Sales

Staff: Good afternoon. How may I help you?

Guest: Good afternoon. I'd like one of your hotel's brochures; I'm interested in your business services.

Staff: Sure. Our brochure has pictures of our conference and banquet halls as well as banquet rooms and gym.

Guest: It looks like a magnificent hotel.

Staff: Thank you. Our specially designed conference hall can fit 500 people. We also have 10 smaller multimedia rooms that can be used for individual sessions.

Guest: That sounds good. We also need an exhibition hall to display our latest products.

Staff: Our exhibition room has a smart video wall display that is convenient for business functions③.

Guest: Good. That'll save us so much time looking for other venues. We'll need more time to discuss the details.

Staff: I can ask our sales manager to contact you and arrange a meeting.

Guest: Wonderful! I'd also like to learn more about your gym.

Staff: Our gym has many opportunities for exercise, and you can check the interactive mirror screen of the kiosk to make appointments for a variety of courses. It also includes city maps for sightseeing, offers several self-service applications and

扫码
听听力

provides useful information.

Guest: Great. I'll take a look at it while I'm waiting.

> Useful Expressions for Better Understanding of Dialogue 3

(1) Our brochure has pictures of our conference and banquet halls as well as banquet rooms and gym.

宣传册中有我们酒店的会议厅、宴会厅、宴会包间和健身中心的图片。

(2) Our exhibition room has a smart video wall display that is convenient for business functions.

我们的展厅配备了视频墙显示屏，智能方便，方便商务使用。

(3) You can check the interactive mirror screen of the kiosk to make appointments for a variety of courses.

您可以在那里查看自助服务终端的互动镜像屏幕，预约不同的课程。

4. **Notes related to check in Dialogues**

①在中西方文化中，商品中的装饰图案会有不同的寓意，例如动物的象征意义有的差异较大。在中国文化中，龙、凤等象征吉祥如意、富贵吉利，甚至在历史上是皇族的象征。而在西方文化中，龙是凶残的怪兽，邪恶的象征，凤凰象征复活。中国文化中白象象征吉祥、太平，喜鹊图案象征好运将至；而在西方文化中，white elephant 这个短语隐含"贵而无用之物"的意思，而喜鹊尤指喋喋不休的人。因此酒店购物中心销售员应具备一定的跨文化意识，补充解释商品中装饰元素的含义，做中国文化故事的传播者。

②酒店客房在旺季、平季和淡季的房价会有所不同，与旅行社或协议单位签订的协议价格也会在合同中标明差别。办理协议价入住时团队领队需出示带团证明、旅行社工作证件，提供预定信息，协议单位人员需出示工作证件。

③商务酒店会议类产品的销售非常重要，顺应现在商务需求电子化的发展，可推荐交互式的展示屏、多功能会议室设施和便于会议使用的新多媒体设备。

Task Four　Procedure, Functional Expressions and Service Culture Points of Shopping Tasks

1. **Greetings**

(1) Good afternoon, sir. Do you need any assistance?

(2) May I help you?

(3) Have you been taken care of?

2. **Introductions and Recommendations**

(1) Which kind of ... would you like?

(2) Which color and style would you like?

(3) Do you like this design? It's very popular right now.

3. Bargaining

(1) I'm sorry, but our prices are non-negotiable.

(2) You can receive a 5% discount if you are a Jingling Elite Member.

4. Packaging and Offering Reminders

(1) The porcelain vase is fragile. Please handle it with care.

(2) The silk should not be hung outside to dry in the sunshine. Please wash it by hand in cold water, and don't wring it.

5. Change and Receipts/Invoices

(1) Please keep your receipt in case your antique is inspected at Customs.

(2) Here's your change and receipt.

(Notes: the above picture is quoted from the following website http://www.xinhuanet.com/tech/.)

6. Culture Points

Quality is born of workmanship. We will promote workmanship and foster a culture of workmanship where workers have a strong work ethic and tirelessly seek for improvement. We will refine our incentive mechanisms and see a large number of Chinese workers exemplify workmanship and more Chinese brands enjoy international recognition. We will usher in an era of quality for China's economic development.

Task Five   Listening Ability Enhancement

1. Listen to the dialogue and fill in the blanks with missing words or phrases

Shop Assistant: Good afternoon, sir. Do you need any assistance?

Guest: Not yet. I'd like to buy something special for my wife.

Shop Assistant: OK. We have pearls, gold, and cloisonne necklaces and bracelets. Would you like to take a look?

Guest: OK. Can you show me the ___(1)___ pearl necklaces?

Shop Assistant: Sure. We have sea pearls and cultured pearls. Which do you prefer?

Guest: Can you explain how they're different?

Shop Assistant: Yes. This is a sea pearl. Its luster is particularly fine and it's very round. Compared with cultured pearls, sea pearls are of much ___(2)___.

Guest: Looks nice. How much is it?

Shop Assistant: It's 2900 yuan, from the South China Sea.

Guest: May I look at the cultured pearls?

Shop Assistant: Certainly. This necklace is made of cultured pearls. These have the same luster and are as beautiful as sea pearls. Part of their ___(3)___ is their wide variety of shapes.

Guest: Oh, I see. Where are they from?

Shop Assistant: They're from Hepu County in Guangxi Province, a very famous ___(4)___ in China. Their price is marked on the label.

Guest: Oh, they're 200 yuan. I prefer sea pearls, but they're very expensive.

Shop Assistant: Yes. How about these cultured pearls? They're very shiny and round. Each strand costs 500 yuan.

Guest: OK, I'll take those. Can you ___(5)___ them for me please?

Shop Assistant: Yes, of course. Thank you, sir. I'm sure your wife will like them.

2. Listen to the conversation and fill in the memo with the information you hear

```
                    Account Appointment Memo
    Account Name: □Mr.    □Mrs.    □Miss    □Ms. _____
    From: □Travel Agency    □Corporation    □Association
          □Government Offices    □Schools    □Others
    (Name): _____
    Time of Meeting: _____
    Date of Meeting: _____
    Purpose of Meeting: _____
```

3. Listen to the conversation and decide whether the following statements are true (T) or false (F)

(   )① Mr. Liu comes to talk with Mr. Lee about this year's reservations.

(   )② The sales manager agrees to provide a bigger discount for room reservations during the peak season.

(   )③ The travel agent guarantees that at least 20 groups will visit the hotel.

(   )④ In three days, the sales manager will send the travel agent a copy of their sales agreement.

🎤 Task Six   Interpretation

(1) The brochure has pictures of our hotel's conference halls, banquet halls, rooms, and gym.

(2) Our exhibition room has a smart video wall display that is convenient for business functions.

(3) We have different rates for groups and fully independent travelers (FIT) throughout the year.

(4) Our prices are non-negotiable. Our porcelain is exquisitely handmade. This piece's quality is well worth its price.

(5) You can check the interactive mirror screen of the kiosk to make appointments for a variety of courses.

(6) We also pay a commission to travel agencies.

(7) 在中国文化中，龙纹是富贵吉祥的象征，有龙纹的瓷器通常供皇室使用。

(8) 瓷花瓶易碎。请小心轻放。

(9) 很荣幸您对我们的业务青睐有加。

(10) 对于团队和常惠客户，价格是可以协商的。

(11) 古董收据请妥善保管，以备海关查验。

(12) 能给我打折么？

Task Seven Role Play

1. Make a situational conversation about shopping at a hotel

Mr. Gary goes to the shopping center at Jinling Hotel in Nanjing. He wants to buy Chinese blue-and-white porcelain with a bamboo pattern. You are the shop assistant who gives him recommendations for suitable porcelain and offers him a 20% discount. Mr. Gary wants to deliver it to one of his friends in Beijing. Please help him purchase this product.

2. Make a situational conversation about the introduction of hotel facilities

Ms. Liu comes to the concierge desk of the Ritz-Carlton in Nanjing to ask about this hotel's gym and restaurants. As a receptionist, provide him with an overview of your hotel's amenities, including its gym, and make recommendations related to its restaurants.

3. Make a situational conversation about sales of conference rooms

Jason Parker is visiting the sales department at the Shangri-La Hotel in Nanjing. He works for ABC Company and wishes to negotiate a price with you, a sales manager in this department. You offer him a 15% discount during the peak season and a 20% discount during the shoulder season. You reach a mutually acceptable agreement.

Task Eight Extended Professional Knowledge Reading

Hotel Shops

Every year, millions of foreigners visit China on business, for sightseeing or

Unit 14　Sales and Shopping Center Service

exchanges in the fields of economy, trade, sports, science and culture. They are not only fascinated by the beautiful scenery, but also fond of the local porcelain specialties. Shopping, therefore, becomes a must of their itineraries. Many of them return home loaded with Chinese souvenirs and gifts.

In China, hotel shops offer a wide range of goods to foreign tourists. Many foreign tourists cannot resist the temptation of the products when they visit China. Chinese arts and crafts are the main products in hotel shops, which are the favorite goods for foreign buyers. The cloisonne, which enjoys a high reputation at home and abroad, is beautiful and elegant in moulding, splendid and graceful in design and dazzling and brilliant in colors. The jade is characterized by its distinct national style of simplicity, gracefulness and delicate lucidity. Lacquerware, exquisite in workmanship, is noted by elegant modeling, beautiful figuration, and lustrous color. Porcelain is perhaps the greatest invention Chinese people made for the world. The chinaware made in Jingdezhen—the capital of porcelain—is known to be "as white as jade, as thin as paper, as bright as mirror and as melodious as Qing (an ancient Chinese musical instrument)". Silk products and embroidery, exquisite in workmanship, harmonious in color scheme, distinctive in national style, are really good buys in China. In fact, tourist shopping has become one of the pillars that support China's tourism industry.

In order to meet the increasing needs of the customers, shop assistants should not only be familiar with the products and have a good command of languages and job procedures, but also have a desire to serve the customers heart and soul. They need to try every means to make every customer feel the value of every coin they spend.

Decide if the following statement are true (T) or false (F) according to the passage

(　　)①Foreign tourists like to buy Chinese souvenirs and gifts when they visit China.

(　　)②Chinese garments are the main products sold in hotel shops and are foreigners' favorite consumer goods.

(　　)③Tourist shopping currently has an important role in China's tourism industry.

(　　)④Shop assistants should be skilled at languages and familiar with their job responsibilities.

The Future of Display Technology in Hospitality

Mirror screen technology is one of the latest ranges to see high profile interest from influencers in hospitality. This extraordinarily flexible technology provides businesses with the opportunity to make their environment shine with a premium glow. Seldom witnessed by the general public, mirror screen technology is not only impressive in principle but also in person, offering a unique and impressive way of modernizing your setting whilst making the most of space that may otherwise be considered wasted when used for an ordinary mirror or traditional LCD screen. Mirror screen technology comes in a variety of formats, each serving the industry from a unique standpoint.

(Notes: the above pictures are quoted from the following website
https://prodisplay.com/category/technology/.)

For slightly more "hands-on" applications, we offer a range of interactive mirror screen products that can meet a surprising array of requirements in the hospitality sector. Interactive Mirror Screens are a popular choice for businesses such as hotels, hairdressers, spas and wellness centers, offering them an opportunity to incorporate the screen as a unique and engaging aspect of the customer journey that will go a long way in ensuring that it is not soon forgotten. Great for allowing customers to browse products or services at their leisure or whilst they are waiting, this technology could also stand the test of time through use of emerging applications such as augmented reality, which would allow customers or guests to interact with objects being displayed on the screen at the same time as reflecting their likeness right back at them, perfect for making their visit to your establishment memorable.

As smart room technology becomes increasingly utilized, other ways of bringing people more in touch with their environment are coming to the surface, demonstrating the best in technological creativity the market has to offer. Few product ranges are as effective as our interactive furniture, which offers display functions at the same time as serving as a piece of practical designer furniture. One of the most popular amongst these is our variety of Interactive Touch Table options, ideal for coffee shops, cafes, restaurants or anywhere where table service would otherwise be used. This incredible table allows customers to place orders without the need to leave their seat or even speak to a member of staff. This can inevitably make the ordering process far more efficient and possibly even more productive, freeing up time for employees to get on with other responsibilities as well as having the opportunity to cross sell more products visually on the screen than table service would ordinarily allow.

(1) Read the passage and write down the benefits of display technology in hospitality.

_____

_____

_____

(2) What are the facilities or applications mentioned in the text? In which departments of a hotel can display facilities be adopted?

_____

_____

_____

Unit 14
练习答案

Unit 15
Events and Recreational Services

Unit Objectives

After studying this unit, you should be able to do the following:
Knowledge & Ability Objectives
1. providing information about meeting rooms;
2. understanding the reservation processes for meeting rooms and wedding banquet halls;
3. talking about events and recreational services;
4. filling out a membership application form.

Quality Objectives
1. become familiar with English words and jargon related to hotel events and recreation services;
2. acquire English knowledge about hotel events and recreation services, and become familiar with management methods and processes for exhibition-related English;
3. mastery of English words and jargon related to hotel events and recreation services;
4. acquire English knowledge about effective communication as well as fluent and correct. Performance in different service scenarios.

Task One Lead-in

Brainstorming

A narrow understanding of hotels is that they provide accommodation and dining. Some hotels, especially five-star hotels, have a wide variety of services. Please discuss with your group members and write down the kinds of services these hotels might offer.

_____

_____

Unit 15 Events and Recreational Services

Task Two Words and Expressions

conference	['kɒnfərəns] n. 会议	layout	['leɪaʊt] n. 布局
banquet	['bæŋkwɪt] n. 宴会	wedding	['wedɪŋ] n. 婚礼；婚宴
participant	[pɑːˈtɪsɪpənt] n. 参与者	recreational	[ˌrekriˈeɪʃnl] adj. 娱乐的；消遣的
cost	[kɒst] n. 价钱；费用	sauna	[ˈsɔːnə] n. 桑拿浴
microphone	['maɪkrəfəʊn] n. 麦克风	shower	[ˈʃaʊə(r)] n. 淋浴
health club	健身俱乐部	locker	[ˈlɒkə(r)] n. 储物柜
U-shape	[juːʃeɪp] n. U字型	corridor	[ˈkɒrɪdɔː(r)] n. 走廊
swimming pool	['swɪmɪŋ puːl] n. 游泳池	stage	[steɪdʒ] n. 舞台
classroom style	[ˈklɑːsruːm staɪl] n. 教室型	theater style	[ˈθɪətə(r) staɪl] n. 剧院型

Task Three Sample Dialogues

1. Dialogue 1 Meeting Room Reservation

Staff: Good morning, this is the Banquet and Conference Department. How can I help you?

Guest: Good morning. I would like to know whether your hotel can cater to a meeting.

Staff: Sure. Sir, may I have your name? When would you like to reserve a meeting room?

Guest: My name's George Karl, and I want to book it for 3 days, from July 27 to July 29.

Staff: Can you tell me how many people will attend your meeting?

Guest: 120.

Staff: Mr. Karl, which kind of meeting room seating layout do you prefer? Our hotel has a theater style, U-shape, and classroom style.

Guest: I have no idea. Do you have any recommendations? We don't need tables.

Staff: I recommend theater style since it's ideal for large groups when writing isn't required.

Guest: Okay, I'll choose theater style.

Staff: Mr. Karl, we recommend that you rent the Yayun Meeting Room. The room's area is 310 square meters for approximately 150 participants. What do you

扫码听听力

think?

Guest: Alright. How much does it cost to rent this room?

Staff: I'll check with our sales manager later about the price, and he'll discuss it with you. Is that okay?

Guest: Yes.

Staff: Mr. Karl, can you provide me with your company's name and contact number?

Guest: My company's name is Tiancheng Technology Co., Ltd., and the phone number is 1690011011.

Staff: Okay, Mr. Karl. I'll give your meeting room request to our sales manager and ask him to reply to you or schedule an appointment to meet with him. Is there anything else I can do for you?

Guest: That's all. Thanks.

Staff: Okay, Mr. Karl. I hope you enjoy your stay. Goodbye!

➤ **Useful Expressions for Better Understanding of Dialogue 1**

(1) Good morning, this is the Banquet and Conference Department. How can I help you.

早上好，会务组，请问有什么可以帮到您?

(2) Sir, May I have your name?

先生，我能知道您的名字吗?

(3) How many people will attend your meeting?

有多少人参加这次会议呢?

(4) Which kind of meeting room seating layout do you prefer?

您预备采用哪种会议室布局?

(5) I recommend theaterstyle.

我会推荐剧院式布局。

(6) How much does it cost to rent this room?

租用会议厅需要多少钱?

(7) Is there anything else I can do for you?

还有什么需要我帮您的吗?

(8) I hope you enjoy your stay.

祝您在我们酒店过得愉快。

2. Dialogue 2   Wedding Banquet Reservation[①]

Staff: Good morning, Banquet and Conference Department. How may I help you?

Guest: My name's Dave Cheng. My daughter's wedding is on June 12, and I would like you to cater to the banquet, please.

Staff: Certainly, sir. Could you please give me some more details? How many guests will there be, sir?

Unit 15　Events and Recreational Services

Guest: Well, the wedding's on June 12, and the guest list's around 130.

Staff: I see. Which do you prefer, Western food or Chinese food?

Guest: Chinese, please.

Staff: Okay. Twelve tables are needed for 120 people, and our hotel can provide 2 additional tables to complete your reservation. Our catering prices are 1500 and 2500 yuan for each table. Which do you prefer?

Guest: I prefer the one for 1500 yuan.

Staff: Okay. Please take a look at this menu (hands him a menu). You can tell me if any of your guests have special dietary needs.

Guest: (Five minutes later) No modifications are needed, but I hope the dishes are light and mild.

Staff: Okay. Do you have any special requests for the layout, music, and banquet?

Guest: I hope that your hotel can create a romantic layout and provide someone to play piano music. My other request is that I would like you to build a stage with an LED screen and microphone because I'll need a video display for a presentation②.

Staff: Okay. Do you have any other requests?

Guest: That's all. Thank you so much.

Staff: Our hotel can provide you with 50 free parking spaces. Would you need to reserve any guest rooms?

Guest: No, thanks.

Staff: Okay, you'll need to pay 10% of the total as a deposit, and we'll charge 15% of the total as a service fee. This is the reservation bill (hands him a reservation bill). Please sign here after you read it.

Guest: No problem.

Staff: (After paying the deposit) Mr. Cheng, please inform us one month before the banquet if you need to make any changes. This is the reservation receipt. We'll issue an invoice after the banquet ends. Do you have any questions?

Guest: No.

Staff: I hope you have a wonderful banquet. Goodbye!

> **Useful Expressions for Better Understanding of Dialogue 2**

(1) Which do you prefer, Western food or Chinese food?
您想吃中餐还是西餐呢？

(2) Our hotel can provide 2 additional tables to complete your reservation.
我们酒店会为您多备两桌酒席

(3) Please take a look at this menu.
这是供您审阅的菜单。

(4) The dishes are light and mild.
菜品可以清淡一些。

酒店英语

(5) Do you have any special requests for the layout?

您对场地的布局还有什么特殊的要求吗?

(6) Our hotel can provide you with 50 free parking spaces.

我们酒店将提供 50 个免费车位给您

(7) You'll need to pay 10% of the total as a deposit.

您将支付总价的 10% 作为定金。

3. Dialogue 3　Sauna Service

Staff: Good evening. Welcome to our Sauna Center.

Guest: Thank you. This is my first time here. Can you tell me more about it?

Staff: Yes. We have a Finnish Sauna and Bath.

Guest: How much do you charge for guests?

Staff: We charge 399 yuan per person.

Guest: I see. Could you please give me more details?

Staff: The dressing room is on the left side. Just beside the dressing room is a large water pool with whirlpools and waterfalls. Before you enter the vapor room, we'll provide you with a tub of cool water, a ladle, iced towels, and any other things you need for the bath.

Guest: Good. Anything else?

Staff: The vapor rooms for the Finnish Sauna are on the pool's left side, the rooms on its right side are for the Finnish Sauna, and the rooms on its right side are for the Turkish Bath. They're all decorated with high-grade wood.

Guest: Where's the shower room?

Staff: There's a big room beside the stairs. That's the shower room. It has complimentary shampoo, soap, and towels.

Guest: How about the lounge?

Staff: The lounge is on the second floor. You can relax there with beer, soft drinks, tea, and fruit.

Guest: It's quite nice. Do I have to pay for them?

Staff: You can have 1 complimentary beer, soft drink, or tea and some fruit, but have to pay if you want more.

Guest: Alright, thank you.

Staff: You're welcome. Have a nice day.

> **Useful Expressions for Better Understanding of Dialogue 3**

(1) Good evening. Welcome to our Sauna Center.

晚上好,欢迎来到我们的桑拿中心

(2) We charge 399 yuan per person.

每个人的收费是 399 元

(3) The dressing room is on the left side.

扫码
听听力

更衣室在左边。

(4) It has complimentary shampoo, soap, and towels.

洗发水、肥皂和毛巾是免费提供的。

(5) The lounge is on the second floor.

休息室在二楼。

(6) You can relax there with beer, soft drinks, tea, and fruit.

您可以喝啤酒、软饮料、茶，吃水果放松一下。

4. Dialogue 4　Health Club Service

Staff: Good morning. Welcome to the health club. Are you going to swim or go to the gym, sir?

Guest: I'm going to swim, and maybe go to the gym.

Staff: Our hotel guests can use the swimming pool and equipment for free. Please show us your room card to register.

Guest: Sure, here you are.

Staff: Thank you. This is the locker key. Please store it securely. The locker room is at the end of the corridor.

Guest: When do you open?

Staff: We're open from 7:30 a.m. to 11:00 p.m.. We provide complimentary bath towels, shampoo, and bath foam.

Guest: I see. Thank you.

Staff: I hope you enjoy your time here. Goodbye.

扫码
听听力

▶ Useful Expressions for Better Understanding of Dialogue 4

(1) Welcome to the health club.

欢迎光临健康会所。

(2) Are you going to swim or go to the gym, sir?

先生，您是去游泳还是健身？

(3) Please show us your room card to register.

请出示您的房卡给我们登记。

(4) This is the locker key.

这是储物柜的钥匙。

(5) The locker room is at the end of the corridor.

更衣室在走廊的尽头。

(6) I hope you enjoy your time here.

我希望您拥有一段愉快的时光。

5. Notes Related to Event Service Dialogues

①婚礼在《礼记·昏义》里面记载为"昏礼"，是中国传统文化的重要组成部分。中国人喜爱红色，认为红色是吉祥的象征，所以传统婚礼习俗总以大红色烘托喜庆、热烈的气氛。吉祥、祝福、孝敬成为婚礼上的主旨，几乎婚礼中的每一项礼仪都渗透着中国

人的哲学思想。酒店在布置婚宴的时候，要注意婚姻寓意，不要选择不合时宜的花朵及颜色。

②受新型冠状肺炎疫情影响，酒店为保障客人的卫生安全做了许多努力。酒店运用先进技术，改变空间设计，调整会议布置和餐饮产品，将原本需要高频次人际接触的服务改成非接触方式。同时，频繁地展开清洁消毒工作，尤其在人流密度大的区域。为了减少人际接触，酒店提供标牌，用来提醒客人保持社交距离。根据防疫政策降低活动场地的座位密度。对高频次人际接触的物品表面经常消毒。酒店为每个宴会活动指定专门的餐饮与茶歇空间（即不与其他活动的与会者接触）。根据宴会活动团体的规模，为客人提供丰富的卫生餐饮选择，比如：便利外带式、罐装食品加瓶装饮料、常规餐盘式。

Task Four　Procedure and Functional Expressions of Meeting Rooms Booking

1. Greetings

(1) Good morning, this is the Banquet and Conference Department. How may I help you?

(2) Good morning, Sir. How may I help you?

(3) Good evening, Mr. Smith. How are you today?

2. Confirm with guests regarding the conference information

(1) Could you please give me some more details about your meeting?

(2) How many guests will there be, sir?

(3) Which kind of meeting room seating layout do you prefer?

(4) I recommend theater style since it's ideal for large groups when writing isn't required.

3. Payment

(1) Our catering prices are 1500 and 2500 yuan for each table. Which one do you prefer?

(2) How will you pay the deposit? Cash, Visa, or Alipay?

4. Receipt/invoice

(1) Here's your receipt.

(2) We'll issue an invoice after the banquet's ended.

Task Five　Listening Ability Enhancement

1. Listen to the membership application dialogue and fill in the blanks

Staff: Good afternoon, sir. How may I help you?

Unit 15 Events and Recreational Services

Guest: Good afternoon. I want to be a __(1)__ of the health club. Could you tell me the __(2)__ ?

Staff: OK, We have 3 kinds of cards, One is only for __(3)__ , one is only for body-fitting and the other is for __(4)__ . The card only for swimming or fitting is 700 yuan for 30 times and available in 3 months. The card for both is 900 yuan for 30 times and __(5)__ in 3 months too. Member card is valid for 2 year from July 27, 2021.

Guest: I see. I'll get the card only for swimming. What's the pool's water __(6)__ and depth of the pool?

Staff: We have a warm massage pool, and the temperature is 36 ℃. The depth of the pool is 1.4 meters. Would you like me to __(7)__ you our club?

Guest: Yes, thank you. I will pay by cash.

Staff: No problem. May I have your __(8)__ and date of birth?

Guest: My name's John Wilson, and I was born on March 23, 1989.

Staff: May I have your telephone number?

Guest: My number is 1671959624

Staff: I've filled __(9)__ the form. Please put your __(10)__ here.

Guest: (Takes the pen) Sure, thanks a lot.

Staff: My pleasure, have a good time.

2. **Listen to the membership application dialogue again and fill in the form**

入会申请表
MEMBERSHIP APPLICATION FORM

会员资料(Member Details):

* 姓名(Name): _____

* 出生日期(Date of Birth) _____ 年 Y _____ 月 M _____ 日 D

* 电话号码(Tel No.): _____

会籍资料(Membership Details)

会员卡类型(Type of Membership Card): _____

起始日期(Start Date) _____ 截止日期(Expiry Date) _____

会费(Membership Fee) _____

支付方式(Payment): □现金(Cash) □信用卡(Credit) □支票(Cheque)

备注(Note): _____

_____

会员签署 (Member's Signature)   财务签署 (Cashier's Signature)

Task Six Interpretation

(1) Sir, Excuse me, the health club will be closing in 5 minutes.

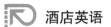

(2) Did you enjoy your stay here?

(3) If there's any way I can help, please let me know.

(4) The fitness center is located on the third floor.

(5) It's free for all of our guests.

(6) The minimum charge for a 200-person dinner party is 10000 yuan, excluding drinks.

(7) 健身房只在下午 4 点到 9 点开放,现在 10 点了。

(8) 我们有可以容纳 10 人的会议室,每小时收费 50 美元。

(9) 先生,请问您想在哪天举行宴会呢?

(10) 请您在这里签字,并且留下电话号码。

(11) 我们可以提供 LED、麦克风及笔记本电脑。

(12) 这是您的更衣柜钥匙,男更衣室在左边,女更衣室在右边。

Task Seven　Role Play

1. Make a situational conversation about the meeting room reservation

William Smith is the head of a technology company. He comes to the Marriott Hotel because his company is going to hold a press conference to introduce its latest product. This conference will have about 100 participants. He asks his company to provide a microphone, LED screen, as well as a stage that must be built and decorated. He estimates that the press conference will last from 9 a.m. to 12 p.m.. The hotel needs to make lunch for 100 people. Please receive the guest as an event manager.

2. Make a situational conversation about the health club

William Smith visits the Hilton Hotel's health club. He wants to know when its gym opens and more about the indoor swimming pool's specifications, including its water temperature, water depth, and available bathing supplies. Please receive the guest as the head of the health club.

Task Eight　Extended Professional Knowledge Reading

Meeting Room Layouts and Conference Table Set Ups

Theater style layout (Theater Style)

Seats or chairs in rows facing a stage area, head table, or speaker (with no conference table).

> Used for

This is the most efficient set-up when the attendees will act as an audience. This set-up is not recommended for food events or if note taking is required.

> Set-up hints

This is a very flexible room set-up. Rows can be circular, semi-circular, straight, or angled towards the focal point. Offset each row so that attendees don't have to look over the person in front of them (this will increase the space required).

If using banquet type chairs, space them 3″[1] to 6″ apart as these chairs are normally narrower than most people's bodies. If you have the space, allow for 24″ between rows to allow attendees easy movement in and out of the row.

> Pros

- Good for large groups when reading/writing is not required

> Cons

- Elevation changes needed for large groups
- No writing surfaces
- Minimal group interaction

U-shape style layout (U-Shape)

A series of conference tables set in the shape of the letter U, with chairs around the outside.

> Used for

This layout style is often used for Board of Directors meetings, committee meetings, or discussion groups where there is a speaker, audio-visual presentation or other focal point.

> Set-up hints

A minimum of 2′[2] of table space is required per attendee.

Skirt the inside of the "U" if attendees are seated only on the outside.

Avoid the "U" set-up for groups greater than 25, as the sides of the "U" become too long and may not promote participation from all attendees.

---

[1] 3″为 3 英寸,1 英寸=2.54 厘米
[2] 2′为 2 英尺,1 英尺=30.48 厘米

➢ Pros

- Good work space
- Good interaction between participants
- Ideal when audio-visual or speakers are involved

➢ Cons

- Not ideal for a larger group

Classroom style layout (Classroom Style)

Rows of conference tables with chairs facing the front of a room (and usually a speaker), providing writing space for each person.

➢ Used for

This room set-up is ideal for note taking, meetings requiring multiple handouts or reference materials, or other tools such as laptop computers. This is the most comfortable set-up for long sessions and allows refreshments to be placed within reach of each attendee.

➢ Set-up hints

Tables that extend beyond the stage or podium should be angled towards the speaker.

Allow for approximately 2' of space per person at each table. (More space may be required depending on the amount of materials).

The minimum space between tables is 3'. Provide 3½' if space allows for ease of movement in and out of rows.

➢ Pros

- Presenter can see all participants
- Accommodates large groups in less space

➢ Cons

- Minimal interaction possible
- Participants only see each other's backs

Decide if the following statements are true (T) or false (F), according to the passage.

(　　) ① U-shape style layout can accommodate as many people as possible in a limited space.

(　　) ② Mini group recommend theater style layout.

(　　)③Classroom style layout is the most comfortable set-up for long sessions and allows refreshments to be placed within reach of each attendee.

(　　)④Theater style providing writing space for each person.

(　　)⑤U-shape style is often used for Board of Directors meetings.

How Hotel Fitness Centers Could be Used to Attract Guests

Older generations enjoy hotel amenities such as free breakfasts and a pool to swim in while they're away from home, but millennials have a different focus. Young people want to travel without breaking their fitness routine, so they consider potential hotels by looking at features such as fitness centers. You must use fitness centers to keep your hotel relevant and attractive to guests. Consider the following ways you can update hotel's fitness center to draw in more guests each quarter.

➢ They emphasize the hotel's value

Whether a guest is a young adult or a retiree, everyone wants to pay for a room rate that has good value. That means they're willing to pay for a space that gives them something in return beyond a place to sleep.

Updated fitness centers show potential guests the hotel is always looking for ways to improve. It's a level of thoughtfulness and care guests will appreciate, showing them they're valued when they choose to book a room.

➢ They include opportunities for self-improvement

A good fitness center is a place where guests can work on self-improvement. They may want to lose weight, gain muscle, or enjoy the self-confidence that comes from working out.

Hotels can hone in on this idea of self-improvement by building their health club. A hotel brand fitness club will draw more guests into the fitness area than a gym that looks thrown together. It also provides hotels with an opportunity to add offerings such as specialized workout equipment or Wi-Fi enabled machinery.

➢ They provide a much needed break

Guests stay at hotels for a variety of reasons, but sometimes they need a break from whatever they're traveling for. They may want to get outside and stretch their legs, which is something any hotel can offer.

➢ They offer guests something new

People who travel often come to expect a routine experience from the hotels they choose to stay with. A new continental breakfast menu or convenience bar item most likely won't impress anyone, so hotels should give guests something new by partnering with local fitness classes.

  Read the passage and write down the viewpoint of how hotel fitness centers used to attract guests.

_____
_____
_____
_____

Unit 16
Handling Complaints and Unexpected Affairs

Unit Objectives

After studying this unit, you should be able to do the following:

Knowledge & Ability Objectives

1. grasp the process of handling complaints and unexpected affairs;

2. be familiar with the terms and sentence patterns of handling complaints and unexpected affairs;

3. know the types of common complaints and unexpected affairs;

4. deal with complaints and unexpected affairs in different situations.

Quality Objectives

1. develop skills and abilities to deal with complaints and unexpected affairs calmly and professionally;

2. understand the importance of guest service and become a highly responsible and helpful hotel employee.

Task One   Lead-in

1. Share your stories

Have you ever lived in a hotel? Were you satisfied? Please share your stories and tell us why you were satisfied or unsatisfied.

2. Brainstorming

Discuss in groups about the common complaints at a hotel. List the complaints you've come up with and group them.

_____

_____

_____

Task Two　Words and Expressions

apologize	[əˈpɒlədʒaɪz]v. 道歉	apology	[əˈpɒlədʒi]n. 道歉
inconvenience	[ˌɪnkənˈviːniəns]n. 不便；麻烦	hesitate	[ˈhezɪteɪt]v. 犹豫；顾虑
immediately	[ɪˈmiːdiətli]adv. 立即，马上	delay	[dɪˈleɪ]n. &v. 延迟；拖延
overcook	[ˌəʊvəˈkʊk]v. 烹调过度	tough	[tʌf]adj. 强硬的；艰苦的；健壮的；艰难的
medium	[ˈmiːdiəm]adj. 半熟；中等的	manager	[ˈmænɪdʒə(r)]n. 经理
spaghetti	[spəˈgeti]n. 意大利面	salmon	[ˈsæmən]n. 三文鱼
disgusting	[dɪsˈgʌstɪŋ]adj. 令人作呕的；令人不快的	expensive	[ɪkˈspensɪv]adj. 昂贵的；价格高的
quality	[ˈkwɒləti]n. 质量；品质	promise	[ˈprɒmɪs]v. &n. 承诺
describe	[dɪˈskraɪb]v. 描述	document	[ˈdɒkjumənt]n. 文件
hand in	上交	repairman	[rɪˈpeəmæn]n. 修理工
stomachache	[ˈstʌməkeɪk]n. 胃痛	bleed	[bliːd]v. 流血

Task Three　Sample Dialogues

1. Dialogue 1　Handling Complaints about the Room①

A guest, Mike Smith, is calling the front desk to complain about the room.

Staff: Good evening, Garden Hotel. What can I do for you?

Guest: This is Mike Smith. I have just checked in but I am not happy with my room.

Unit 16　Handling Complaints and Unexpected Affairs

Staff: I'm sorry, sir. May I know the problem?

Guest: The bathroom is smelly and the bathtub is not clean. There is hair in the bathtub!

Staff: I'm sorry to hear that. I will send a housekeeper to your room right now. Would you please tell me your room number?

Guest: Yes. 1209

Staff: Room 1209. Is that right?

Guest: Yes.

Staff: Thank you, Mr. Smith. I do apologize for the inconvenience. Please wait a moment, and a housekeeper will come to your room soon.

Guest: OK. Thank you.

Staff: You're welcome, Mr. Smith. Is there any other problem?

Guest: Yes. Could you send a bath towel to my room? There is only one bath towel and it's not enough for me.

Staff: I am very sorry for the inconvenience. I'll ask the housekeeper to send a bath towel.

Guest: Thank you.

Staff: You're welcome. Is there any other problem?

Guest: No.

Staff: Thanks for calling, Mr. Smith. The housekeeper is coming to your room. If there is anything else we can do for you, please don't hesitate to call us.

➢ **Useful Expressions for Better Understanding of Dialogue 1**

(1) I have just checked in but I am not happy with my room.

我刚刚入住，但是我对房间不满意。

(2) May I know the problem?

请问有什么问题吗？

(3) The bathroom is smelly and the bathtub is not clean. There is hair in the bathtub!

浴室有臭味，而且浴缸不干净。浴缸里有毛发！

(4) I'm sorry to hear that.

很抱歉发生这种事。

(5) I will send a housekeeper to your room right now.

我现在就叫一个客房服务员去打扫您的房间。

(6) Would you please tell me your room number?

方便告知您的房号吗？

(7) I do apologize for the inconvenience. / I am very sorry for the inconvenience.

对于造成的不便，我向您道歉。/很抱歉给您造成不便。

(8) Please wait a moment, and a housekeeper will come to your room soon.

请稍等，客房服务员马上就到。

(9) Is there any other problem?

请问还有其他问题吗？

(10) Could you send a bath towel to my room? There is only one bath towel and it's not enough for me.

可以送条浴巾到我房间吗？这里只有一条浴巾，对我来说不够用。

(11) I'll ask the housekeeper to send a bath towel.

我会叫客房服务员送一条浴巾给您。

(12) If there is anything else we can do for you, please don't hesitate to call us.

如果有什么我们能够效劳的，请尽管打给我们。

2. Dialogue 2　　Handling Complaints about the Food & Beverage Service

Guest: Waiter. I ordered my meal at least 15 minutes ago but it hasn't come yet. Why is it taking so long?

Staff: I'm very sorry, sir. I will check your order with our chef immediately. Would you like some drink while you are waiting?

Guest: Fine! Please hurry up! I have a meeting at 2:30 p.m..

Staff: Wait a moment, please. (The waiter brings the dishes in 10 minutes.) Here's your meal, sir. We do apologize for the delay. Please enjoy your lunch.

Guest: (5 minutes later) Waiter!

Staff: Yes, sir. How may I help you?

Guest: The steak is overcooked. It is too tough to eat. I ordered the steak medium but you served it well done.

Staff: I'm awfully sorry about that, sir. I will check it with our chef. I will talk to our manager and see if we can get you another steak for free. Would you like to have the spaghetti first?

Guest: Alright, but I don't want to have any steak now. This one is disgusting.

Staff: I'm very sorry. Would you like some salmon instead? It goes well with the spaghetti.

Guest: OK, I'll try the salmon.

Staff: OK, sir. (The waiter takes the steak and talks to the manager. The manager agrees, and 10 minutes later, the waiter brings the salmon.) Sorry to have kept you waiting, sir. This is the salmon. Please enjoy it.

▶ **Useful Expressions for Better Understanding of Dialogue 2**

(1) I ordered my meal at least 15 minutes ago but it hasn't come yet.

我十五分钟前点菜，但是到现在还没上菜。

(2) I will check your order with our chef immediately.

我马上和厨师核实一下。

(3) We do apologize for the delay.

Unit 16　Handling Complaints and Unexpected Affairs

很抱歉我们上菜慢了。

(4) The steak is overcooked. It is too tough to eat.

牛排煎老了，很硬，不好吃。

(5) I ordered the steak medium but you served it well done.

我点的牛排是五成熟，但是你们上的这个是全熟了。

(6) I'm awfully sorry about that, sir.

对此非常抱歉，先生。

(7) I will check it with our chef. I will talk to our manager and see if we can get you another steak for free.

我会和我们的厨师确认。我也会请示经理给您免费重新做一份牛排。

(8) Would you like to have the spaghetti first?

您可以先吃意大利面吗？

(9) Sorry to have kept you waiting, sir.

抱歉让您久等了。

3. Dialogue 3　Handling Complaints about the Bill

(At the restaurant)

Guest: Waiter!

Staff: Yes, sir. How may I help you?

Guest: I'd like to have my bill, please.

Staff: Sure, sir. Here's the bill.

Guest: Thank you. Excuse me, I think there may be something wrong with the bill.

Staff: Oh, yes?

Guest: The wine is far too expensive!

Staff: Well, sir, the wine price is the same as it is listed on the menu. Our wine is from France and of high quality.

Guest: OK, fine! The wine tastes good, indeed. One more thing, I remember that I ordered Caesar salad②, but it's Chef salad on the bill.

Staff: Well, let me see… Oh, yes. You ordered a Caesar salad. Sorry, sir. I do apologize for this mistake.

Guest: That's fine.

Staff: Is there any other problem?

Guest: No.

Staff: OK. Wait a moment, please. I will give you another bill. Sorry again for our mistake. We promise that we will be more careful in the future.

Guest: That's fine.

扫码
听听力

➢ **Useful Expressions for Better Understanding of Dialogue 3**

(1) I'd like to have my bill, please.

我想结账。

(2)Excuse me, I think there may be something wrong with the bill.

不好意思，我的账单有点问题。

(3)The wine is far too expensive!

红酒太贵了！

(4)The wine price is the same as it is listed on the menu.

红酒价格和菜单上列出来的是一样的。

(5)Our wine is from France and of high quality.

我们的红酒是法国进口的，品质极高。

(6)I remember that I ordered Caesar salad, but it's Chef salad on the bill.

我记得我点的是凯撒沙拉，但是账单上是厨师沙拉。

(7)We promise that we will be more careful in the future.

我们保证今后工作会更加细心。

4. Dialogue 4　Helping Guest Find Missing Items

Staff: Good afternoon, madam. How can I help you?

Guest: I left a bag on the sofa in the lobby, but it's missing now.

Staff: I'm sorry, madam. I will try my best to help you find it. Please calm down. Could you describe your bag?

Guest: Yes. It's a white paper bag with a red logo. There are some documents in the bag. The documents are very important to me.

Staff: Could you tell me when you left it in the lobby?

Guest: Around 2p.m.. I forgot to take it when I went out to take a taxi.

Staff: OK. I will check whether someone has handed it in to us. Please wait a moment.

Guest: OK.

Staff: (A moment later) Madam, one of our staff found this bag when she did the cleaning in the lobby. There are some paper documents in it. Is it your bag?

Guest: Yes, it is! Thank you very much.

Staff: You're welcome. It's my pleasure.

➢ Useful Expressions for Better Understanding of Dialogue 4

(1)I left a bag on the sofa in the lobby, but it's missing now.

我落了一个包在大厅沙发上，现在不见了。

(2)I will try my best to help you find it.

我会尽力帮您找到。

(3)Please calm down.

请冷静。

(4)Could you describe your bag?

您可以描述一下您的包吗？

扫码
听听力

Unit 16　Handling Complaints and Unexpected Affairs

(5)It's a white paper bag with a red logo.

是一个白色的纸袋子，上面有个红色的商标。

(6)Could you tell me when you left it in the lobby?

您是什么时候把袋子落在大厅的呢？

(7)I will check whether someone has handed it in to us.

我查看一下是否有人上交了这个袋子。

(8)One of our staff found this bag when she did the cleaning in the lobby.

我们的一个员工在大厅做保洁工作时发现了这个袋子。

5. Notes Related to Handling Complaints and Unexpected Affairs Dialogues

①客人投诉客房有问题，应予以重视并立即提出相应措施或找相关部门解决。如果是短时间内难以解决的问题，可以请示经理给客人换房。妥善处理好投诉，可改善顾客与酒店的长期关系，使顾客成为酒店的好顾客、常客；处理不好，酒店失去的不仅是一位客人或几位客人，还有可能是他们身后的亲友、同事、上下级等潜在顾客。

②凯撒沙拉(Caesar salad)是西餐中受欢迎的一种沙拉，其他沙拉包括厨师沙拉(Chef salad)、田园沙拉(Garden salad)、希腊沙拉(Greek salad)、卷心菜沙拉(Colslaw)和土豆沙拉(Potato salad)等。

Task Four　Procedure, Functional Expressions and Service Culture Points of Handling Complaints and Unexpected Affairs

1. Learn about the complaints or unexpected affairs

(1) Greet the guests and listen to them carefully about their complaints or issues.

①Good morning/afternoon, sir/madam! May I help you?

②Hello, Mr. /Mrs. ×××, how can I help you? /what can I do for you?

(2) Listen to guests carefully and understand their needs.

2. Show empathy and apologize

(1) Show your empathy.

①I am very sorry to hear that.

②That sounds too bad.

(2) Apologize.

①I/We do apologize (for ...)

②I am/We are very sorry for ...

③Please accept our apologies for ...

3. Take actions or give explanations

(1) Ask for more details.

①Could you tell me more about ... ?

②Could you describe ... ? /Could you make a description of ... ?

③Could you give me more details?

④What exactly is the problem?

⑤Is there any other problem? /Is there anything else?

(2) Give explanations.

①This is due to/because of …

②The reason is that …

③This was caused by …

(3) Take actions.

①I will send a housekeeper/repairman/someone to your room immediately.

②Let me check … /with …

③We will come to you soon.

④I will ask … to …

4. Future actions and follow up

(1) Future actions.

①In the future, we will …

②Please rest assured that this will not happen again.

③We will make sure that …

(2) Follow up.

①How's your room/new dishes … ?

②Are you feeling better now?

5. Culture Points

Guest service is the primary responsibility for a hotel employee. Each letter of the word "service" has a specific meaning. "S" means smile. It means that hotel staff should always smile to guests. The first "E" means excellent. Its meaning is that hotel staff should do the job very well. "R" means ready. It means that hotel staff should be ready to provide services to guests at any time. "V" means viewing. Its meaning is that hotel staff should treat every guest fairly. "I" means invitation. It means that hotel staff should actively invite guests to come again. "C" means creating. Its meaning is that every staff should have the spirit of innovative service. The last "E" means eye. Its meaning is that every staff should always pay attention to the guests with enthusiasm and let the guests feel it. Service is very important in the hotel industry, and if you do the above, you will be a good hotel staff with a high sense of service and responsibility.

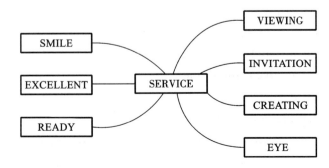

Unit 16 Handling Complaints and Unexpected Affairs

Task Five Listening Ability Enhancement

1. Listen to the dialogue of handling complaints about the room and fill in the blanks

Staff: Good evening, ___(1)___. May I help you?

Guest: Yes. There's something wrong with the TV. It doesn't work. The ___(2)___ doesn't work, either. My hair is still dripping!

Staff: I'm sorry to hear that. I will have a ___(3)___ fix it right now. Could you please tell me your room number, sir?

Guest: Yes. It's ___(4)___.

Staff: Room ___(5)___. Thanks for calling. I ___(6)___ for the ___(7)___ again. The repairman is coming to your room now.

Guest: Thank you.

Staff: You're welcome. If you have any other problem, please don't ___(8)___ to call us.

(5 minutes later)

Staff: Housekeeping. May I come in?

Guest: Come in, please.

Staff: Good evening, sir. I have come to ___(9)___ the TV and the hair drier, and it may take a few minutes to fix them. Also, I have brought a new hair drier. You can use it now.

Guest: Thank you. I really need it right now.

(A few minutes later)

Staff: The TV is alright, sir. You can watch it now. This old hair drier is ___(10)___, and I have to take it away.

Guest: OK. Thank you.

Staff: Have a good night, sir.

扫码听听力

2. Listen to the dialogue of dealing with a sick guest and fill in the blanks

Staff: Good afternoon, ___(1)___. What can I do for you?

Guest: My husband has a ___(2)___. Do you know where the nearest ___(3)___ is?

Staff: Oh, shall I call an ___(4)___?

Guest: No, I think we can go to the hospital ___(5)___. His condition is not too bad, and we think we just need to see a doctor and get some ___(6)___.

Staff: OK, I will call a taxi for you, and I will tell the driver to go to the nearest hospital.

Guest: Thank you.

Staff: You're welcome. The driver is coming now. Do you need help to

扫码听听力

go ___(7)___?

Guest: No, thanks. We can ___(8)___ to take the elevator.

Staff: OK. I will be at the elevator door.

Guest: Thank you. We're coming now.

Staff: OK. See you soon.

Task Six Interpretation

(1) The room is smelly and the wardrobe is in a mess.

(2) I do apologize for the inconvenience.

(3) If there is any other problem, please don't hesitate to call us.

(4) I have ordered my meal 20 minutes ago and it still doesn't come.

(5) I am very sorry for the mistake.

(6) I will send a housekeeper to your room right away.

(7) 抱歉让您久等了。

(8) 我们保证今后工作会更仔细。

(9) 我马上和经理核实一下。

(10) 牛排太硬了,无法下咽。

(11) 方便告知您的房号吗?

(12) 可以描述一下您丢失的衣服吗?

Task Seven Role Play

1. Make a situational conversation about handling complaints on dishes

David Smith complaints to the waiter. He has ordered a salad with no egg, but he still gets it with an egg. Also, he is not pleased with the steak because it is a bit cold. You are the waiter. Please handle Mr. Smith's complaints.

2. Make a situational conversation about handling complaints on the room

David Smith is calling the Front Office and asking for changing a room. His room is facing the street, and he thinks it's too noisy to sleep at night. You are a staff at the Front Office. Please handle Mr. Smith's complaint.

3. Make a situational conversation about dealing with an accident

David Smith is calling the Front Office for help. He has hit his head on the wardrobe, and his forehead is bleeding. You are a staff at the Front Office. Please offer Mr. Smith your help.

Task Eight   Extended Professional Knowledge Reading

Four Principles of Dealing with Complaints

(1) Understanding, Tolerance, Sincerity and Care——the Key to Win Guests' Understanding.

When guests encounter dissatisfaction, certain weaknesses of their human nature will be relatively exposed. There are guests who love to show their brilliance, want to be paid special attention to or like to give orders like a leader. Most of the guests are for the sake of face.

(2) "Guests are Always Right"—the Guiding Principle for Handling Guest Complaints.

Why insist on the principle of "guests are always right"? The guests are the source of the hotel's benefits. Adherence to this principle is good to maintain guest self-esteem, alleviating staff and guest conflicts and improving guest satisfaction. It can bring word-of-mouth benefits on the basis of guest satisfaction.

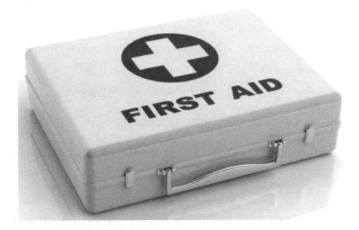

(Note: the above picture is quoted from the website
https://ns-strategy.cdn.bcebos.com/ns-strategy/upload/fc_big_pic/part-00413-3615.jpg.)

How to adhere to this principle? If the guest is not wrong, then of course the guest is right. If the guest is wrong, as long as the guest's words and deeds are legal and do not interfere with the interests of other guests, all the legitimate needs of the guest should be met. It is necessary to fully understand what the guests need and think so as to understand the guests' misunderstandings and faults.

(3) Fairness, Impartiality and Equal Treatment—the Basic Guarantee for the Correct Handling of Guest Complaints.

Treat guests equally, regardless of age, gender, occupation, social status, race, or belief. Don't judge people by their appearance.

(4) To Maintain the Hotel's Interests—the Key to the Long-term Development of the Hotel.

High-quality service must achieve "double satisfaction": maximizing the benefits of the hotel on the basis of maximizing guest satisfaction; the basic mission of the hotel staff is to create value for guests and the company as well. When guests complain, staff should not blame each other. They should avoid conflicts between departments for the overall interests of the hotel.

Read the passage and discuss the following questions.

①Why do guests complain to the hotel?

②What are the four principles of handling guest complaints?

③Do you agree with the above four principles? Why?

④What are other principles or methods of handling guest complaints?

Plan for Hotel Emergencies (Excerpt)

(1) Emergency Response Team.

Team Leader: General Manager

Deputy Team Leader: Executive Deputy General Manager

Members: General Manager's Office, Finance Department Manager, Security Department Manager, Front Office Manager, Food and Beverage Department Manager, Housekeeping Department Manager, Sales Department Manager

In the event of an emergency, the manager on duty is responsible for handling the incident before the members of the rescue team arrive.

(2) Emergency measures to deal with various emergencies.

Emergency measures for food poisoning incidents

If any person is found to be poisoned in the hotel, whether by mistake or deliberately, in addition to immediately calling the police, the following measures shall be taken.

A. Call the emergency center number "120" for help. If the medical staff does not arrive in time, the poisoned person is in danger. The poisoned person should be sent to a nearby hospital for rescue, and the poisoned person's relatives and friends should be notified.

B. Protect the site of the poisoned person, and do not allow anyone to touch toxic or suspicious toxic items (such as medicines, containers, drinks and food, vomit, etc.).

C. Arrange parking places for police cars and ambulances when they arrive and leave.

D. Register and hand in the personal belongings of the poisoned person to the police.

E. To prevent onlookers of idle and miscellaneous personnel.

Unit 16 Handling Complaints and Unexpected Affairs

F. Register the relevant information (including the time of arrival and departure of police cars and ambulances, the name of the person in charge of the police, etc.) for the record.

G. If a poisoner or suspicious person is found, he shall be handed over to the police immediately.

① Read the passage and summarize how to deal with food poisoning.
_____
_____
_____

② Try to write down the emergency measures for the guest being sick.
_____
_____
_____

Unit 16
练习答案

教学支持说明

为了改善教学效果,提高教材的使用效率,满足高校授课教师的教学需求,本套教材备有与纸质教材配套的教学课件(PPT 电子教案)和拓展资源(案例库、习题库、视频等)。

为保证本教学课件及相关教学资料仅为教材使用者所得,我们将向使用本套教材的高校授课教师和学生免费赠送教学课件或者相关教学资料,烦请授课教师和学生通过邮件或加入酒店专家俱乐部 QQ 群等方式与我们联系,获取"教学课件资源申请表"文档并认真准确填写后发给我们,我们的联系方式如下:

E-mail:lyzjjlb@163.com

酒店专家俱乐部 QQ 群号:710568959

酒店专家俱乐部 QQ 群二维码:

群名称:酒店专家俱乐部
群　号:710568959

教学课件资源申请表

填表时间：_____年___月___日

1. 以下内容请教师按实际情况写，★为必填项。
2. 学生根据个人情况如实填写，相关内容可以酌情调整提交。

★姓名		★性别	□男 □女	出生年月		★职务		
						★职称	□教授 □副教授 □讲师 □助教	
★学校				★院/系				
★教研室				★专业				
★办公电话			家庭电话			★移动电话		
★E-mail（请填写清晰）						★QQ号/微信号		
★联系地址						★邮编		

★现在主授课程情况	学生人数	教材所属出版社	教材满意度
课程一			□满意 □一般 □不满意
课程二			□满意 □一般 □不满意
课程三			□满意 □一般 □不满意
其 他			□满意 □一般 □不满意

教 材 出 版 信 息						
方向一		□准备写	□写作中	□已成稿	□已出版待修订	□有讲义
方向二		□准备写	□写作中	□已成稿	□已出版待修订	□有讲义
方向三		□准备写	□写作中	□已成稿	□已出版待修订	□有讲义

请教师认真填写表格下列内容，提供索取课件配套教材的相关信息，我社根据每位教师/学生填表信息的完整性、授课情况与索取课件的相关性，以及教材使用的情况赠送教材的配套课件及相关教学资源。

ISBN（书号）	书名	作者	索取课件简要说明	学生人数（如选作教材）
			□教学 □参考	
			□教学 □参考	

★您对与课件配套的纸质教材的意见和建议，希望提供哪些配套教学资源：